FEAR

FEAR ACROSS THE DISCIPLINES

EDITED BY Jan Plamper and Benjamin Lazier

University of Pittsburgh Press

Published by the University of Pittsburgh Press, Pittsburgh, Pa., 15260
Copyright © 2012, University of Pittsburgh Press
All rights reserved
Manufactured in the United States of America
Printed on acid-free paper
10 9 8 7 6 5 4 3 2 1

Library of Congress Cataloging-in-Publication Data

Fear : across the disciplines / edited by Jan Plamper and Benjamin Lazier.
    p. cm.
  Includes bibliographical references and index.
  ISBN 978-0-8229-6220-5 (pbk. : alk. paper)
  1. Fear. I. Plamper, Jan, 1970– II. Lazier, Benjamin, 1971–
  BF575.F2F385 2012

  152.4'6—dc23   2012030695

CONTENTS

ACKNOWLEDGMENTS

THIS EDITED VOLUME emerged from the workshop "Fear: Multi-disciplinary Perspectives," held at Princeton's Shelby Cullom Davis Center for Historical Studies on April 12, 2008. "Fear" was the Davis Center's theme for 2007–2008. For the invitation to convene the workshop, we are very grateful to Gyan Prakash, the director of the center at the time, and to Stephen Kotkin. Jennifer Houle, the manager of the Davis Center, took care of the logistical side of the workshop with stunning efficiency. The crime novelist Henning Mankell and the philosopher Vincent McCarthy also participated in the workshop, and we are most grateful to them. We would further like to thank Lorraine Daston, Carla Hesse, Ruth Leys, and William Reddy for comments and for answering queries.

Michael Laffan, another Princeton historian, not only reviewed the manuscript but also coedited with Max Weiss a monodisciplinary historical volume on fear that can be read in conjunction with ours:

Facing Fear: The History of an Emotion in Global Perspective (Princeton: Princeton University Press, 2012).

At the University of Pittsburgh Press Peter Kracht took on this risky multidisciplinary project and shepherded it to production with assistance from Amberle Sherman, Ann Walston saw it through production, and Alex Wolfe expertly edited the manuscript. The index was prepared by Stefanie Gert with assistance from Karola Rockmann at the Center for the History of Emotions, directed by Ute Frevert at the Max Planck Institute for Human Development in Berlin. We are grateful to them all.

<u>FEAR</u>

INTRODUCTION

Benjamin Lazier and Jan Plamper

WE HABITUALLY SAY that we see fear, that we smell it, touch it, breathe it. But how, after all is said and done, do we *know* it?

The chapters in this edited volume help us with just this question—how fear is variously constituted as an object of knowledge.[1] The contributions to this book emerged from a workshop in which a distinguished group of scholars (representing the fields of neuroscience, clinical psychology, philosophy, political theory, literary studies, film studies, economic history, intellectual history, and history of science) and one novelist gathered to reflect on the predispositions they and their disciplines bring to bear on the phenomenon of fear, broadly construed. Some opted to present synoptic overviews; others, case studies. The unstated presumption of the workshop was to break down barriers between social-scientific, humanistic, and natural-scientific approaches to fear and to leave behind the binary distinction between nature and culture that has long underwritten their differences. These hopes were animated by recent works that combine the universalism of cognitive psychology with the attention to cultural particularity found in much anthropological research.[2] It therefore came as a surprise to discover, at the workshop, how these boundaries were at times so readily reconstituted. As Lorraine Daston has remarked, developing a language beyond the terms of the hoary nature/culture distinction "would require nothing less than the functional equivalent of a discipline's collective psychotherapy."[3]

What would such therapy entail? And what new view would it produce? Supposing, for a moment, that humanities scholars, social scientists, and life scientists joined one another on the proverbial couch, what kind of landscape would reveal itself after the old edifice had been destroyed and the rubble cleared away?

Destroying the old edifice requires first that we reveal it for what it is—a toxic bequest, of use in its time but no longer. Most proximately, this bequest can be traced to a change in the understanding of emotions over the course of the nineteenth century. That is when emotions appeared for the first time as "hardwired," as evolutionarily determined bodily reactions to objects or outer stimuli. In the work of Darwin, and later Carl Lange and William James, fear in particular became the "alpha emotion in the hierarchy of human affects."[4] It was at once the most archaic and most modern of emotions. As Darwin wrote in *The Expression of the Emotions in Man and Animals*, "fear was expressed from an extremely remote period, in almost the same manner as it is now in man."[5] This new view overturned earlier ideas, in which fear was often regarded as a passion subject to volition, imagination, and an ethical will.[6]

There are indications, however, that the phobic regime born of the nineteenth century is coming to an end.[7] Life scientists, for example, are recovering conceptual resources for their work in eras prior to the rise of Darwin, Lange, and James. Some, like the renowned developmental psychologist Jerome Kagan, have mobilized philosophers as historically and intellectually diverse as Aristotle, Descartes, and Kant to argue against the approach to emotions currently favored by experimental psychology. "Definitions of emotion that relied on taped verbal reports, filmed behaviors, or recordings of biological reactions," Kagan says, are comparatively impoverished next to the "robust" knowledge about feelings produced by thinkers now retrofitted into the tradition of the humanities.[8] In part, this is because the methods of the life sciences have sometimes constituted fear as an object of knowledge in a fashion that denies the complexity of the phenomenon—the language of the laboratory can sterilize the recalcitrant messiness of lived experience. Summing up a lifetime of experimental research, Kagan offered this suggestion: "Let us agree to a moratorium on the use of single words, such as *fear*, . . . and write about emotional processes with full sentences rather than ambiguous, naked concepts."[9]

The chapters in this edited volume follow Kagan's lead. They also trace a loose thematic arc. The first two contributions, by Richard McNally (an experimental psychologist and clinician) and Arne Öhman (a neuroscientist), together provide an overview of contemporary psychobiological approaches to fear, with particular attention to anxiety disorders. The third chapter, by Ruth Leys, situates the first two in an account of post-1960s psychological scholarship on affect, highlighting their historical contingency. In the process Leys mounts an attack on the work of Paul Ekman, a leading psychologist whose work on facial expression has enjoyed tremendous popularity in venues ranging from the Fox Broadcasting Company to the Department of Homeland Security. The next two chapters take the historicizing impulse still further. First, Jan Plamper extends Leys's account by describing how emotion became an object of investigation for the life sciences, in this instance by way of the theories and practices of Russian military psychologists around the beginning of the twentieth century. Then, Jan Mieszkowski looks to the history of late Enlightenment discussions about the terror of encounters with the sublime to account for some of the peculiarities of fear in the modern theater of war. Whereas Mieszkowski focuses on the *spectacle* of fear in war, Corey Robin, a political theorist, follows with a contribution on the *politics* of fear in times of war and crisis. The economic historian Harold James rounds out this series of pieces on fear and calamity with an account of the psychology of mass panic in moments of economic collapse, with special attention to the origins of the Great Depression. The book then concludes with a chapter by Adam Lowenstein (a film scholar), who addresses the fear induced by horror films.

All told, the chapters gathered here go a long way toward contesting the phobic regime to which we are heir. They also reveal alternative categories—in the instance of this book, intentionality and admixture, temporality, spectacle, and politics—through which to think about fear across the disciplines.

INTENTIONALITY AND ADMIXTURE

Everyday experience would seem to confirm Kagan's point about the admixture of feeling. Any visit to an amusement park roller coaster will do. Faces marked at once by pleasure and terror attest to a composite *Angstlust* in vivo.[10] Or at least they seem to. What facial expression can actually tell us is a matter of heated academic debate and biopolitical significance. For example, facial testimony animates the work of the psychologist Paul Ekman, associated with the most prominent contemporary effort to identify "basic" emotions independent of time and place. Ekman gained notoriety for a series of studies in which he traversed Papua New Guinea asking isolated villagers to identify the emotions on the faces of photographed persons from cultures they had never before encountered. Later, he was made editor of Darwin's *The Expression of the Emotions in Man and Animals*. And he has more recently become an expert in facial-recognition techniques, feted in the popular press and highly sought after by law enforcement agencies. He has the peculiar distinction of having become at once a foremost resource in the global "war on terror" and the author of a series of self-help books designed to aid the aggrieved half of fractious couples to determine when their partners lie.[11]

The article by Ruth Leys calls both the conclusions and presuppositions of Ekman's foundational experiments into question. Leys focuses on the role of photographs in Ekman's studies. In fact, her contribution might be read as one prolonged plea for taking the mediality and temporality of Ekman's photos more seriously. Of course, these problems long preceded Ekman's own experiments. Doubts about the ability of photography to capture the display of emotions on the site of the human face set in, Leys reports, with Darwin himself. Exposure times of cameras in the 1860s lasted several seconds, which meant that the subject had to keep still and "conserve" the emotion on her face. The problems with such an approach are numerous. For one, if the face truly is an embodiment of emotion, then such faces were at best embodiments of staged emotions, embodiments of feigned affect—the faces, in other words, of the fake. As Leys points out, this was one of several methodological deficiencies plaguing Ekman's early experiments, a deficiency that endures, albeit in more complicated fashion, both in the filmic evidence at the core of Ekman's later work and in one of the dominant natural-scientific approaches to visually registering emotions today—the "still" photographs of functional magnetic resonance imaging (fMRI) and positron emission tomography (PET) brain scans.

The dispute about what such photographs and films can tell us hinges on a deeper set of arguments about the kind of entity that fear is and the kind of self that experiences, expresses, or lives it. Roughly, following Leys, we might speak of two competing positions: so-called intentionalist and nonintentionalist theories of fear. The first describes fear as a process, the second as an entity. The first is sometimes associated with psychoanalysis and phenomenology, the second typically with neuroscience. The first foregrounds questions of meaning and belief, the second tends to separate feeling from cognition. In sum, the two positions hinge on competing understandings of self and world. Nonintentionalist theories are thought to posit a discrete subject over and against a world of objects. Intentionalist theories, by contrast, speak of a porous, open, socially mediated self and of fear as always attached to the specific objects with which they are associated.

The distinction is itself a fairly recent innovation in the history of Western thought, in part because nonintentional theories gained real purchase only in the second half of the nineteenth century.[12] Until then, the dominant trend described fear as a subjective state of feeling, not a bodily response to an external stimulus. Aristotle, for example, held that fear (*phobos*) entailed a moment of evaluation (must I fear something and does it truly pose a threat?), and that it was subject to *moral* education (how do we teach the young a fear that will enable them to contribute to the good life?), not just the physical conditioning now associated with the name Pavlov.[13] Thomas Aquinas was also keen to distinguish human fear (*timor*) from animal fear. Fear in humans, he held, entailed an element of intellectual appraisal (*cogitativa* and *ratio particularis*), while animals instinctively fled or fought.[14] Even Descartes, whose distinction between cognition and emotion is sometimes thought to have prefigured the anti-intentionalism of the nineteenth century, spoke of volition in the management of fear as a "mastery of the passions," involving the focus "on useful thoughts designed to generate one passion (e.g., courage) to counteract another (e.g., fear)."[15] Not until modern psychology came to dominate scholarly and public discussions about fear did the intentionalist approach lose sway.

We see both psychologists in this book grappling with this legacy. Richard McNally begins his chapter with a fascinating account of the felt need to produce a nonintentionalist theory in the first place. Psychologists eager to establish their discipline as (hard) science, he argues, were understandably uneasy with a tradition of thinking about emotion that privileged subjective experience over objectifiable, measurable indicators such as verbalization (cries of terror), physiological changes (a racing heart), and motor actions (flight). This approach had virtues: it inspired ways to measure fear beyond the self-reporting of the fearful, which in turn produced public and observable sets of data. But the approach raised as many questions as it resolved, and McNally casts his lot with those psychologists who believe in patient self-reporting to get at individual, subjective states of feeling (or, in the psychological term of art, *qualia*).

We can begin to fathom the infrequency of such openly intention-alist partisanship once we consider Arne Öhman's contribution. Like McNally, Öhman acknowledges the importance of self-reporting, at least as one among many ways to get at the "multi-component responses" that comprise all emotions (a definition he adopts from the experimental psychologist Keith Oatley). But Öhman is fundamentally interested in the biology of fear, and he presents us with a survey of the findings that have made biological approaches to fear so powerful. He focuses on the role of the amygdalae—small, almond-shaped collections of nuclei in the anterior medial temporal lobe of the brain—in mediating functional rela-tionships between threats and defensive behavior. This is important: the fact that the "fear network" is located in parts of the brain that evolved at the junction between reptiles and mammals indicates that it is extremely primitive. In evolutionary terms, the amygdala is anterior to the cortex, where the kind of cognitive processing associated with intentionality in fear—"willpower," "subjective feeling"—is thought to take place.[16] For those impressed by these findings, there is therefore something inescap-ably "nonintentional" about fear. But others such as McNally call into question this bottom-top hierarchy (amygdala over cortex), along with the linkage of one particular area of the brain with fear.

The argument about intentionality is not conducted only in the reg-ister of the natural sciences and their history. It figures also in the work of humanists. Take Adam Lowenstein's chapter, which addresses *Land of the Dead* (2005), the fourth horror film in director George Romero's leg-endary *Dead* series. Lowenstein takes the film as an occasion to inveigh against so-called cognitivist approaches to thinking about audience terror —elicited by the horror genre in particular and in more occulted fashion by the medium of film in general. "No physiological sensors or strategic interviews or questionnaire results can ever tell the whole story about . . . how exactly spectators interact with a film," he writes. Indeed, he thinks it is folly to say that the fear induced in moviegoers is a matter of stimu-lus generalization: that our fear of zombies in the theater is just another version of the fear we feel in the real world at the sight of the monstrous, distorted, deformed, and impure.

Instead, Lowenstein suggests we think of horror films as enacting a "cinema of attractions" (in the critic Tom Gunning's phrase). Or better, *recalling* such a cinema: for the cinema of attractions was one of the roads not taken once Hollywood's cinema of narrative pleasures marginalized its competitors. Against the temporality of narrative, this argument has it, the cinema of attractions prized deferral, belatedness, and retrospection —a dramatization, say, of a Freudian psyche hard at work rearranging and retranscribing memories or strategically deferring action on experiences impossible for the subject to integrate at the moment of their occurrence. If Hollywood privileged the time of narrative, the cinema of attractions preferred what Lowenstein calls the "allegorical moment."

There is a certain irony in Lowenstein's use of the phrase "cinema of attractions." It recalls, after all, Sergei Eisenstein's notion of a "montage of attractions"—a theory of film that held that moviegoers could be transformed into proletarianized subjects not, or not only, with suitably ideological stories (for example, *Battleship Potemkin*) but on the assumption that the formal elements of a film could "train" viewers by means of a Pavlovian mechanism of stimulus and response. In other words, the montage of attractions imported the laboratory into the theater, whereas Lowenstein's work implicitly asks us to think, as does Leys, about how the phantasmatic and theatrical constructions of fear reassert themselves within the sterile confines of the lab.

Here, then, is where Lowenstein can help us think about Ekman and the approach to fear he represents. As Leys points out, Ekman's early work was roundly criticized, in part for its use of staged faces frozen in the form of synchronic snapshots. Ekman answered his critics, Margaret Mead among them, by turning to faces invested with diachrony and movement instead—in other words, to faces on film. His later experiments monitored the facial expressions of test-subjects exposed to traumatic or disturbing films, on the assumption that involuntary "micromovements" reveal the truth of our feelings. But Lowenstein works on a medium whose success as an art form would seem to hinge on the ability to fake just what Ekman claims cannot be feigned. And if we take Lowenstein seriously, we realize that there is much more of the theater in the lab than we are accustomed to think. To describe what transpires in the lab requires that we consider how the phantasmatic and theatrical temporalities of fear play out in laboratory experiments predicated on their exclusion.

TEMPORALITY

This brings us to a second motif in the book—temporality. Or to pose it in the form of a question: *When* does fear happen? The life sciences provide us with several answers. At first glance, fear is triggered by an immediate threat, and the function of fear is to induce the organism to freeze, fight, or flee in defense. But things quickly become more complicated. There is first the evidence provided by the Pavlovian conditioning of animals, who are trained to respond with fear to a stimulus that in and of itself presents no threat. What this evidence means is up for debate. Some think it indicates animals are capable of anxiety about something that has not yet come to pass. The implication: even in animals, the temporality of fear involves a manifestation of expectation (the future) and experience (the past) in the present. Others, and here McNally comes to mind, warn against such a conclusion: rodents, he holds, are confined to the "temporal prison of the present" because they lack the capacity for self-representation that allows for the projection of the self into an imagined future or the recollection of the self from a lived past. Laboratory mice are presentists. Hence, one argument goes, models of fear developed in the animal lab are presentist too and cannot account for the temporal play at the heart of the human experience of fear.

There is a second way in which the life sciences insert temporality into understandings of fear, and that is in discussions of evolution. At first glance, this sounds counterintuitive. The life sciences are often accused of having no sense for history: not just the history of disciplines but for the ways historical developments have produced the objects of investigation for those disciplines. But there is a difference between history and temporality; the methodological stress on evolution might be hostile to the first but not to the second. After all, to stress the evolutionary background to fear is also to insist on the enduring importance of the distant past—call it "prehistory"—in the present.[17] It is also to insist on open futures (since evolution brooks no end or conclusion save extinction), albeit in most cases distant ones (given a pace of change generally too slow to register in a human lifetime).

To understand the role of more proximate historical horizons in manifestations of fear, it helps to consider the chapters by Harold James and Jan Plamper. James provides a careful, lucid analysis of the stock market panic of 1929: first, a review of the economic explanations that have been marshaled and rejected to account for it, and second, a survey of the strange temporalities at work in the psychology of mass panic. James concludes that it was not this or that economic event so much as a sense of history—a sense for radical alternatives to the present embedded in a dystopian, concocted fantasy of the past—that accounts for the course of events. "History actually induced the sense of crisis," James reports, as "fear arises when deep historical experience suddenly reemerges and becomes alive as a possible version of the present."

By "history" James means something more like "historical imagination"—and a radically unstable, phantasmatic one at that. To take one example: observers of the crash unwittingly conflated the events of their day with a historical predecessor, the collapse of Friday, September 24, 1869. As James points out, this seems to be the only way to account for one of the most curious dimensions of the panic—the fact that the collapse, which transpired on Thursday, October 24, came to be known, quickly and erroneously, as Black Friday. Those who watched the market crash, it turns out, shared something with Lowenstein's moviegoers: a febrile, temporal imagination in which present could be past, past future, and future already lived. If there is an economic logic here, James suggests, it is difficult indeed to discern. The nature of fear means that market panics may not be amenable to market explanations (or at least not to those inspired by the "efficient markets hypothesis"). Ben Bernanke once claimed that "to understand the Great Depression is the Holy Grail of macroeconomics."[18] But if James is right, the social scientists and policy makers are doomed to failure. Their search is more like the Grail quest—"fundamentally futile"—than they may care to admit, and this futility is born of erroneous ideas about what fear is and how it is best known.

James focuses on the role of the historical imagination in the felt experience of fear. Jan Plamper's chapter, in turn, broaches the question of what happens to fear as an object of knowledge when it is submitted to the temporalities of historical analysis. Plamper tracks the transformation of talk about fear among Russian soldiers from the early nineteenth century to the early twentieth century. Discussions of fear were few in the war of 1812, and, when they did surface, were conducted in the lexica of morality and ethnicity (understood in terms of religion and sometimes climate, but not genetic inheritance). Half a century later talk of fear exploded in the wake of the Crimean War. This explosion took place across genres: in belles letters (Leo Tolstoy), in military theory, and above all in the newly established science of military psychology. In the hands of military psychologists, fear was transformed into a symptom of disease and sometimes into a disease proper ("shell shock" and its Russian variants), which was in turn to be submitted to medical-scientific practice (diagnosis, therapy, prophylactics). Like Leys, then, Plamper provides us with a story about how fear became an object of scientific inquiry. Implicitly, both raise the question of whether fear might even be understood as a stable, enduring experience across time. To judge by the qualia or self-reporting of Russian soldiers—to use McNally's language for a moment—the answer appears to be no.

SPECTACLE

A third motif in this book hinges on the spectacular dimensions of fear. Literally: spectatorship seems to be intrinsic to the fear experience. Take first the example of the fear provoked by horror films, in which the spectacular nature of the experience is front and center. As Lowenstein points out in his chapter, there are very good reasons to make a sharp distinction between fear induced in the theater and fear encountered in the world. But it is worth considering the tantalizing, if counterintuitive alternative: that the horror show reveals a deep truth about fear, both within the theater and beyond.

The prospect is counterintuitive, because moviegoers are not confronted with an actual threat to life or limb. Theirs, it seems, is a faux fear, a simulation, manufactured for the purposes of titillation and delight. Fear is enjoyable, provided it is not the real thing, experienced from the perspective afforded by a safe place. But the prospect of taking the horror film as a model is also tantalizing, for two reasons above all. First, it asks us to think more carefully about the artifice and the spectacle at work in other instances of manufactured fear. Ekman's findings, for example, were acquired by monitoring the facial movements of test subjects exposed to frightening or disturbing films. These test subjects were watching their own "horror show" in their own safe place—not the theater but the lab. More recent experiments using fMRI function similarly. It is common, especially in the popular scientific press, to conclude that such imaging provides access to the deep, biological truth of emotions. We are not watching the face, after all, but the brain. In truth, however, such experiments do just what Ekman did, only with a change of locus. Emotional reactions are still induced in test subjects (we are still watching those induced to fear), and there is still an elision between the laboratory and life.[19]

Taking the moviegoer as a model is tantalizing for a second reason. As Jan Mieszkowski suggests in his intellectual-historical reconstruction of what it has meant to be a witness to war, there is a sense in which even the most fearful of places, the battlefield, is experienced as a theater, not just by observers but by soldiers. Curiously, however, it is an experience of a theater staging a threat to the lives of others—not the self. The startling suggestion is that in war even combatants can never be afraid *enough*; a part of our psyche will always apprehend war as spectacle, as a horror show about someone else.

To make this argument, Mieszkowski first turns to a tradition of late Enlightenment thought about aesthetics. Figures like Edmund Burke and Immanuel Kant famously invoked the category of the sublime to account for the pleasure we feel when exposed to terror, even scenes of others' demise, provided we view such spectacles from the vantage of a "safe place." They had in effect elaborated a new model of spectatorship, prompted by some of the horrific events of their day (the Lisbon earthquake of 1755 for Kant, the French Revolution for Burke). But there were good reasons to wonder about the ethical palatability of such a model. As Samuel Taylor Coleridge described it, Britain had given birth to a mass audience that consumed the stories of the suffering of others for breakfast: "Boys and girls, / And women, that would groan to see a child / Pull off an insect's leg, all read of war, / The best amusement for our morning meal!"[20] In other words, their safe place had become a bit too safe. According to Mieszkowski, fear was thereby banished from the experience of the sublime, "leaving in its wake only the imaginative artifice of Burke and Kant's staged terror—faux fear without the fear."

This tradition of thought took a curious but telling turn in Sigmund Freud's reflections on the origins of the First World War. How are we to account for the fact of modern mass war? Given the terrors it visits upon combatants and civilians alike, why do we make such easy recourse to armed conflict? Freud conjectured that something about the fear of death made it impossible to take its threat seriously enough. In the unconscious, he held, we are convinced of our own immortality. It is therefore impossible to imagine our own death—or rather, "whenever we attempt to do so we can perceive that we are in fact still present as spectators."[21] Even those in battle inevitably construed themselves in part as observers immune to the threat of death. Mieszkowski therefore concludes that for Freud, "all fear is a product of a staged scenario in which there is no need to offer a qualifying 'providing we are in a safe place' because, emotionally speaking, we invariably feel that we already are." Mieszkowski leaves us to consider whether this disquieting conclusion holds not just for Freud but for us—and in particular for Americans left unmoved by sights of war from Afghanistan and Iraq.

POLITICS

There is a final, important series of questions animating the contributions to this book. Who rules? Who sets the tone in contemporary debates about fear? And to what effect? In recent years, the natural sciences have displaced, occluded, even excluded humanist discussions of fear. This trend, in which debates on "eternal" questions of humanity (free will, the self, emotions) moved from the domain of the humanities to the domain of the life sciences, only accelerated after 9/11. It is not difficult to understand why. Whatever the contemporary status of C. P. Snow's "two cultures," the natural sciences offer a seductive promise that the humanities cannot: empirically derived certainties for society of the kind manufactured within the confines of their experiments. Ekman's faces, for example, have moved out of laboratories and into our airports in the form of Screening Passengers by Observational Techniques (SPOT) machines stationed at fourteen U.S. airports to register the "micro-expressions" of passengers, now coded as potential terrorists.[22] Critics of SPOT, Ekman writes,

> have said that it is an unnecessary invasion of privacy, based on an untested method of observation, that is unlikely to yield much in the way of red-handed terrorists set on blowing up a plane or flying it into a building, but would violate fliers' civil rights. I disagree. I've participated in four decades' worth of research into deception and demeanor, and I know that researchers have amassed enough knowledge about how someone who is lying looks and behaves that it would be negligent not to use it in the search for terrorists. Along with luggage checks, radar screening, bomb-sniffing dogs and the rest of our security arsenal, observational techniques can help reduce risks—and potentially prevent another deadly assault like the attacks of September 11, 2001.[23]

To be sure, there was the counterbalance of writings—across the disciplines, spanning political science to medicine—on the politics of fear, penned with the aim of shifting public attention to fear as it is manipulated and produced.[24] But on the whole, the natural sciences have been spectacularly adept at exporting their laboratory principle to society as a whole. Just as fear must be stimulated or simulated in the lab in order to measure it, so fear must be nourished and then contained or, more precisely, nourished in order to be contained by a government at the ready.

Need this be the case? It is a difficult question to answer. If we follow the argument of the political scientist Corey Robin, the answer may unfortunately be yes. Robin aims to demonstrate how the language of security mobilizes fear to justify the limitation of rights the state was theoretically constituted to protect. In itself, this is not news. But Robin goes further. He explains why recourse to such language is so tempting. He also suggests that liberal conceptions of the state in fact encourage the use of coercive power in the name of national security. Liberal stalwarts such as John Locke, John Stuart Mill, and Oliver Wendell Holmes may have articulated reasons for limiting the power of the state to use coercion on matters of religion, morality, and politics. But the exceptions they invoked in which coercion might be justified—"the security and safety of the commonwealth" (Locke), harm (Mill), "clear and present danger" (Holmes)—ensure that when states do exercise such power, they will do so on behalf of security.[25]

Still worse, the nature of the fear stoked by such language is peculiarly resistant to reasoned discussion or debate. As Robin points out, such language is frequently articulated in the conditional and therefore inhabits a grammatical space beyond the distinction between fact and fiction. When the television journalist Diane Sawyer asked former president George W. Bush to distinguish between the claim, stated as fact, that "there were weapons of mass destruction" and the hypothetical possibility that Saddam Hussein "could move to acquire those weapons," Bush answered: "What's the difference?" Robin holds up just this response as the most straightforward and revealing statement Bush ever made about the war. Like no other, it demonstrates that the conditional is a mood "where evidence and intuition, reason and speculation combine to make the worst-case scenario seem as real as the realest fact." And the perverse corollary is that the greater the threat, the less proof we demand on behalf of the claim that the threat is real.

The pathology Robin identifies is endemic, he thinks, to the liberal political order. It is a congenital defect. Life scientists such as Arne Öhman have a similar point to make, if in a different key. Öhman concludes his chapter with an impassioned plea against the understandable impulse to avoid danger—taken to an extreme, after all, avoidance is a hallmark of anxiety disorder, and it curiously reaffirms the gravity of the problems it is meant to solve. As Öhman points out, however, a version of such avoidance plagues many who do not fulfill any of the typical diagnostic criteria for the disease, and here he is thinking of America after 9/11. The extraordinary measures undertaken on behalf of national security and safety, he argues, hide a "sad truth": that we in fact have little control over the things we fear most, such as illness, accidents, or, in this instance, terrorist attacks. Such measures also stoke the fires of the very fear they are meant to quench. Like Robin, Öhman would have us submit the question of security to arenas, like politics, better suited to contention and choice. Doing so might enable us to rescue ourselves from the Pavlovian conditioning of color-coded terror alerts. It might allow us to consider anew whether public resources are better expended on SPOT machines or on schools.

Or it might not. Whatever the new insights offered by the disciplines represented in this book bring into the process of how we know and live fear, it remains to be seen whether such insights can be of use in public discussion. If the chapters presented here are any measure by which to judge, this question ought to receive a qualified yes. How these insights are to insinuate themselves into the public arena in the first place, however, is a question that must remain unresolved for now.

FEAR, ANXIETY, AND THEIR DISORDERS

Richard J. McNally

THE PSYCHOLOGY OF fear is haunted by the ghost of Descartes. The traditional view of fear as a subjectively distinct feeling state accessible only to the person experiencing it seemingly implies a Cartesian dualism that harkens back to psychology's prescientific past. Accordingly, psychologists keen to establish a science of fear have endeavored to exorcise Descartes's ghost by reconceptualizing fear (and anxiety) in ways that eliminate its subjective aspect. This effort has been driven by the mandate that data in science must be public and observable.

In a landmark paper, Peter Lang proposed "an alternative to the view that anxiety can best be understood as a phenomenon of human experience."[1] He reconceptualized anxiety as an observable response that occurs in three loosely coupled systems: verbal, physiologic, and motoric. Hence, a snake phobic person encountering a snake in the woods might respond by verbalizing fear, exhibiting a sudden increase in heart rate, and fleeing the scene as quickly as possible. The person's cry of terror, racing heart, and rapid flight are all public events that can be seen, heard, or otherwise recorded by others. Lang also emphasized that objective data from each of these systems need not covary. A soldier might report intense anxiety and exhibit heightened arousal prior to combat but fight rather than flee the battlefield. Approach toward threat despite activation in the verbal and physiologic systems corresponds to the lay concept of courage.

Lang's three-systems approach to fear and anxiety has had an immense heuristic impact on psychology. It encouraged innovative ways to measure fear in addition to self-report. It ensured that the database of fear was public and observable. Lang's approach was counterintuitive in that it expelled inner feelings from the science of fear. It rejected what for most people is the very essence of fear: how it feels to the person experiencing it. On the other hand, many theoretical advances in science have run counter to everyday intuitions. Untutored observation indicates that the Sun revolves around the Earth, not vice versa. Hence, a scientific theory need not comport with common sense to be true.

Yet Lang's approach had its own limitations. Two of his former PhD students, Michael Kozak and Gregory Miller, elucidated some of the conceptual problems inherent in regarding fear as a response evinced in three loosely coupled systems.[2] They pointed out that if fear is nothing but a summary of a set of observable responses, then the concept possesses no additional meaning beyond its indicators and cannot serve any explanatory function. It loses its status as a hypothetical construct extendable to new circumstances.

Kozak and Miller also observed that the very discordance among the three systems raised the question about what the systems share in common that qualifies them as evincing fear. What is it about these empirical measures, often poorly covarying, that justifies them as measures of the same thing? Something must transcend the measures themselves, uniting them conceptually as variant manifestations of the same underlying process.

Kozak and Miller addressed this problem by posing an alternative formulation to Lang's. Instead of defining fear as a response, they argued that fear is a functional state expressed in observable responses in the three systems. Fear is not a response itself; fear is the mediating psychobiological state that produces the observable phenomena. What ties the observable reactions of fear together is that they are variant expressions of this adaptive, defensive functional state. Because the meaning of fear is not exhausted by its observable manifestations, scientists can investigate the mediating psychobiology that generates its observable manifestations.

FEAR AND FUNCTIONALISM

The doctrine of functionalism, invoked by Kozak and Miller to reconceptualize fear, originated in philosophy as a solution to the mind-body problem.[3] Like Lang's original three systems view, functionalism was an attempt to exorcise Descartes's ghost. Rather than construing the mind as a kind of nonmaterial stuff, functionalists conceptualized mental states as functional states defined by their input, their output, and their relation to other functional states. They likened cognition to computation, viewing the mind as software running on the hardware of the brain or any other suitable device. Because mentality was defined computationally, the medium of its instantiation did not matter. Cognition could be studied in its own right, independent of the brain.

Although the philosophers of mind who developed functionalism seldom addressed emotions, one could sketch functionalist definitions of terms such as "fear" and "anxiety," as implied by Kozak and Miller. These two terms are often used interchangeably, but their functions are distinct. Fear is a state triggered by an immediate threat whose function is to mobilize the person to defend against the threat by freezing, fleeing, or fighting. Anxiety is a state triggered by the prospect of future threat whose function is to motivate the person to take steps to prevent the threat from materializing. Neither of these definitions appeals to the subjective, inner experience of fear and anxiety—the *qualia* of fear and anxiety.

FUNCTIONALISM'S MISSING QUALIA

A functionalist construal of fear and other states avoids Cartesian dualism. On the other hand, functionalism ignores qualia—the irreducibly subjective aspects of functional states, as realized in human brains.

Consider pain. A functionalist definition of pain would specify its input (e.g., tissue damage), its output (e.g., grimacing, verbal complaints, reaching for a bottle of aspirin), and its relation to other states. We might elucidate the neurophysiologic processes occurring as a person is writhing in pain, including performing functional magnetic resonance imaging (fMRI) of the person's brain, and we might even program a robot to mimic pain. All of these procedures yield objective, publically observable data accessible to any third party. But none disclose what it is like for the person who is experiencing the pain itself. Cognition and emotion, construed functionally as programs capable of running on diverse devices, leaves out important objectively real, but subjective, aspects of the empirical world.

As John Searle has argued, consciousness is an emergent property of the brain just as solidity is an emergent property of H_2O when the temperature falls below 32 degrees Fahrenheit.[4] Hence, qualia—feelings of fear, pain, and so forth—are biological facts about the empirical world, albeit ones inaccessible to observers other than the person experiencing them.

Scientific skepticism about the reality of qualia arises from the mistaken assumption that for something to be real it must be accessible to all observers.[5] This mistake arises from the conflation of two senses of objectivity and subjectivity.[6] Scientists are told to eliminate subjectivity from their work. They must strive to be objective by rooting out personal prejudice, bias, and so forth as they seek to discover truths about the world. But this desirable epistemic objectivity does imply that all aspects of the world are ontologically objective. Qualia are real emergent properties of the brain, but they are ontologically subjective. The irreducibly subjective character of the qualia of fear, pain, and so forth is a factual matter about the empirical world. If a man says that he has a headache, that statement is objective in the sense that it is made true by certain facts in the world. Yet the headache itself has a subjective mode of existence.[7]

To acknowledge that not all aspects of the empirical world are accessible to third-party observers does not entail relapse into Cartesian dualism. Consciousness (qualia) is not another kind of stuff, distinct from the physical. It is merely a higher-level, emergent property of the brain. Yet this subjective mode of existence will forever elude observation by third parties. Even the most sophisticated neuroimaging devices can only track the observable correlates of qualia. These methods can disclose the neural correlates of conscious states but not their intentional content.

SELF-REPORTING THE QUALIA OF FEAR

If what it feels like to feel fear is an irreducible, biological fact, then we ought to address it as best as we can in our psychological theories rather than ignoring it. Jerome Kagan, for example, does not hesitate to emphasize the importance of feelings to an adequate theory of emotion. A consciously detected change in feeling possessing sensory qualities that the person interprets semantically are core features of emotion.[8] He recognizes that some scientists will balk at including such elements into a scientific theory of emotion, especially because of the difficulty in measuring qualia. Yet he stresses these irreducible features of human emotion, in part to resist that tendency of some scientists to equate brain states, detected via neuroimaging, with emotion itself. As he put it, "a colored photograph of a brain state created with the help of a brain scanner is no more equivalent to an emotion than a picture of an apple represents the texture and taste of the fruit."[9]

Self-report is the best, albeit fallible, method of tackling the qualia of fear. Self-report's unsavory reputation among scientists arises because of its association with introspection, a method discredited in early twentieth-century psychology.

But self-reports of qualia do not presuppose the operation of a special faculty called introspection. This presupposition arises from a mistaken analogy with vision. In vision, there are two things: the act of perceiving and the thing perceived. But this is not the case when we "introspect."[10] There are not two things: the act of gazing inward and the object, consciousness, of this inner gaze. Hence, the metaphor of (inner) vision does not work. There is no introspective faculty akin to vision, and when people "introspect," all they are doing is thinking about their mental states and reporting on them. This activity does not involve a special inner vision that detects a hidden object called a mental state. Indeed, to think about a mental state is a mental state.

None of the foregoing implies that self-reports are infallible. A person may lie or may use words in idiosyncratic ways. For example, some patients with anxiety disorders will say that they had a panic attack for an entire day. Further probing and clarification reveals that what they mean is that they were suffering from intense anxiety all day but did not experience the crescendo of intense terror and cardiorespiratory symptoms that characterize panic and distinguish it from very high anxiety.

ANIMAL MODELS OF FEAR AND ANXIETY

Functionalism recognizes uniformity in diversity. It holds that the same program can be instantiated in the most diverse media—in computers, in the brains of people, or in the brains of animals. Functionalism encourages the view that fear is the same state irrespective of its mode of instantiation.

This view dovetails nicely with the Darwinian emphasis on cross-species continuity. That fear is an evolved adaptation that fostered fitness in ancestral populations implies that the machinery of fear has been largely preserved throughout the course of mammalian evolution. This suggests that we can learn much about fear from studying it in mice, rats, and other animals. Hence, arguments arising from the very different fields of philosophy of mind (and computer science) and evolutionary biology motivate research focusing on what is common in fear in people and in animals.

This approach has enabled us learn much about the neural circuitry of learned fear.[11] These experiments have often involved mice or rats exposed to Pavlovian (classical) fear conditioning procedures. For example, researchers have presented neutral tones prior to the delivery of electric shocks to the animal's feet through the floor grid of the cage. The tone is thereby established as a conditioned stimulus capable of eliciting the conditioned response of freezing or suppression of ongoing behavior (e.g., pressing a lever for food). The unconditioned stimulus is the shock and the unconditioned response is flinching. The conditioned response provides an index of conditioned fear.

Without denying the importance of basic animal conditioning research to our understanding of fear, Kagan has issued cautions about the risks of assuming the functional equivalence of fear as studied in animals and fear as studied in people: "Because rats and mice, and perhaps apes as well, do not interpret their bodily changes, scientists should not equate the emotions of animals and humans. Although some scientists attribute 'fear' to both rats and humans, the psychological states in the two species are far from identical. Some scientists say that mice that freeze in a place where they had been shocked a day earlier or do not enter a brightly lit alley are 'anxious.' But readers should understand that the brain state of the mice is quite different from that of adults who refuse to fly because of anxiety over a possible crash."[12]

Animal models have other limitations that make it impossible for them to capture certain features of human fear and anxiety. Because adult human beings possess the capacity for self-representation, they are vulnerable to experiencing anxiety in ways unavailable to other animals. A mouse may exhibit "timidity" in its wary refusal to enter certain settings, but this term denotes something entirely different in a shy person who avoids social gatherings. At a very abstract level of analysis, both the mouse and the person exhibit avoidance behavior. But the motivational basis, the cognitive content, and the mediating brain states will differ. For the shy person, it is the social self, not the physical self, that is "endangered" by attending a party.

Moreover, self-representational capacity enables people to project themselves into the future and into the past. In contrast, rodents are trapped within the temporal prison of the present and thus are free from worries about the distant future or from being haunted by memories of past trauma. Indeed, because the term "anxiety" implies the capacity to envision the future, nonhuman animals are incapable of experiencing this state.

NEUROSCIENCE AND FEAR

Brain activity detected by scanners provides the foundation for emotional states, but they are not the emotions themselves. For example, the amygdala "lights up" in response to certain threats, but this activation is not equivalent to fear. As Kagan observed, "the corpus of evidence suggests that a primary function of the amygdala is to respond to unexpected, unfamiliar, or ambiguous events, whether they are safe, pleasant, aversive, or potentially dangerous."[13] Hence, we cannot assume that heightened amygdala activation in response to pictures of people displaying the facial expression of terror means that subjects in the scanner are themselves experiencing fear.[14] Indeed, Scott Rauch and his colleagues reported that Vietnam veterans with posttraumatic stress disorder (PTSD) exhibited heightened amygdala responses to fearful faces relative to happy faces even when these pictures were presented too rapidly to be consciously identified.[15] Because most people encounter terrified faces far less frequently than smiling ones in everyday life, heightened responses to the physical configuration of a terrified face likely reflects novelty, not fear in the subjects themselves.

The term "fear" does not have a unitary referent, and the source of evidence for assigning this predicate (e.g., self-report, brain scans, peripheral psychophysiology, behavioral avoidance) requires specification, as does the species and the context.[16] Fear denotes a family of related states, not a single, unvarying state occurring unaltered across contexts, inciting stimuli, and species.

WHEN DOES FEAR BECOME DISORDERED?

Psychologists recognize that fear and anxiety are usually adaptive states that likely fostered survival throughout the course of evolution. Accordingly, the presence of fear or anxiety does not itself signify disorder.

So, if these emotions are ordinarily adaptive, when do they become anxiety *disorders*? Clinicians recognize that the boundary between normal and abnormal fear is fuzzy. But they have articulated guidelines for making this distinction. First, the degree of anxiety or fear is disproportionate to the magnitude of the threat. Hence, the person either overestimates the likelihood of the feared event's occurrence, exaggerates how bad it would be if it did occur, or both. That is, the degree of threat is a multiplicative function of the probability of an event and its negative valence (its "badness"). Anxiety-disordered people either explicitly or implicitly overestimate probability, exaggerate negative valence, or both.

Consider a person with obsessive-compulsive disorder (OCD) who fearfully avoids touching a public toilet seat because of concern about contracting AIDS. Although the negative valence of contracting AIDS is, indeed, marked, the probability of one becoming infected in this manner is vanishingly small. Or a person with social phobia may dread speaking in public because of concern that others will notice his sweating and trembling hands. Yet even if the audience members do detect these signs of fear, their having done so is not the catastrophe envisioned by the socially anxious speaker. Hence, fear or anxiety is excessive when the person either overestimates the probability of the event, exaggerates its negative valence, or both.

Yet even if a person's fear and anxiety is disproportionate to the magnitude of threat, he or she still does not qualify for an anxiety disorder. According to the fourth edition of the *Diagnostic and Statistical Manual of Mental Disorders (DSM-IV-TR)*, the fear, anxiety, and avoidance of threat must be persistent, and it must either cause significant distress for the individual, impair his or her functioning in everyday life, or both.[17] For example, a man might have an intense fear of driving an automobile in snowy weather because of concern about losing control and crashing. This persistent fear could severely impair his life as long as he lives in northern New England, thereby qualifying him for a diagnosis of specific phobia of driving. Yet if he were to move to Miami, he would suddenly be cured of his anxiety disorder because his intense fear would have no impairing impact on his life in Florida.

On the face of it, reliance upon impairment seems a bit strange. In other areas of medicine, doctors conduct laboratory tests to confirm or rule out the presence of disease. Moreover, a person could be entirely asymptomatic and still have a disease. Consider a woman with a silent, undetected cancer. Despite the absence of current impairment, we would not hesitate to diagnose disease following a positive biopsy. Psychiatric disorders are not like this, at least not yet. We do not have confirmatory tests, and many symptoms lie on a continuum with normal emotion. In the case of cancer, our knowledge about the likely progression of a malignant tumor permits us to forecast the subsequent emergence of serious impairment.

The *DSM-IV-TR* permits diagnosis of anxiety disorder when people endorse sufficient persistent symptoms and either significant impairment results or the person experiences significant distress about the symptoms ("meta-distress"?). The latter proviso is also a bit odd, and it differs from what we find in the rest of medicine. Whether someone is distressed about a malignant tumor has no bearing on our diagnosing disease.

WHAT ARE THE TYPES OF ANXIETY DISORDER?

All anxiety disorders involve disproportionate, persistent, impairing fear and anxiety. Yet these features can appear in distinct ways, as embodied in the different categories of anxiety disorder. Many people with anxiety disorders, especially in clinical settings, qualify for more than one disorder, and many have suffered from depression as well. In the sections below, I briefly describe salient features of certain anxiety disorders, and I mention certain aspects that illuminate our understanding of fear in general.

Panic Disorder and Agoraphobia

Panic disorder is the prototype of disordered fear.[18] It is characterized by panic attacks, episodes of terror that seemingly "come out of the blue" and that do not seem to be caused by any obvious external precipitant. Panic attacks begin abruptly and reach peak intensity within seconds or minutes.

Panic attacks are marked by intense physiological sensations, including dyspnea (difficulty breathing and feelings of suffocation), a pounding or rapid heart rate, dizziness, faintness, nausea, feeling disconnected from one's body (depersonalization) or one's environment (derealization), hot or cold flashes, paresthesias (tingling sensations), and thoughts that one is about to collapse, faint, die from a heart attack, or "go crazy."

Panic attacks do not last very long. Most wane within minutes, leaving the person emotionally drained and shaken. Yet despite their brevity, panic attacks can dominate a person's life. Or, more precisely, anxiety about being mugged by subsequent attacks can ruin the quality of a person's life, especially if the sufferer begins to avoid public situations where panic might occur.

Panic disorder usually begins with these sudden, "spontaneous" panics that strike out of the blue. Yet after awhile, people with panic disorder notice that attacks are more likely to occur in some places rather than others. They may develop anticipatory anxiety about having a panic attack when they enter shopping malls, drive on the expressway during rush hour, attend movies, concerts, or church, use a crowded elevator, fly on an airplane, or travel unaccompanied by a trusted friend or family member. What unites these otherwise diverse settings is that they are difficult to escape from gracefully should panic suddenly strike. When avoidance becomes widespread, a diagnosis of panic disorder with agoraphobia is warranted.

The term "agoraphobia"—fear of the agora, or marketplace—is a misnomer. Agoraphobic individuals do not fear marketplaces or other open spaces; they fear having a panic attack in them. That is why psychologists call agoraphobia a "fear of fear."[19]

Agoraphobia at its worst can result in the person being housebound. But even remaining in the safety of one's home does not preclude panic attacks. Many people with panic disorder will awaken from sleep in the midst of panic.

There are several theories about what has gone wrong in panic disorder, but none commands universal assent in psychiatry and clinical psychology. According to David Barlow, panic is misreleased fear.[20] The psychobiological mechanisms that activate the fight or flight defensive response of fear are triggered despite the absence of danger. A spontaneous panic attack is a kind of false alarm. Individuals with panic disorder then learn to respond fearfully to bodily sensations associated with previous panics, and this can lead to subsequent panic attacks or learned alarms.

According to Donald Klein, spontaneous panic is not simply fear.[21] Rather, he argues, it results from derangement in a suffocation alarm system. Klein says that spontaneous panics, in contrast to ordinary fear, are marked by intense dyspnea, and that these feelings of suffocation incite hyperventilation and fear. In other words, terror and rapid breathing are expectable reactions to stimuli signifying imminent suffocation. So, for example, if patients with panic disorder are asked to inhale air enriched with carbon dioxide, they experience dyspnea and often panic. Klein suspects that brainstem circuits mediating respiration are the source of the dysfunction and correcting these with medication resets the suffocation alarm system, preventing it from inappropriately firing and resulting in panic.

In contrast to Klein's physiocentric theory of panic, David Clark believes that panic attacks result from the catastrophic misinterpretation of benign bodily sensations as harbingers of imminent danger.[22] For example, a person might notice skipped heartbeats and misconstrue them as indicative of an impending heart attack. This catastrophic misinterpretation will increase fear, which, in turn, worsens the palpitations, thereby seemingly confirming the correctness of the appraisal. A vicious circle of sensation, misinterpretation, fear, and worsened sensation eventually culminates in a full-blown panic attack. According to Clark, the dysfunction is a cognitive one, not a physiologic one. Retraining people to interpret their bodily sensations in a more benign fashion ought to correct the problem, thereby preventing further panic attacks.

Not everyone is equally likely to respond fearfully to his or her bodily sensations and panic. People scoring high on the Anxiety Sensitivity Index, a questionnaire tapping fears, concerns, and negative beliefs about the meaning of bodily sensations associated with fear, are especially likely to panic.[23] Just as some people are more prone than others to experience episodes of anxiety (i.e., elevated trait anxiety), so are some people more prone than others to experience fear in response to anxiety symptoms themselves (i.e., elevated anxiety sensitivity).[24] Moreover, although often worsened by the experience of panic, elevated anxiety sensitivity often precedes the experience of panic, thereby constituting a cognitive risk factor for panic and other anxiety disorders.[25]

For a diagnosis of panic disorder, panic attacks, including spontaneous ones, must be persistent, and the person must live in dread of subsequent attacks or restrict his or her life as a result of them. In other words, panic attacks per se do not equal the diagnosis; the fear of panic must also be present.

Depending on one's theory, panic attacks may or may not be instances of objectless fear. Klein's suffocation false alarm theory regards the state of terror as a natural consequence of dysregulated respiratory mechanisms signaling the absence of oxygen. The automatic triggering of fear is a consequence of an evolved adaptive mechanism that is not working properly.

Barlow's false alarm theory likewise implies the faulty triggering of an adaptive mechanism. He does not conjecture, however, where the problem may lie and accordingly comes close to redescribing the very phenomenon he endeavors to explain. To say that a spontaneous panic attack results from the misfiring of our adaptive fear mechanism does not provide a deeper account of what has gone wrong.

Clark's cognitive theory differs from Klein's and Barlow's by specifying the reasons, not just the causes, of panic. Panic results from a logical deduction from an incorrect premise. The incorrect premise is that certain bodily sensations indicate the imminent occurrence of a catastrophe. The dysfunction in panic is interpretive, and it presupposes (faulty) knowledge about how heart attacks occur. No animal model can capture this process.

Of course, the appraisal of bodily sensations as harbingers of impending collapse, heart attack, and so forth may play no causal role at all in the emergence of a full-blown panic attack. The cognitive aspects of panic may merely be the epiphenomenal correlates accompanying an autonomous, unfolding biological process.

Social Phobia (Social Anxiety Disorder)

People with social phobia fear and avoid situations or activities where they may suffer embarrassment, humiliation, or negative evaluation by others. Fearing that others will see them as anxious, weak, and incompetent, they experience intense symptoms of fear whenever they are about to enter a social evaluative situation. Characteristic symptoms include trembling, blushing, "butterflies" in the stomach, and feeling tongue-tied and inarticulate. Their fear that others will notice their distress only tends to make the symptoms worse.

The focus of dread in social phobia is negative evaluation by others. Any situation that may result in critical scrutiny by others can be very difficult for people with social phobia. So, for example, many people with this disorder avoid doing things in the presence of others, such as drinking, eating, or signing credit card slips. They fear that they will make a fool out of themselves by spilling food or drink or that others will regard them with scornful contempt should their hands tremble while they write.

Although some people with social phobia fear and avoid only circumscribed situations, such as public speaking, many others experience intense anxiety in a wide range of social interactional contexts, such as asking for directions, asking someone out for a date, engaging in conversation, attending parties, meeting strangers, and interacting with authority figures. People with this generalized form of social phobia may have deficits in social skills and exhibit awkwardness and uncertainty about what to say and do in social settings.

Once deemed rare, recent epidemiologic studies suggest that social phobia is common in the general population.[26] The massive increase in the prevalence of the disorder has provoked skeptical critiques. Some skeptics believe that mental health professionals, epidemiologists, and especially officials of the pharmaceutical industry are medicalizing shyness.[27]

However, unambiguous cases of social phobia exhibit marked impairment in their educational, occupational, and personal lives. Longing to bond with others but fearful of rejection, people with social phobia suffer from aching loneliness and can develop depression.

Animal models of social phobia have limited relevance. Rodents lack the cortical machinery essential for self-representation. The capacity to develop and evaluate cognitive representations of oneself is essential for the emotions integral to social phobia. People with social phobia do not fear physical harm from others. They fear experiencing embarrassment, shame, and rejection by others. A mouse, however timid, cannot experience embarrassment or shame.

Specific Phobia

Specific fears and phobias are common in the general population but much less so in the clinic. Most people with this problem either endure it with distress or find ways to avoid their phobic stimulus in everyday life. Only when their fear becomes intolerable or seriously impairing do they seek treatment.

There are several subtypes of specific phobia. The *animal* subtype includes phobias of spiders, mice, insects, dogs, and snakes. People with animal phobia usually say that they have feared the animal for as long as they can remember, thereby implying an early childhood onset. Although in rare instances, the person might have had an actual painful encounter with the animal (e.g., being bitten by a dog as a child), this is usually not the case.[28] More often, the person recalls having experienced inexplicable terror upon encountering the creature early in childhood.

Psychologists have often assumed that animal phobias result from Pavlovian fear conditioning episodes. They have drawn parallels between a state of fear in a rat evoked by a tone that had previously preceded electric shock and a state of fear evoked in a person who has stumbled across a snake in the woods. There is, however, one key difference. The rat fears the tone because it has predicted electric shock. Yet most people with animal phobias have never been exposed to the real-life counterpart of the electric shock. The animal they now fear has attacked few. This fact has provoked disagreement about what counts as a Pavlovian fear conditioning episode sufficient to establish a phobia for spiders, for example.[29] Some psychologists regard the original, sudden outburst of terror exhibited by the child when he or she first encounters the animal to count as a conditioning episode. Other psychologists argue that this claim begs the question: Why did the child exhibit terror in the first place? There is nothing in these episodes like the electric shock experienced by the rat in the laboratory. Indeed, this would be akin to a tone eliciting fear in the rat before the tone was ever paired with shock.

According to the preparedness theory of phobias, fears of snakes and spiders reflect an evolved disposition for people to acquire fears of stimuli that would have posed threats to our ancestors throughout the course of natural history. Rapidly learning to fear these creatures presumably conferred fitness benefits. The preparedness theory, however, still requires some kind of conditioning episode and thus encounters the problem of the missing unconditioned stimulus. Moreover, some widely feared creatures pose little threat to human beings.[30] Only 0.1 percent of all varieties of spiders pose dangers for human beings.[31] Spiders are at far greater risk for dying at the hands (or feet) of people than vice versa.

The nonassociative theory of fear provides yet another evolutionary account of these phobias.[32] These fears are deemed innate and hence require no unconditioned stimuli to establish them. Nonassociative theorists do not ask why some people have acquired these fears but rather ask why some people have failed to lose these early childhood fears. However, a problem with this account is that it seems to redescribe rather than solve the problem. Saying that the fear is innate seems to be merely another way of saying that no conditioning episode has been detected in the lives of phobic individuals.

Yet another possibility is that certain perceptual features may be hardwired to elicit fear. Among these might be discrepancy from the human form and rapid or otherwise unpredictable movement.[33] These perceptual features may themselves have evolved as elicitors of fear, and their chance coalescence in the form of spiders may render this category of animal especially feared despite its relative harmlessness. Another possibility is that emotions other than fear per se, such as disgust, motivate fear of spiders and other insects. Of course, why they might incite disgust remains a matter of speculation.[34]

Animal phobia is the prototype of the irrational fear. The phobic person knows that the spider is harmless but nevertheless responds with terror. Why? Investigators have queried patients with animal phobia regarding what they fear might happen should they have an unavoidable encounter with their feared animal. Their responses are illuminating. In one study, less than half said that they feared that the animal might harm them.[35] Others said they simply feared experiencing terror itself, a fact that leaves unexplained why they would experience fear in the first place when no threat is present. Others reported distress at the physical properties of the animal itself, such as its perceived sliminess, its abrupt movements, or the prospect of it touching one's skin. These reactions are akin to noncognitive sensory aversions (e.g., the distress experienced by someone scratching fingernails on a chalkboard or the shivers experienced by some people upon touching a peach or cotton). Of course, the reasons that people generate for their behavior need not illuminate the true causes of the phobia.

Blood phobia is relatively common in the clinic as well as in the community. People with this problem often faint upon encountering blood-related stimuli, and hence their fear and avoidance of these stimuli have a rational basis. These individuals fear fainting in the presence of blood, and faint is precisely what they do.[36]

Unlike other people with anxiety disorders, those with blood phobia experience a sudden drop in blood pressure and heart rate (after first experiencing a brief increase) upon encountering their feared stimuli. It is the sudden drop in blood pressure that triggers fainting.

Having blood drawn is the prototypical phobic situation for people with this problem. Others include receiving injections, having dental work done, seeing a child's bloody nose, and viewing a gruesome film. Blood phobia can be impairing because it can motivate avoidance of needed medical and dental treatment, and it can cause problems for those seeking a career in health services. Its impairing consequences notwithstanding, it stands out among the anxiety disorders as having a rational basis.

Fear of flying in airplanes is another common situational phobia. Although both claustrophobic and agoraphobic people also fear and avoid flight, their motivation for doing so differs from that of the situationally phobic person.[37] What their fears are about differ. Those with specific phobia of flying dread crashing, whereas those with agoraphobia dread panicking while aloft.

Flight phobia illustrates how the intentional content of fear—what it is about—can vary dramatically, behavioral and physiological similarities notwithstanding. It also illustrates how poorly people calculate risk of harm. Actuarial estimates indicate that if one were only able to die in an airplane crash, and therefore continue living until this fatal crash occurred, the average person would live to be one million years old.[38]

People with flight phobia are not the only ones who miscalculate risk. During the autumn of 2001, many Americans opted to drive rather than fly, apparently out of fear of another airborne terrorist event. Yet driving is far more hazardous than flying. Although there were no more al-Qaeda plane hijackings that fall, traffic fatalities skyrocketed.[39] Indeed, human beings tend to overestimate the probability of dangers that are salient, horrific, and that easily come to mind.

Obsessive-Compulsive Disorder

OCD is characterized by intrusive, recurrent thoughts, images, or impulses that heighten anxiety, fear, or distress. Usually the person realizes that the obsessions are absurd, repugnant, and unrealistic. The most frequent obsessions concern contamination (e.g., coming into contact with germs by handling a doorknob, contracting AIDS by touching a toilet seat), doubt (e.g., fearing that one may either have failed to perform an important action, such as locking the door before leaving home or turning off the gas on the stove, or thinking one may have inadvertently performed a terrible act, such as running over a pedestrian while driving one's car), symmetry (e.g., concern that the pictures on the wall are misaligned), aggressive impulses or images (e.g., fear that one may murder one's infant), blasphemy (e.g., feeling that one is about to curse aloud in church), or sex (e.g., recurrent images of personally repugnant sexual activities). Although people with OCD acknowledge that their obsessions have arisen in their own mind rather than believing that they have been inserted by some alien force as do psychotic patients, they nevertheless regard them as ego-dystonic or alien to their character.

Obsessions are experienced as involuntary, whereas compulsions are somewhat under the person's control. Compulsions are thoughts or actions that the person feels compelled to perform to reduce the distress associated with an obsession, to prevent a feared disaster from occurring, or both. Hence, people with contamination obsessions repeatedly wash their hands. People with doubting obsessions will repeatedly check to ensure that the door is truly locked or repeatedly retrace their driving route to ensure that they have not run over any pedestrians. People with symmetry obsessions continually rearrange things so that these objects are ordered just so. Those with harming obsessions may think certain thoughts that "neutralize" their homicidal obsessions, and these cognitive compulsive rituals have the same anxiety-reducing function as do behavioral rituals such as washing and checking.

OCD illustrates why self-reports are essential for understanding anxiety and the anxiety disorders.[40] The content of obsessions can only be ascertained this way. Neuroimaging methods, behavioral observation, and so forth cannot distinguish between the intrusive thought that one may murder one's infant and intrusive thoughts about contamination.

Generalized Anxiety Disorder

People with generalized anxiety disorder (GAD) suffer from excessive and unrealistic worry about numerous matters. To qualify for the diagnosis, a person must have experienced anxiety and worry on more days than not for at least six months, and he or she must have at least three of the following symptoms: feeling on edge, keyed up, or restless; becoming easily fatigued; having difficulty concentrating or having one's mind go blank; irritability; tense muscles; and having difficulty either falling asleep or staying asleep or failing to be rested after having slept. Finally, they must experience difficulty controlling their worry.

Although many people with other anxiety disorders also qualify for GAD, for a diagnosis of GAD to be warranted, the person's worry must not be restricted to the primary concern of another disorder (e.g., being embarrassed in social phobia; having a panic attack). The concerns that trouble people with GAD are usually similar to those of most people (e.g., relationships, career, children, finances). However, in GAD the anxious expectation of harm is disproportionate to the likelihood of the threat materializing, and worry is difficult to control.

GAD is resistant to animal modeling. The capacity to envision one's self being exposed to threats lying in the future is a capacity that lies beyond the abilities of mice and rats. To be sure, unpredictable shocks might produce an aversive state of arousal in rats trapped in the context where the shocks have been occurring. But they are also continuously exposed to stimuli associated with the shocks. GAD, in contrast, involves creating cognitive representations of the future and its threat irrespective of the immediate stimulus context. The person with GAD suffers in ways unavailable to a mouse.

GAD illustrates the difficulties distinguishing between normal distress and psychopathology. That is, it raises the question of whether GAD is merely an extreme point on a continuous dimension of trait anxiety or whether it is a discrete categorical syndrome, as the *DSM-IV-TR* characterizes it.

Posttraumatic Stress Disorder

PTSD can develop in people exposed to terrifying, often life-threatening events, such as combat, violent assaults, including rape, and natural disasters. Seeing others exposed to these events can sometimes cause PTSD in the witness. Unlike the other anxiety disorders, PTSD specifies an etiologic event essential for assigning the diagnosis: exposure to trauma. And the person must also have reacted to this event with fear, horror, or helplessness during the trauma.

PTSD is a disorder of pathological memory.[41] Without a memory of trauma, there can be no PTSD. Thus, the person is exposed to a trauma, encodes it in memory, and then this memory produces the characteristic signs and symptoms of the disorder. There is no convincing evidence that people "repress" or become incapable of recalling their most horrific experiences.[42] Indeed, in PTSD, they remember them all too well.

PTSD symptoms are grouped in three clusters. The reexperiencing cluster comprises intrusive, distressing thoughts about the trauma; trauma-related nightmares; heightened distress and physiological reactivity (e.g., increased heart rate) in response to reminders of the trauma and "flashbacks"—recollections so vivid that it seems as if the event were occurring once again.

The second cluster comprises symptoms of avoidance and numbing. Sufferers of PTSD do not relish being haunted by recollections of trauma, and so they try their best to avoid reminders of the trauma. Hence, war veterans may avoid talking about combat, or rape survivors may avoid wearing clothes they wore during the assault. Some individuals with PTSD may experience a foreshortened future, believing that the hazardous unpredictability of life precludes them imagining how their lives will unfold months or years later. They may also report emotional numbing characterized by difficulty experiencing positive feelings toward others and by difficulty enjoying previously pleasurable activities.

The third cluster includes symptoms of heightened arousal. Among these are irritability, exaggerated startle reactions, problems concentrating, and difficulty falling or staying asleep.

Symptoms must be present for at least one month and must result in functional impairment, marked distress, or both to warrant the diagnosis. These requirements are designed to distinguish normal emotional reactions to horrific events from a pathological response characterized by impairing symptoms that persist long after the event has occurred.

PTSD differs from the other anxiety disorders in that it concerns the past rather than the future. Panic disorder, social phobia, GAD, and so forth involve distress in the present evoked by the person's envisioning a future threat about to occur very soon (e.g., collapse in panic disorder) or later (e.g., fear that one's job is in peril in GAD). The temporal focus in PTSD is the past and, more specifically, the past as intruding on the present.

This brief survey of how fear is conceptualized by clinical psychologists and psychiatrists is perforce synoptic. Moreover, my highly selective review of issues and controversies barely scratches the surface of this diverse and ever-changing field. Indeed, space limitations preclude discussion of the cognitive-behavioral therapies that now dominate the therapeutic landscape of anxiety disorders. None is a panacea, but all enjoy the evidential support of randomized controlled trials, the gold standard for gauging treatment efficacy in medicine.[43] Medications remain popular, but their efficacy rarely surpasses that of cognitive-behavioral therapy in the short term, and their lasting benefit remains uncertain.

The American Psychiatric Association is in the midst of revising the *DSM-IV-TR*, ostensibly guided by the massive amount of data published since the fourth edition of the manual appeared in 1994. The fifth edition is scheduled to appear in May 2013. At the outset of the revision process, some scholars hoped that neuroimaging, genomics, and cognitive science would permit the conceptualization of mental disorders in terms of their etiology and pathophysiology as well as their signs and symptoms.[44] It appears that this is unlikely to occur. Science has advanced but not to the extent whereby findings in neuroscience, genomics, and so forth replicate with the consistency needed to transform the diagnostic system from a purely descriptive one to one emphasizing etiology and pathophysiology. However, tinkering with diagnostic criteria will likely occur, as every *DSM* committee seems committed to putting its distinctive stamp on how we diagnose mental disorders.

One of the most persistent problems in psychiatric nosology, especially in the anxiety disorders area, concerns comorbidity. For the sake of expositional clarity, I discussed each discrete syndrome as a self-contained categorical entity, reflecting how they appear in the *DSM-IV-TR*. Yet most people suffering from one anxiety disorder qualify for others as well. Such rampant comorbidity has raised questions about whether a person who meets criteria for social anxiety disorder and GAD, for example, "really" has two distinct disorders or whether he or she suffers from some more fundamental entity, such as heightened negative affectivity, that manifests itself in diverse ways. Some scholars believe that anxiety disorders vary along certain dimensions, differing by degree rather than by kind.

Until very recently, no one has offered a convincing resolution to the category versus dimension debate in psychiatric nosology until Denny Borsboom and his colleagues cut the Gordian knot by reconceptualizing disorders as networks of functionally interrelated symptoms rather than as inferred latent entities (categories or dimensions) that serve as common causes producing clusters of functionally independent symptoms.[45] Their work is too new to permit judgment of its impact on a field accustomed to interpreting symptoms as arising from an underlying, unseen, and inferred disease entity.

2

THE BIOLOGY OF FEAR
EVOLUTIONARY, NEURAL, AND PSYCHOLOGICAL PERSPECTIVES

Arne Öhman

FORMER U.S. PRESIDENT George Herbert Walker Bush and federal funding agencies dubbed the 1990s the Decade of the Brain.[1] Indeed, thanks to an increase in funding and publicity there was a rare explosion in knowledge and research techniques about what is conventionally called "higher nervous activity." Partly as a follow-up, partly out of a concern that other aspects of brain activity had gotten short shrift during the so-called Decade of the Brain, and partly to shift attention back to the Decade of Behavior (2000–2010), a group of leading U.S. scientists in 2007 published a manifesto in *Science*, demanding a Decade of the Mind for the years 2010–2020. The premise for this initiative of scientists from disciplines as varied as cognitive science, psychology, neuroscience, medicine, computer science, engineering, and mathematics is that "a deep scientific understanding of how the mind perceives, thinks, and acts is within our grasp"; the initiative further proposes that "research should be encouraged on all aspects of the mind believed to be uniquely human, such as the notion of self, rational thought processes, theory of mind, language, and higher order consciousness."[2]

Emotion is part and parcel of "how the mind perceives, thinks, and acts." Our understanding of emotion, and particularly the emotion of fear, has been revolutionized during the last couple of decades. Before research on fear gets another boost during the Decade of the Mind, it makes sense to take stock and survey what has been done so far. The purpose of this chapter, then, is to present the current knowledge of fear in psychology, neuroscience, and the theory of evolution. The chapter is organized topically around a number of propositional statements about fear, some of which are primarily conceptual and theoretical, while others grew out of empirical research.

FEAR IS AN EMOTION

Fear is a state that is all too familiar to many of us. Fear is an emotion—few would argue with this proposition. But what kind of emotion? According to one contemporary definition of emotion, they "are multi-component responses to challenges or opportunities that are important to the individual's goals."[3] A "multi-component response" in this context refers to components of feeling (conveyed through verbal reports), bodily activation (e.g., heart-rate changes), and behavior (e.g., approach or avoidance). Fear is the paradigmatic emotion evoked by challenges perceived as threatening. The dominating feeling of fear is an intense urge to get out of the situation.[4] Thus, flight is a dominant behavioral response to fearful circumstances, and because it taxes metabolic resources, fear typically includes an activated body. In humans, flight does not have to mean "running away"; it can also occur on a symbolic level, as in attempts to evade a disturbing thought by trying to focus attention on something else.

FEAR IS FUNCTIONAL

Many of us would prefer a life with much less fear because we perceive most of the fear that we experience as irrational, as limiting our choices, and as detrimental to our well-being. Indeed, a hallmark of anxiety disorders, which may afflict up to 25 percent of human populations, is that they involve fear that is out of proportion to the objective danger of the situation. Nevertheless, in a broader perspective fear is functional: it is deeply rooted in biological evolution.[5] The primary function of fear is to foster coping with stimuli that are perceived as dangerous in a psychological or physical sense. Fear is predicated on a perception or a belief that something can be done about the situation, and it motivates coping behavior that is appropriate in view of this perception. Fear, if you will, includes an element of hope. If nothing can be done to alleviate the threat—in situations of helplessness—fear turns into a different emotion that is best termed "anxiety."

The Evolutionary Origin of Fear

The pillar of biological evolution is the transport of genes across generations. Hence our preoccupation with procreation: partners, sex, pair-bonding, children. But to enjoy these delights we must survive in often hazardous environments. Microorganisms can invade us, substances mistaken as nutritious can poison us, predators can attack us, we can drown in water, get crushed by falling rocks and trees, burned by fire, or caught in avalanches, and last but not least, other humans can attack, abuse, or even kill us. Thus, a repertoire of defense responses is a prerequisite for individuals to survive and maintain their capacity to project genes into coming generations. Such defense behavior provides the evolutionary origin of fear. Indeed, predation is a central force in evolution, not only an origin in what we experience as fear. At many junctures in evolution, small predators have served as pioneers of new adaptations that conferred selective advantage to predation.[6] These innovations put pressure on prey animals to evolve new defenses, and in this way predator-prey arms races have been repeatedly initiated, resulting in accelerated general evolutionary change.

Ernst Mayr, a leading theorist of evolution, suggested that behavior may be classified according to the type of environment it was historically directed toward: physical surroundings; members of other species (e.g., predators, prey); individuals of one's own species (e.g., sex, offspring, social hierarchies).[7] One of his points was that the two first categories were likely to depend on learning about the environment, whereas the third category, social behavior, was likely to be more rigidly genetically programmed because it relies on social signaling that must be unequivocally understood for necessary social activities to function smoothly. Sex is a case in point because it rests on the mutual understanding of an often subtle language of social signals, which effectively excludes those that fail to master it from access to the gene pool of the species.

Humans, to be sure, are eminently flexible, and this flexibility, epitomized in language, makes human social behavior unique. And yet, humans not only talk to each other but they also communicate on a more basic nonverbal level. This communication often takes place outside of awareness but may nonetheless have important consequences for the mutual understanding resulting from an encounter. There is, for example, significant evidence that human facial expression includes a set of basic emotions that are cross-culturally recognized and understood.[8]

More to the point for the present discussion, Mayr provides a classification of defense and fear that partly overlaps with contemporary classifications of phobias ("irrational, debilitating fear of specific situations or events") and is hence worth citing: nature phobias (e.g., thunder and lightening, heights, water, fire); animal phobias (e.g., snakes, spiders, cats, dogs); social phobia (e.g., superiors, situations of social evaluation such as social gatherings, public speaking, and so on). This is consistent with the idea that phobias result from evolutionarily primed learning to fear situations and events that have incurred significant danger on life and safety throughout evolution.[9]

Fear Provides Motivation for Defensive Action

The evolutionary perspective situates the origins of fear in prehistoric times and assigns to it a central role in the defense against life threats to organisms. With very primitive organisms, it is reasonable to talk about fearless defense, because their defense maneuvers were primitive and highly reflexive (and their nervous systems incapable of anything remotely resembling organized emotion). The evolution of more advanced mammalian brains brought about the insertion of motivational states between the perception of potentially threatening circumstances and the activation of defensive responses. Fear is such a motivational state. Its functional advantage is to allow more flexible exploitation of the actual situation before a defense strategy is chosen. And yet there is a delicate balance to strike here. Clearly, time is a central factor for the success of a defense maneuver; the faster its activation, the better its chances of success. However, if, for instance, very rapidly activated flight inadvertently delivers the animal into the claws of a previously unnoticed partner of an attacking predator, disaster is likely. Still, if the evoked fear is very intense, our brains bet on its evolutionary, time-proven strategies by downregulating its most advanced part, the frontal cortex, thus delegating to more primitive subcortical structures the organization of rapid defense.[10] This is why a panic-stricken person gives bad advice.

At first glance the proposition that fear is an emotion and the statement that fear provides motivation for action may seem hardly distinguishable. Clearly, "emotion" and "motivation" are related terms, and indeed, the present zeitgeist favors the blurring of the distinction between the two. I believe, however, that the two ought to be separated. Motivation is best understood to refer to internal states that activate and channel behavior in functional directions. Emotion, on the other hand, typically refers to responses to stimuli that are relevant for the present concerns of the individual. For example, we respond more emotionally to food items when we are hungry than full. Indeed, it has been proposed that the basic function of emotion is to give value to stimuli.[11] Thus, while motivation pushes, emotion-evoking stimuli pull (or repel). Seen this way, motivation and emotion can be understood as different aspects of processes that are crucial for honoring goals that are central to adaptive functioning.

Defensive Behavior

Remnants of primitive defense reflexes are still observable in the classification of mammalian fear behavior. Immobility or "freezing" is a stop, look, and listen response, which may go back to the diving reflex of early amphibians.[12] It gives camouflage because primitive predators primarily responded to movement, and it allows time to scan the environment for escape routes. Flight is the typical response when fear is elicited. Its functional significance is obvious: it introduces distance and preferably obstacles between the organism and the source of threat. If possible, the escape route is not random but directed toward safe havens, a nest, kin, hiding places. If flight is not possible and the threat acute—say, a predator or member of one's own species is about to attack—the remaining option is to fight. Defensive aggression is a very old evolutionary invention emerging from the interaction between prey and predator. This context is critical here because it presumes that this type of aggression is based on fear. Often there is oscillation between flight and fight within a fear context. For example, when a chase results in the cornering of the victim no option remains but to resort to violence, the goal of which is to pave the way for new episodes of flight that may end in new fights and so on. In humans, this type of fear-driven oscillation between evasion and attack often takes place at a symbolic, linguistic level.

Defensive aggression should be distinguished from the within-species aggression inherent in social hierarchies in which high-ranking members assert their dominance by threatening gestures or actual aggressive acts. The targets of these acts show signs of (often intense) fear, but rather than resorting to defensive aggression they typically respond with gestures suggesting subordination, submission, and withdrawal, eventually, perhaps, to flee the scene. Thus, there is a ritualistic, symbolic aspect to fear and aggression in the intraspecific context of dominance conflicts that is lacking in the interspecific context of encounters between prey and predators. Indeed, most scientists reserve the term "aggression" for the emotion and behavior expressed by dominant individuals (and individuals seeking dominance) in the intraspecific context. Predation is not driven by aggression but by the reward value of a meal.

Conflicts between Evolutionary and Cultural Agendas

The evolutionary agenda may come in conflict with the individual's plans and what he or she perceives as the immediate requirements and opportunities of a given situation. Because evolution has given us emotions to make sure that we stick to its agenda, this type of conflict invades the emotional arena; it is typically experienced as a battle between wants and wishes originating in our bodies on the one hand and the restrictions imposed by society on the other hand. For example, a married person who happens to encounter an overwhelmingly attractive potential erotic partner has to resist the emotionally charged evolutionary imperative of procreation, seeking less spectacular emotional support from the socially sanctioned institution of marriage to refrain from adultery. In our cultural settings this type of conflict has often been cast in terms of "lower" emotions versus "higher" reason. In the case of fear this means cowardice versus courage; a coward yields to but a hero resists the flight promoted by the evolutionary shaped emotion of fear. Rather than choosing the response that "comes naturally," the courageous person sacrifices his or her own interest, both in an immediate and long-term genetic perspective, in the service of a higher (but nonetheless often quite obscure) goal. There is a long tradition of interpreting the individual resistance to emotion-driven actions as a mark of wisdom. According to the Stoics, more than two thousand years ago, the good life was to enjoy food, drink, and intellectual exchange in the context of cultivating friendship. But it does not involve being seduced by emotions associated with insatiable desires for ephemeral things—such as wealth, fame, and power.

FEAR MOBILIZES THE BODY: BODILY RESPONSES AND THEIR CONSEQUENCES

Because the basic function of fear is to mobilize defense behavior, an important component of fear is to activate the autonomic nervous system to assure metabolic resources for vigorous action.[13] The autonomic nervous system is composed of the sympathetic and the parasympathetic branches. The former mobilizes metabolic resources, the latter restores them. This psychophysiological side of fear activation provides access to objective measures of fear. For example, rising fear is related to increases in heart rate and blood pressure, as well as increases in palmar sweating, which can be measured electrically via skin conductance responses. But these objective correlates of fear activation also have an experiential side. When in fear, we may feel our heart beating faster and more vigorously than usual.

What is more, these perceived bodily changes can serve as an important source of information for experienced fear. Indeed, in the 1880s William James, the famous American philosopher and psychologist, and Carl Lange, a more obscure Danish physiologist, independently of each other proposed a theory claiming that perception of the bodily response in emotional circumstances actually *is* the emotion: we do not flee the bear because we fear it, but we feel fear because we flee, and it is not sorrow that produce our tears but the tears that produce the sorrow.[14]

This inversion of psychological common sense has had a mixed history in the psychology of emotion. While at certain times it seemed utterly defunct, it later reappeared in different disguises.[15] At present, it is met with increased interest because of findings suggesting a neural substrate for bodily feedback in the anterior insula in the frontal lobes of the brain.[16]

There is also a body of empirical research that suggests a more general role of physiological arousal in emotion. For example, the experience of unexplained arousal (because of an adrenaline injection coupled with false instructions about its effect) appears to make research participants, eager to explain their jerked-up state, very sensitive to environmental context.[17] Strong arousal may subtly spill over to be interpreted in terms of other emotions. For example, in a social psychology experiment young males were met by an attractive young female, allegedly for an interview on scenic attraction as part of a student project, after having crossed a long, narrow, suspense bridge that swayed alarmingly over rocks and

rapids of a river two hundred feet below. Compared to control participants, who had crossed a low, wide, and fixed wood bridge upstream the
river, or who were met by a male interviewer after the suspense bridge,
those met by the female interviewer after the suspense bridge produced
more sexual imagery on a projective test and were more likely to take
advantage of an offer for more information by phoning the interviewer.
Because fear, as we shall see in a moment, can be quite subtly evoked, it
may have a subsidiary role by providing emotional charge to situations
of different valence.[18]

FEAR IS GENERATED BY A SPECIFIC NETWORK IN THE BRAIN

Fear is controlled by a specific neural circuit in the brain that has
been evolutionarily shaped to mediate functional relationships between
threats and defensive behavior. The circuit is organized around the
amygdala (or in the plural, amygdalae), a collection of nuclei in the
anterior medial temporal lobe, which is strategically placed to mediate
between emotional input and output (see fig. 2.1). Its lateral nucleus
receives input from all sensory modalities. Sensory information accesses
the amygdala via two different routes, "a high road" and "a low road."[19]
The high road is the well-known pathways from the sensory receptors
via sensory thalamic nuclei to the primary sensory cortices and associated areas of the cortex, including the prefrontal cortex, that convey
deeply processed information about the world to the brain. However,
lesion studies in animals have demonstrated that cortical processing is
not necessary for auditory or visual information to reach the amygdala
and activate fear responses, thus providing a basis for the concept of a
low road to the amygdala.[20] Human brain imaging data concur that there
is a direct, fast route to the amygdala via thalamic nuclei, which provides
a pathway of crudely processed information that alerts the amygdala to
deal with potentially significant stimuli.[21]

On the basis of the information conveyed by the low road, the amygdala (and particularly its basolateral nuclei) performs a very quick, crude
assessment for threat potential, which is continually updated by incom-
ing information from the high road. This information is conveyed to the
central nucleus, which has efferent connections to nuclei in the hyopo-
thalamus and brainstem that activate emotional output. For example,
emotional behavior (flight, fight, freezing) is controlled from areas in
the upper midbrain. Autonomic responses, mediated by the sympathetic
branch, are activated through connections between the central nucle-

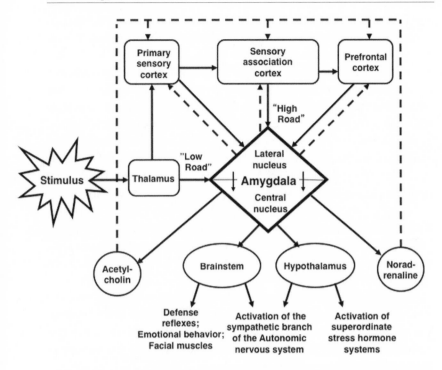

Figure 2.1. A schematic representation of the fear network of the mammalian brain

us and the hypothalamus, an area for control of internal bodily states, whereas parasympathetic effects primarily are mediated from areas in the brainstem. Defensive reflexes (e.g., the startle reflex) and responses of the facial muscles are controlled by connections from the central nucleus to other brainstem nuclei. There is an important link preparing the body for demanding fight or flight that results in the secretion of superordinate stress hormones through the hypothalamic-pituitary hormonal axis. Finally, via connections to nuclei in the forebrain and brainstem, the central nucleus may produce widespread activation of the cortex via activation of cholinergic and noradrenergic pathways, respectively.

FEAR CAN BE ACTIVATED BY STIMULI OF WHICH WE REMAIN UNAWARE

The primary location of the fear network in parts of the brain that emerged at the junction between reptiles and mammals suggests that it is primitive, because the creatures in which it evolved had very little cortex, making little room for cognitive control in its original design. Thus, at the basic level it should be automatic and relatively impenetrable to cognition. Indeed, as Joseph LeDoux has pointed out, there are much more extensive connections from the amygdala to the cortex than the other way around, which suggests that the amygdala has larger impact on the cortex than the cortex has on the amygdala.[22] For example, the amygdala can tune cortical processes at all stages of sensory processing from the primary sensory to the prefrontal cortex, thus biasing interpretation of stimuli and exerting control of attention (broken arrows from amygdala to different cortical regions). Moreover, the concept of the low road suggests that information about potential danger in the world around us may bypass the cortex (and presumably awareness) to activate an internal state of fear and a readiness to respond with fear-related behavior. Nevertheless, there are important connections from the prefrontal cortex to the amygdala that may be used for cognitive based modulation and regulation of fear.

Psychologists have devised several techniques to manipulate research participants' perceptual awareness of stimuli to which they are exposed. One technique that they frequently use is backward masking. It involves a very short (on the order of a few hundredths of a second) presentation of a target stimulus of interest immediately followed by a masking stimulus. For example, the target stimulus could be a word and the masking stimulus a set of letter fragments covering the same area as the word. With a suitable onset difference between these two stimuli (again in the order of one to three hundredths of a second), the mask will block perception of the word. Nevertheless, effects of the masked emotional words can be documented in other measures as increased readiness to interpret stimuli in terms of a congruent emotion. More to the point for the present context, effective fear stimuli, such as pictures of snakes and spiders for snake and spider phobic individuals that are presented and then masked by stimuli of similar colors and texture but without a perceivable central object, elicit both autonomic responses and activation of the amygdala as assessed in a brain scanner, which are substantially larger to the feared than to non-feared control stimuli.[23] These findings have been confirmed by studies using alternative techniques for preventing awareness of stimuli.[24] There are also studies of patients with lesions in areas of primary visual cortices, which make them blind for stimuli falling in these areas—suggesting, again, that cortical processing is not necessary for fear activation. Nevertheless, even though such patients deny perceiving emotional faces presented to a blind cortical field, the amygdala recruits emotional responses to such nonperceived stimuli.[25]

FEAR CAN BE INDUCED BY MANY STIMULI
Situations Feared by Humans

Fear can be elicited by an enormous number of stimuli that often are idiosyncratic for individual persons, which suggests that learning is an important mechanism of selection for what people fear. Conversely, there are few stimuli that researchers can agree are inborn fear stimuli. Nevertheless there are recognizable recurrent themes among fear stimuli, and these themes tend to represent situations of relevance for human evolution in the sense that they are more or less directly related to survival threats. Such themes can be isolated from questionnaire studies of what people report as frightening in large samples of respondents from different countries.[26] One of the most prominent themes, which we have already discussed and that attests to the central importance of the social scene for humans, is "fears concerning interpersonal events or situations." It includes fears of social rejection, criticism, evaluation, and conflicts, but also of being the target of aggression and witnessing scenes of sexual and aggressive content. A second theme is "fears related to death, injuries, illness, blood, and surgical procedures." This theme centers on ailments, illness, life threats, and death. A third theme, which we also already have discussed as predatory fear, concerns "fear of animals," including common domestic animals (dogs, cats, etc.), other small, often harmless animals, and creeping and crawling animals such as insects and reptiles. A fourth theme concerns what might be called "fears of separation from a safe base." It involves fear of entering public places (such as stores or shopping malls) and crowds but also fear of closed spaces (such as elevators, or middle seats in rows at theaters or churches), going to school among children, or places lacking an escape route to a safe haven (such as bridges and tunnels and traveling alone in trains, buses, or airplanes).

Learning to Fear New Stimuli

In spite of the evolutionary ring of these themes, they are not likely to represent inborn fears. Rather they may be cases of evolutionary primed or prepared learning that facilitate fear conditioning to situations that have provided recurrent threats to survival over mammalian and human evolution.[27] Because the function of fear is to promote flight and avoidance of danger and threat, it follows that it must have been advantageous in an evolutionary perspective to be able to acquire fear of stimuli represented in these categories.

In the natural environment danger may be heralded by subtle cues. For example, a predator may provide clues to its presence by faint sounds or odors. When organisms learn that a relatively innocuous stimulus (e.g., a sound) signals the occurrence of a dangerous and potentially life threatening stimulus (e.g., an attacking predator), fear and defense elicited by the predator (the unconditioned stimulus) become transferred to the sound (the conditioned stimulus).[28] In this way an association is formed between the two stimuli such that the conditioned stimulus, when encountered at a later occasion, retrieves a memory of the unconditioned stimulus and a state of fear is activated. This is called Pavlovian fear conditioning after its discoverer, the brilliant Russian Nobel laureate I. P. Pavlov. It is now clear that the molecular machinery of Pavlovian fear conditioning is housed in the basolateral amygdala, and there is an extensive literature documenting that the amygdala is critical for fear conditioning in humans as well as in other animals.[29]

Pavlovian fear conditioning is more open to stimuli that can be viewed as threatening in an evolutionary perspective. For example, when pictures of common phobic objects such as snakes or spiders are presented in conjunction with a mildly aversive stimulus, human research participants show more persisting autonomic conditioned responses than control participants conditioned with the same unconditioned stimulus to neutral pictures.[30] Similar results are obtained with angry as opposed to happy or neutral faces.[31]

Observational and Instructional Fear Acquisition

Fear conditioning may appear a costly method to learn which stimuli signal danger because it appears to require a direct encounter with a potentially deadly unconditioned stimulus. However, such direct conditioning experience is not necessary because similar learning can be obtained simply by observing another individual who is subjected to the contingency between a conditioned and an unconditioned stimulus. Such observational fear conditioning has been extensively documented both in monkeys and humans.[32]

In humans, similar results can be obtained by simply instructing research participants that a particular stimulus will be followed by an aversive event.[33] Indeed, in humans most things feared are likely to have acquired their fear-evoking power primarily through instructions and more often through observational rather than direct Pavlovian fear conditioning. However, while direct and observational learning appear to conform to similar principles, the situation is less clear for instructional learning of fear.[34] Evidence suggests that both direct and observational conditioning accesses a deep fundamental level of fear, which includes the amygdala and does not require conscious mediation. However, this is less clear for instructional fear. Indeed, one interesting possibility is that the learning of fear requires that the situation involves some level of fear expression. Being subjected to pain oneself or seeing someone in pain are situations that involve some degree of emotionality. Instructions, however, may be quite emotional (e.g., through fear expressed by the instructor), but they sometimes may be unemotional or neutral. Indeed, it could be speculated that an origin of the performing arts might be the need to convey what is and what is not emotionally relevant to an audience. By being artfully designed to evoke emotion this message could reach emotions inaccessible to consciousness, and hence it could be more likely to promote learning at the emotional level.

Fear Can Be Conditioned and Expressed to Stimuli That Are Not Consciously Perceived

The discussion of differences between the effects of different types of fear learning relates to our previous discussion that fear can be elicited by stimuli of which one remains unaware. This is consistent with the subcortical low road to the amygdala that provides a neural explanation for the independence of fear evocation and awareness of the eliciting stimulus. From this perspective it should come as no surprise that human conditioned responses can be elicited by conditioned stimuli that have been masked to prevent conscious recognition. A bit more surprising, perhaps, is a finding suggesting that fear can be conditioned to stimuli that are masked from conscious recognition.[35] Thus, after having been exposed to masked presentations of pictures of faces that were followed by a mildly aversive unconditioned stimulus, research participants for whom the masked faces were angry showed enhanced autonomic responses to these pictures when they were presented without masks. Participants exposed to masked happy faces during conditioning, however, did not show such enhanced responses to subsequently presented unmasked faces.[36] Similar results were obtained with potentially phobic pictures such as snakes and spiders (as opposed to neutral stimuli such as pictures of flowers and mushrooms).[37] Thus, somewhat echoing Carl Gustav Jung's concept of archetypes, these data suggest that beasts and angry humans have special access to unconscious mechanisms for evoking and learning about stimuli that are threatening in an evolutionary perspective.

LEARNED FEAR CAN BE EXTINGUISHED

By learning through Pavlovian conditioning and other mechanisms of fear learning, organisms acquire knowledge that allows them to predict when dangerous stimuli will occur. This is a fundamental requirement for improving the coping with danger. However, environments change so that stimuli once predicting potentially harmful events no longer do so. Having fear evoked by such stimuli is wasteful both to mood and metabolic resources.

Adaptive functioning requires a complementary process to Pavlovian fear conditioning for inhibiting fear to stimuli that have lost predictive power in relation to dangerous events. This process, also discovered by Pavlov, is called "extinction," and it is, at the surface level, deceptively simple: Pavlovian conditioned responses wane if the conditioned stimulus is repeatedly presented in the absence of the unconditioned stimulus. This is a powerful principle that is behind the success of different varieties of exposure treatments of anxiety problems.[38] For example, specific phobias for objects that are easily available like small animals (snakes, spiders) or injection needles, which may exclude the sufferer from desirable activities such as nature walks or necessary injections, may be cured within a few hours of intense training to approach and handle the phobic stimulus.[39] Such treatment requires great courage from clients, who will be required to face their fear, and persuasiveness and sensitivity from the therapist to bring the client into treatment and match the tempo of approaching the most fear-inducing acts such as touching the feared animal to the fear expressed by the client.

However, extinction tends to be more ephemeral than conditioning. For example, an extinguished fear response may reappear spontaneously if the conditioned stimulus is reencountered after some period of time. Furthermore, contrary to conditioning, which results in fear to the conditioned stimulus that transcends the context of learning, extinction tends to be specific to the situation of extinction training. It is as if conditioning results in learning a general expectancy that "this cue signals danger," whereas extinction involves the more restricted expectancy that "this cue is safe in this particular context." Consequently, when brought back to the original context of learning, an individual who has extinguished fear in a different context typically shows a full strength conditioned response. This is called "renewal" of the conditioned response. Permanent extinction, therefore, requires that the procedure is carried out in several contexts. An extinguished conditioned response can also be made to reappear by a few presentations of the unconditioned stimulus alone, a procedure that is termed "reinstatement."[40] Collectively, the characteristics of extinction of fear suggest the concept of "evolutionary conservatism,"[41] involving the implicit generalized assumptions that a conditioned fear stimulus is always dangerous but that the lack of danger of an extinguished conditioned fear stimulus is always conditional on context.

Consistent with the concept of spontaneous recovery, renewal, and reinstatement, fear may sometimes return after successful exposure treatments of phobias. Experimental tests demonstrate a significant renewal of self-reported fear after intense exposure therapy with change of treatment room and therapist and a change from one context to another.[42] Therefore, these principles suggest that exposure therapy preferably should be performed in several different contexts.

FEAR LEARNING PROMOTES AVOIDANCE OF DANGER

Pavlovian fear conditioning is a powerful mechanism for extending the range of events that can elicit fear. Because the exposure of the conditioned stimulus retrieves the memory of the unconditioned stimulus before it actually occurs, defense such as flight can be anticipatorily initiated before the danger materializes. For example, animals become able to activate flight on the basis of cues (e.g., smells, sounds) that they have learned announce a predatory attack, which gives an important edge in escaping. By promoting avoidance of stimuli that threaten survival, fear conditioning significantly favored prey at an early stage in the predatory-prey arms race.

Although evolutionarily critical, avoidance guided by conditioned fear is not invariably beneficial. A successful avoidance response saves the organisms from the potentially hazardous effects of the unconditioned fear stimulus. However, this benefit has a price, because it prevents challenges to the belief that the unconditioned fear stimulus will have to be endured unless the response is made. Thus, the organism will not stay long enough in the presence of the conditioned stimulus to discover if the unconditioned fear stimulus is omitted. Therefore, the expectation that avoidance produces in safety is always confirmed. This provides a bias toward playing it safe by always avoiding, and the avoidance response not only avoids the unconditioned stimulus but also the opportunity to check whether the danger is still there. Once one gets started on the track of avoidance, there is a risk of extending this strategy to ever-new situations that have to be avoided, which in the long run will result in severe limitations of one's choices in life.

Extensive and often extreme avoidance is a hallmark of anxiety disorder. But it plagues also many of us who do not fulfill any diagnostic criteria of anxiety disorder. It may breed a false sense of security: if we perform all the rituals of safety nothing bad will happen. We put on helmets when biking, life vests when boating, stop smoking, refrain from alcohol, and exercise diligently, not to speak of the protective measures we impose on our children. But these safety measures hide the sad truth that we have little control over important events in our lives. There is little we can do about the things and events that we fear most: illness, death of kin, accidents, terrorist attacks, and so on. The Swedish comedian Tage Danielsson (who died of cancer) once remarked that nuclear power disasters were comfortably improbable, but at Three Mile Island near Harrisburg the probability of an incidence at that specific place suddenly jumped to 100 percent. In fact, as is readily seen in the aftermath of 9/11, the often draconian defense measures to avoid further terrorist deeds are justified not only by reference to the general fear in the population but also support its maintenance by their intrusiveness. If there is not something to fear, why is it that we are subject to security measures that even run contrary to the democratic principles our leaders say they strive to protect? To paraphrase President Franklin D. Roosevelt, fear itself is often more of a danger than its perceived causes.

HOW DID FEAR BECOME A SCIENTIFIC OBJECT AND WHAT KIND OF OBJECT IS IT?

3

Ruth Leys

WHEN ON SEPTEMBER 11, 2001, terrorists killed more than three thousand people in their attacks on the World Trade Center in New York City, for Americans in particular the world suddenly became a much more frightening place. Insecurity became the norm as the Bush administration's new Department of Homeland Security used its color-coded terror alert system to orchestrate and manipulate the public's fears. Among the many consequences of 9/11 has been the flow of federal funds to scientists committed to finding ways to identify terrorists before they can act. One of those is Paul Ekman, a psychologist who has devoted his career to studying facial expressions and is working on methods of surveillance designed to read the telltale involuntary facial signs that betray the potential terrorist's deadly intentions. Ekman's goal is to reassure us that we don't have to be frightened by the tendency of human beings to dissimulate, because science can be counted on to reliably distinguish authentic facial expressions from false ones, genuine from feigned.[1]

In this chapter I examine the theoretical assumptions and methods informing Ekman's approach to the emotions and facial expression. I offer my analysis as a contribution, from the perspective of the history of the human sciences, to our understanding of one major strand of research in the United States that has helped shaped the science of fear. Ekman's is not the only game in town; in fact, as we shall see, there are signs today of a growing opposition to his research program from within psychology. But for the last thirty years he has exerted, and indeed continues to exert, a powerful influence. Not only do psychologists and neuroscientists routinely cite his experimental findings but, as a consequence of the striking recent growth of interest in the emotions and affect in the humanities and social sciences, his work has begun to attract the attention of scholars in philosophy, political theory, cultural studies, literature, and related fields. Among those who share many of Ekman's presuppositions is the celebrated neuroscientist Antonio Damasio. In the course of this chapter I shall be discussing an important case, investigated by Damasio, Ralph Adolphs, and others, of a young woman who, it has been claimed, is unable to experience fear because she has an abnormal brain. More precisely, the patient suffers from a genetic disorder that causes bilateral calcification of her amygdala, a subcortical group of neurons widely held to be implicated in rapid emotional responses, especially fear. Crucial to Damasio's interpretation of the case has been his use of methods developed by Ekman to test a person's ability to judge emotional expressions. In particular Damasio has employed a set of pictures of people intentionally presenting, that is, posing, such expressions drawn from Ekman's portfolio of such items in order to evaluate the deficits in his amygdala-damaged patient's skill in judging threatening faces.

I find Ekman's pictures at once interesting and puzzling (figs. 3.1 and 3.2). One of my aims is to make such images historically intelligible while also bringing out what seems to me their sheer strangeness as scientific documents.

EMOTIONS AS NONINTENTIONAL STATES: TOMKINS'S AFFECT PROGRAM THEORY

When in the 1960s Ekman began studying nonverbal behavior, including facial expressions, the emotions after years of neglect were just beginning to become a topic of renewed concern among scientists. Ekman started his investigations at a time when one psychologist in particular, Silvan S. Tomkins, was proposing a new way of thinking about the affects. Influenced by several important trends in the human sci-

 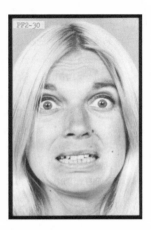

Figures 3.1 and 3.2. From Paul Ekman and Wallace V. Friesen, *Pictures of Facial Affect* (Palo Alto: Consulting Psychologists Press, 1976), reproduced by permission

ences, especially a resurgent interest in Darwinian evolution and the rise of cybernetics, Tomkins turned his back on the then-reigning orthodoxies of psychoanalysis to advocate instead a Darwinian-inspired biological theory of the emotions.

Tomkins argued that there exists a small number of basic emotions defined in evolutionary terms as universal or pancultural adaptive responses of the organism.[2] He proposed that there were eight or nine such basic emotions, namely, fear, anger, distress, disgust, interest, shame, joy, and surprise. (He later added contempt.) Tomkins described the basic emotions as discrete, hardwired, reflex-like "affect programs" located in the subcortical parts of the brain. He believed that each discrete emotion manifested itself in distinct physiological and behavioral responses and especially in characteristic facial expressions. Central to Tomkins's approach was the idea that although the emotions can and do combine with the cognitive and other information-processing systems in the brain, they are essentially separate from these. In other words, he posited a disjunction between our *emotions* and our *knowledge* of what causes and maintains them by treating feeling and cognition as two separate systems. He thus argued that there is a "radical dichotomy between the 'real' causes of affects and the individual's own interpretations of these causes."[3] In short, according to Tomkins the affects have no inherent knowledge of, or relation to, the objects that trigger them—which is why, he thought, we are so liable to be wrong about our feelings and ourselves.

By separating the affects from cognition Tomkins broke with the paradigm that had previously governed much of the work on the emotions. According to Tomkins's predecessors, emotions are intentional states: they are directed toward objects and depend on our desires and beliefs about the world. In Sigmund Freud's case of "Little Hans," to take one famous example, the five-year-old Hans becomes terrified of horses and refuses to go anywhere near them. The immediate, precipitating cause of his fear was his experience of seeing a horse fall down, as if dead. But what interests Freud is not the contingent role of the event of the falling horse but the *meaning* the horse has for Hans, especially the meaning it has for him as a substitute object for his conflictual desires, wishes, and beliefs. In the course of Freud's narrative of the case it emerges that the little boy not only fears horses but also unconsciously identifies with them, to the point of wanting to *be* the very object of his terror. According to Freud, the reason the horse became so salient or important for the child is that it had once been an object of interest and desire for him. The child had liked horses and enjoyed playing at being a horse before the onset of his phobia. By identifying with or becoming the horse in play, he can "bite" the father whom he (loves and) dreads. As Freud would later argue, the child's unconscious yielding to, or identification with, the powerful, aggressive father solves the problem of the child's conflictual wishes and intentions toward him, albeit at the price of the child's experiencing the incorporated paternal aggression in the form of a guilty, anxious conscience. Hence Freud joins together fear, the phobic object, identification, guilt, anxiety, and the subject in a single explanatory complex. And of course for Freud the wishes and intentions that underlie the phobic reaction can only be brought into the subject's awareness through the transferential narrative process of the "talking cure."[4]

I am not concerned here with the validity of Freud's analysis of the case of Hans, which has been widely dismissed in scientific circles ever since J. Wolpe and S. Rachman in 1960 critically reviewed it and reinterpreted phobia as a conditioned response.[5] My purpose is simply to indicate that psychoanalysis—and more generally "cognitivist" or "propositional" or "appraisal" or "phenomenological" approaches to the emotions—operates within an intentionalist paradigm that makes questions of meaning and belief of fundamental importance.[6] The intentionalist approach contrasts strikingly with that of Tomkins, for whom the affects are, crucially, nonintentional states. His account of fear goes something like this: If I run from a snake I do not do so because I believe there is a dangerous object in front of me and desire or intend not to be bitten by it. I run because I am terrified of snakes. The threat of the snake lies out there in the object: snakes make me frightened because they were once terrifying to our ancestors in evolutionary history. The snake on this model does not function as an object of my beliefs or desires but as a "trigger" or trip wire for an involuntary, hardwired response that is rapidly discharged without the affect system's knowledge of the object that triggered it.[7] As Donald Nathanson has recently stated in support of such an approach to the emotions:

> The affects bear no intrinsic relation to any triggering source. . . . If we are frightened, some other mechanism will have to tell us what has become not just too much, but more too much. . . . The affects are completely free from inherent meaning or association to their trigger-ing source. There is nothing about sobbing that tells us anything about the steady-state stimulus that has triggered it; sobbing itself has nothing to do with hunger or cold or loneliness. Only the fact that we grow up with an increasing experience of sobbing lets us form some idea about its meaning.[8]

Tomkins's affect theory thus suspends or displaces considerations of intentionality and meaning in order to produce an account of the emotions as discharges of facial behaviors and related autonomic responses that are fundamentally corporeal in nature.[9] With this model of fear, the nervous system is understood to be "wired directly to the onset of the danger."[10]

For Ekman in the 1960s the most intriguing aspect of Tomkins's affect theory was his claim that emotions are universal categories or "natural kinds" that are accompanied by distinct facial expressions.[11] Tomkins's views were at odds with the prevailing consensus among psychologists and particularly anthropologists, who doubted that facial behaviors had the same meaning in all cultures. The contradictory results of more than five decades of experimental research on the recognition of facial expres-sion reinforced their skepticism on this point.[12] But Tomkins was deter-mined to prove them wrong.[13] According to Ekman's "neurocultural" version of Tomkins's theory, socialization might determine the range of elicitors that can trigger the affect programs and can moderate facial movements according to social norms or "display rules," but the underly-ing emotions might nevertheless "leak out."[14] He was therefore convinced it ought to be possible to find ways of distinguishing or separating out the involuntary, biologically determined facial expressions from those that are influenced by learning and culture. With Tomkins's encouragement and help, Ekman in the late 1960s embarked on a series of highly influential cross-cultural judgment studies aimed at determining whether the basic emotions, as manifested in photographs of posed facial expressions, can be universally recognized by literate and preliterate people alike.

PHOTOGRAPHING EMOTIONS

The use of photographs for the scientific study of expression goes back to the pathbreaking work of the French scientist Duchenne de Boulogne and of course to Charles Darwin's *The Expression of the Emotions in Man and Animals* (1872). Early on in *The Expression of the Emotions in Man and Animals,* Darwin—among the first to use photographs for scientific purposes—describes the challenges confronting anyone wishing to study the face in an objective way. In a brief but telling passage he observes: "The study of expression is difficult, owing to the movements being often extremely slight, and of a fleeting nature. A difference may be clearly perceived, and yet it may be impossible, at least I have found it so, to state in what the difference consists. When we witness any deep emotion, our sympathy is so strongly excited, that close observation is forgotten or rendered almost impossible."[15]

One implication that was drawn from this state of affairs was the need for "instantaneous" photography because, it was thought, only high-speed photography would be capable of capturing objectively—that is, of arresting and "freezing" in time—the rapid play of facial muscles in a single image.[16] It might be objected that Darwin's statement has rather different implications. For instance, one might want to argue on the basis of his remarks that expressions are all about movement, especially the subtlety and volatility of the movements of the muscles of the face, and that these movements—perhaps *actions* would be a better word—are what we ordinarily mean by emotion. From this point of view any technology for objectifying the movements of the face in a freeze-frame is likely to be useless, because by freezing an expression the camera isolates a single, static moment in an overall flow of events that alone gives that moment its meaning. Another implication of Darwin's remarks would seem to be that there is an ineluctable sympathetic-identificatory dimension to our perceptions of other people, a dimension that will inevitably be ignored or suppressed by techniques of observation based on the assumption of an absolute separation between subject and other, between the viewer and the object of his gaze.

For the photographers to whom Darwin turned for help to illustrate

Figure 3.3. Oscar Rejlander posing the emotion of surprise, from Charles Darwin, *The Expression of the Emotions in Man and Animals*, 3rd ed. (New York: Oxford University Press, 1998), 287

the expressions of emotion, however, the solution to the difficulty was to be found in the use of "instantaneous" photographic techniques capable of capturing and fixing once and for all the subtle, transient movements of the face invisible to the naked eye. But as Phillip Prodger has observed, although advances in photochemical technology had reduced exposure times, thereby making it possible for the camera to capture relatively small movements in time, by contemporary standards "exposure times were still long: in the order of tens of seconds."[17] This meant that the subject was required to remain completely still for several seconds while his or her picture was taken. One consequence of this, of course, was that the subject was fully aware of being observed. In its fidelity to the scene, the photograph inevitably registered this fact, which was perceived in terms of an aspect of artificiality, conventionality, exaggeration, or "theatrical-

Figure 3.4. "Terror," from Charles Darwin, *The Expression of the Emotions in Man and Animals*, 3rd ed. (New York: Oxford University Press, 1998), 301

ity" in the sitter's expression as he or she self-consciously held the desired pose.[18] Darwin accepted the need for posing and indeed for photographic manipulation and editing in order to produce convincing portraits of the emotions. Figure 3.3, for example, shows a picture of the Swedish photographer, Oscar Rejlander, well known for his mastery of photographic manipulation, himself posing the emotion of surprise in one of the thirty photographs Darwin included in his book. Figure 3.4 shows Darwin's picture of fear or terror. The latter is not a photograph; rather, it is a slightly altered engraving after a photograph. The original was taken by the French scientist Duchenne de Boulogne (fig. 3.5). In it one can see that the muscles of the man's face have been artificially stimulated by electrical currents to produce the facial movements allegedly expressive of terror; in the engraving he commissioned for his book Darwin had the electrodes removed in order to give the face a more natural appearance.[19]

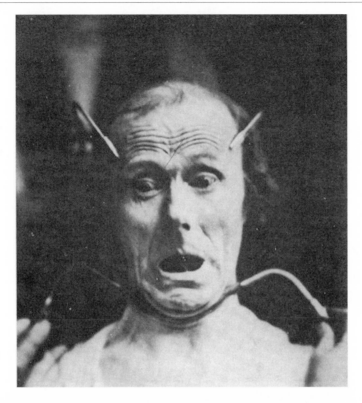

Figure 3.5. "Horror and Fear," from G.-B. Duchenne de Boulogne, *The Mechanism of Human Facial Expression*, edited and translated by R. Andrew Cuthbertson (Cambridge: Cambridge University Press, 1990), plate 61

Prodger has remarked that Darwin "considered the fleeting nature of expression to be the principal difficulty in observing facial movements," as if for Darwin the problems he encountered were merely technological. This seems to be Prodger's view as well, since he observes in this connection that "the limitations of photographic technology precluded objective recording of facial expressions."[20] There is an important sense, of course, in which the limitations Darwin confronted were not merely or only technological but had a deeper, more philosophical or, say, ontological cause. A passage in a text by Johann Caspar Lavater, a famous eighteenth-century predecessor in the physiognomic tradition to which Darwin, Tomkins, and Ekman can all be seen to belong, bears directly on this point. "I want to discover in the mild-mannered person the traits of this manner, in the humble person the signs of humility," Lavater observed in 1772, exactly a hundred years before Darwin. He goes on:

But my observations must be exact, they must be repeated and tested often. How can that be possible if I have to make these observations on the sly? Isn't it presumptuous to analyze faces? And if a humble person notices that she is being observed, won't she turn away and hide her face? Indeed, it is here that I encountered one of the greatest obstacles to my studies; anyone who notices that he or she is being observed either puts up resistance or dissimulates. How can I get around this problem? Perhaps in part in the following way.

I retire into solitude; I place before me a medallion or a piece of antique sculpture, the sketches of a Raphael, the apostles as depicted by Van Dyck, the portraits of Houbraken. These I can observe at will, I can turn them and view them from all sides.[21]

On the one hand, in this passage Lavater recognizes that the spectatorial gaze of the observer is *itself* the problem, since it inevitably makes the subject aware of being seen. From this it follows that the risk of a certain posing or conventionalizing of expression inheres in the very situation of being beheld, which is to say that the problem of posing can't be solved by technological means, such as the invention of the high-speed camera. On the other hand, and this is the point I especially want to stress, Lavater's belief that the truth shows itself on someone's face when the person believes he or she is alone is what might be called a theoretical or ideological claim. It does *not* follow from the fact that the face is a privileged site of expression for us that if only it could be seen in solitude it would tell us the deep truth about ourselves. To believe this is to succumb to the view that a distinction can be strictly maintained between authentic and artificial signs, based solely on the state of awareness of the subject in question. More precisely, it is to surrender to a physiognomic ideology that claims we can draw an absolute differentiation between the masks we allegedly put on for others and the genuine faces we have when we are alone and no one is watching. (One limit case here, I suppose, would be to photograph persons when they are asleep. The expressions of blind people have also been imagined as free from all social taint, which is why they have figured in discussions of the Tomkins-Ekman affect program theory.) It's as if we were to imagine that we cannot find out the truth about people in the course of interacting with them in daily life, or by discovering how they act in an emergency, or on the basis of intimate conversations with them, but only when they are entirely removed from human intercourse. But if someone is untrustworthy, or inconsistent, or indeed honorable, is it plausible that the truth about that person will emerge simply because he or she is alone?

And of course if you think this way, if you believe that the answer to this question is yes, then you will have to worry about whether the expressions you have recorded by photographic means for scientific observation really are natural and unposed. You will find yourself continually haunted by the suspicion or charge that the images you are studying are not truly spontaneous because you have not adequately isolated them from the contamination of others.[22] As we have seen, Lavater in the pre-photograph era thought one solution to the problem of the subject's consciousness of being beheld was to study artistic illustrations of expression in the privacy of his study. His idea seems to have been that since the subjects of such artist's representations were not physically present to him, the problem of posing could not arise. Lavater's solution could hardly satisfy Ekman, and it is not surprising that in the latter's discussion of methods for recording emotional expressions he ruled out of consideration the results of *any* experiments that had made use of artists' drawings and illustrations, precisely on the grounds that such pictures were likely to be too stereotyped or subjective for scientific purposes.[23]

But Ekman *was* committed to the project of distinguishing between nature and culture, between the "natural signs" of emotional expression that might be so small or rapid as to be easily overlooked and the culturally coded displays or "artificial signs" that he thought tended to mask or disguise them.[24] The whole point of his Tomkins-inspired "neurocultural" theory of the emotions was to reconcile the warring sides in the dispute between the universalists and the culturalists by developing a framework capable of explaining the occurrence of *both* universal and culturally specific facial expressions.[25] According to Ekman, the display rules of any given culture are the social norms that govern the way a person manages and controls his or her emotions. Thus when a person is fearful he or she might exaggerate, constrain, or neutralize feelings and expressions in conformity with the felt requirements of the social context. (Ekman had been reading Erving Goffman on the performance of social roles.) But Ekman believed that it should be possible to identify the pancultural or universal signs of emotion behind the culturally determined display rules and even outright dissimulations ("lies") that mask the truth.[26] For these purposes, photographs of persons posing expressions were for him an indispensable research tool because, by fixing expressions in still images, they made possible the testing of people's ability across the world to recognize and identify particular emotions. Still pictures were also crucial if Ekman was to realize his project to identify and code the component muscle movements responsible for the facial expressions supposedly linked to each of the hypothesized basic emotions—not an easy project, as he recognized, since facial movements seemed to lack natural divisions and the selection of variables was unclear.[27]

EKMAN AND THE PROBLEM OF THE POSE

Starting in the late 1960s, then, Ekman set out to test the idea that the emotions could be correctly judged by everyone, literate and preliterate people alike. On the basis of studies purporting to demonstrate that American, Brazilian, Japanese, and other observers, including observers from among the last of the isolated, preliterate cultures of New Guinea, could all successfully distinguish the primary affects as represented in photographs of people posing expressions, he concluded that such facial expressions must contain universal or pancultural elements linked to the hypothesized "basic emotions." In order to uncover the pancultural elements, he needed photographs of facial movements that, as he put it, were free of cultural differences because of learned evokers, display rules, and consequences. He therefore attempted to select such photographs in order to prove that observers from different cultures recognized the same affect from the same photograph. In other words, to test the validity of the universality thesis, Ekman preselected photographs of posed expressions that he theorized were *already free* of cultural influence. The Facial Action Scoring Technique, or FAST, which he and Tomkins developed at this time as a system for measuring facial expressions held to be characteristic of the hypothesized affect categories, played a role in this preselection process. For, partly on the basis of FAST (and partly on the basis of personal intuition), the two men chose only those photographs, from among more than three thousand such pictures of posed expressions employed by themselves or others in previous experiments, that had obtained the highest agreement about the emotion portrayed and that seemed to them to exhibit the affective expressions in their specific ("unmixed") and unacculturated form.[28] Since posed facial expressions were critical to establishing FAST in the first place, posing was institutionalized in Ekman's first system of measurement from the start. His procedures were therefore highly recursive, to say the least.[29]

I can sum up Ekman's situation by saying that photographs of posed emotional expressions were central to his research enterprise, even as he was also committed to maintaining that such photographs were unconventionalized, unacculturated representations of the universal truth of the primary emotions. It was especially urgent for him to argue this point, since the status of still, posed expressions had been a topic of much contention during the previous decades of emotion research. Ekman's concern with this theme is especially evident in his book *Emotion in the Human Face: Guidelines for Research and an Integration of Findings* (1972), in which he and his coauthors reanalyzed many of the experiments on the judgment of facial expression performed between 1914 and 1970 and presented their own findings in order to argue that, contrary to the opinion of the majority of his contemporaries, the preponderance of the data yielded consistently positive evidence in support of the universality thesis. But the problem of posing never really disappears from his work.[30] Although Ekman moves with seeming confidence in this terrain, his arguments are marked by considerable tension and even, at times, incoherence. In effect, he adopts two different, apparently competing responses to the problem of posing.

Ekman's first response to the problem of posing was to argue on the basis of the empirical evidence that, since people all over the world regardless of their cultural origins and background consistently labeled photographs preselected to depict the basic emotions the same way, facial expressions must be universal. Ekman wrote that "observers in both literate and preliterate cultures chose the predicted emotion for photographs of the face, although agreement was higher in the literate samples. These findings suggest that the pan-cultural element in facial displays of emotion is the association between facial muscular movements and discrete primary emotions, although cultures may still differ in what evokes an emotion, in rules for controlling the display of emotion, and in behavioral consequences."[31] In other words, the fact that, as his cross-cultural experiments seemed to demonstrate, literate and preliterate people alike could agree when looking at photographs that certain facial expressions connoted the same emotional categories argued against the idea that posed expressions were determined by conventions, as the cultural relativists claimed. Rather, posed expressions must contain pancultural elements and must be in some way "based on the repertoire of spontaneous facial behaviors associated with emotion."[32]

Ekman granted that posed and spontaneous expressions were not completely identical. Rather, as he explained, posed expressions were similar in appearance to "that spontaneous behavior which is of extreme intensity and unmodulated, although it may differ in onset, duration, and decay time."[33] Thus, according to Ekman, if posed expressions do look a bit strange, odd, or extreme, this is just because they are what spontaneous expressions would look like if they were not fixed in time or not blends or not altered or modified ("modulated" or "moderated") by culturally inflected display rules. His idea seems to have been that social constraints suppress or damp down or deflect our facial expressions from conveying the inward "truth" of our feelings and that the emphatic nature and single-mindedness of posed expressions (that is, their exaggerated, caricatural, even comic-book quality) are the outcome of the successful avoidance or outflanking or overcoming of that suppressive effect, though it is not clear how that feat is managed. For him, the tendency of such expressions to look exaggerated is not the result of convention but exactly the opposite: the absence of those conventions that in everyday life constrain or moderate or mask behavior. In effect, Ekman weirdly claimed that *posed expressions in their very caricatural intensity are among the best examples we have of what we would look like if we were entirely alone*: "Our view is that posed facial behavior is similar to, if perhaps an exaggeration of, those spontaneous facial behaviors which are shown when the display rules to deintensify or mask emotion are not applied. . . . Posed behavior is thus an approximation of the facial behavior which spontaneously occurs when people are making little or no attempt to manage the facial appearance associated with intense emotion."[34] It follows for Ekman that when an investigator asks someone to pose an emotion, all he is doing is implicitly requesting the subject to show that emotion without attempting to "deintensify, mask, or neutralize his facial appearance" as the display rules would normally require. The subject simply interprets the instruction as an "occasion to display an uncontrolled version of the emotion."[35] I repeat, how this is supposed to work is a mystery; it's as if Ekman imagined that the poser ordinarily follows a set of explicit rules and conventions about how he or she is meant to act but is able to suspend these at will when asked to do so—or indeed when asked to pose!

But Ekman also dealt with the problem of posing in a different way. According to what I am calling his *second response*, and in an apparently contradictory gesture, he admitted that the subject's consciousness of being beheld when posing for the camera inevitably introduced what was, according to the logic of his project, a problematic component of conventionality. Ekman not only knew and accepted this, he even used the issue of the subject's awareness of being observed in certain experiments as a reason for rejecting some of his predecessors' findings in the field. He also recognized that so-called candid photos, widely understood as solving the problem of posing because the subject was assumed to be oblivious of the camera, might not be so candid after all. In other words, he conceded what he elsewhere denied, that posed facial expressions are conventionalized behaviors.

We can track Ekman's arguments on this point by noting that in 1940 a psychologist named Norman L. Munn had objected to some experiments by Carney Landis on the grounds that what the latter had taken to be spontaneous emotional expressions of his subjects responding to various situations created in the laboratory, such as witnessing a rat having its head cut off, might not have been so spontaneous after all because the subjects had been filmed and therefore might have been "self-conscious, and hence not so spontaneously expressive as under more natural circumstances."[36] This is an objection with which Ekman agreed, and he did so precisely on the grounds that Landis's subjects knew they were being photographed. As Ekman wrote: "A number of aspects of the experimental setting indicate the operation of display rules either to neutralize the facial responses or to mask them with a positive affect. All of Landis' subjects knew him; most were psychologists who had had other laboratory experiences. Not only did they know they were being photographed, but, because Landis had marked their faces with burnt cork in order to measure the components of facial behavior in his other use of these records, they knew Landis was interested in their facial behavior."[37] In short, Ekman here endorsed the idea that in posed expressions the subject's awareness of being photographed was likely to induce the operation of masking conventions or "display rules"—the very idea that according to his first response to the problem of posing he appeared to reject.

In order to meet the criterion of "spontaneity without conventionalization" Munn had decided that "candid" photographs might do the job.[38] Ideal material of this kind, he felt, would comprise candid shots of the same persons in a variety of emotional situations, together with verbal reports of the emotions they had experienced in each case. Munn remarked, though, that to obtain many different expressions of the same individual under such conditions would be practically impossible because "the subject, aware of the photographer's purpose, would be no more naturally expressive than are subjects in the laboratory." He therefore resorted to the use of "candid-camera" images published in *Life* and other journals of the day. He characterized such candid shots as "obviously unposed emotional expressions" and reported significant agreement among experimental subjects concerning the emotions those candid pictures were thought to express.[39] But Munn's solution to the problem of posing was soon held to be no solution at all when in 1941 Hunt complained that most of Munn's "candid" photographs involved social situations where conventionalization could be expected. "Even the man holding the drowned person's hand," Hunt commented, "seems aware of the camera."[40] He therefore dismissed findings based on the use of posed expressions that appeared to support the thesis of the universal recognition of emotions. In Hunt's view, emotions were not defined by distinct universal facial expressions or even distinct physiological responses but were situational reactions involving a complex, learned relationship between the individual and his environment.

To Ekman, Hunt epitomized everything that was wrong with the culturalists' approach to the emotions and facial expression. Nevertheless—and this is what I want to emphasize—he did not question the validity of Hunt's criticisms of the candid shot. On the contrary, Ekman acknowledged as a methodological limitation in Munn's experiments the fact that, as he observed, "the behavior studied (candid photographs taken from magazines) may not all actually have been spontaneous. The person shown in the photographs may have been aware of the photographer, or, even worse, might have completely re-enacted or staged the behavior for the press."[41] With this admission one might have expected Ekman to reconsider his use of posed expressions in his research. But he did not. Instead, he sidestepped the difficulty, essentially by changing the topic. That is, he proceeded as if after all the real problem was not that of posing *per se* but the merely methodological-technical one of the representativeness of findings based on the use of posed expressions. The result was a tendency on Ekman's part to divert attention from the problem of posing and to justify the continued use of posed expressions in experiments on emotion, as long as the latter were carried out with the appropriate methodological safeguards.[42] Above all, he returned to the (by now familiar) argument that "posed behavior is not a specialized, language-like set of conventions" unrelated to authentic emotional behavior on the grounds that he had shown that facial expressions could be accurately judged across cultures. "For these findings to emerge," he wrote, "the behaviors occurring during posing must have developed in the same way across cultures. One reasonable explanation of such development would be that they are in some way based on the repertoire of spontaneous facial behaviors associated with emotion."[43] In other words, Ekman's conclusion once again was that posed expressions are simply slightly exaggerated because they are unmodulated or uncontrolled versions of expressions of the kind that occur naturally when subjects are alone.

There would come a moment when Ekman had to respond to criticism on precisely this point. In 1975, in a scathing review of Ekman's work, the anthropologist Margaret Mead, no lover of the universalist thesis, protested that all Ekman appeared to have demonstrated with his cross-cultural studies was that *"simulated"* expressions of emotion—by which she meant pantomimed, or highly theatricalized, facial movements—could be recognized across cultures.[44] This was not a trivial rebuke in light of Ekman's commitment to distinguishing between natural and artificial expressions and hence to isolating authentic faces hidden behind the codes of convention. Nor did Ekman dismiss her objection.[45] On the contrary, he acknowledged as a drawback of his cross-cultural studies precisely that the expressions he had studied were not authentic or the real thing.[46] But Ekman had a solution to the difficulty. The physiognomist Lavater in the passage I quoted earlier had remarked: "But my observations must be exact, they must be repeated and tested often. How can that be possible if I have to make these observations on the sly? . . . Anyone who notices that he or she is being observed either puts up resistance or dissimulates." In response to the problem of posing raised by Mead, Ekman now pointed to the results of an experiment he had already carried out using a device for recording facial expressions "on the sly" that had been unavailable to Lavater: *the device of the hidden camera.* By secretly recording the emotional expressions of subjects as they watched stressful films, Ekman felt he had discovered the key to detecting authentic, spontaneous expressions. As he replied to Mead's objection to his use of posed expressions: "The next type of research design answered this criticism."[47] Or as he also stated: "We avoided the display rule pitfall by videotaping when the subjects thought they were completely alone and unobserved."[48] It is to Ekman's "next type of research design," involving the use of a hidden camera, that I now turn.

SPONTANEOUS EXPRESSIONS

In the 1960s, in an interesting and important series of research studies, the psychologist Richard S. Lazarus began using films in a systematic way to evaluate and measure the response of various subjects to stress. One film used extensively by him for this purpose was called *Subincision.* It was a short, silent, black-and-white anthropological film (with a running length of seventeen minutes) that showed naked Aborigines in the Australian bush undergoing puberty initiation rites involving scenes of extensive cutting of the penis with sharp stones, of bleeding wounds, and of the adolescents wincing and writhing in pain. The boys appeared to volunteer for the initiation procedure, which was carried out by older men.[49] Lazarus demonstrated that the film induced subjective and autonomic signs of stress in a variety of student and other viewers. But by varying the sound track of the film in ways designed to minimize or, alternatively, to enhance the threatening content, Lazarus was also able to show that the film became less or more disturbing to watch. He argued on the basis of these results and related considerations that the film's threat could not be considered simply "out there as an attribute of the stimulus" but depended on the viewer's appraisal process, which is to say, on the "person's beliefs about what the stimulus meant for the thwarting of motives of importance to him." Thus the same stimulus could be threatening or not, depending on the "interpretation the person makes concerning its future personal significance."[50] In terms of the opposition between intentionalist and nonintentionalist accounts of the emotions with which I began this chapter, Lazarus was on the intentionalist side.[51]

In spite of their apparently different theoretical orientations, Lazarus lent Ekman considerable research help when the latter decided to make use of *Subincision* and other stress films to test his ideas about the universality of emotions. In a variant of Lazarus's experiments, first published in 1972 and carried out with his collaborator Wallace V. Friesen, Ekman used a hidden camera to secretly videotape the facial expressions of American and Japanese students as they watched brief sections of *Subincision* and three other stress-inducing or "neutral" films when each student was alone in the viewing room. Japan was selected for comparison with the United States, Ekman explained, because of the common belief that Japanese facial behavior was sufficiently different from that of Americans to mitigate against finding universals.[52] Ekman reported on the basis of his findings that the emotional responses of American and Japanese students to the stress films were very similar. But according to him, when an "authority figure" from the student's own culture (actually a graduate assistant dressed in a white coat) was introduced into the room and interviewed the student about his feelings while the latter was viewing additional stress material, the facial behavior of the Americans and Japanese diverged. Ekman stated that the Japanese students masked their negative feelings about the stress films more than did the Americans when in the presence of the authority figure. Slow-motion videotape analysis, allowing for direct scoring of the facial movements, he declared, demonstrated at a microlevel the occurrence of the Japanese students' spontaneous negative emotional expressions before these were covered over by the culturally determined display rules controlling for false, polite smiles (unfortunately, no video frames showing this transition were published). Ekman thus claimed to have proven that the universal, biologically based feelings remained intact behind the culturally determined behavior and hence to have demonstrated the validity of his neurocultural theory of the emotions.[53]

Ekman's study of apparently spontaneous expressions in American and Japanese students and their inhibition by display rules, presented by him as an answer to Mead's worries about the problem of posing, has become canonical in the field. It is routinely cited today in works on emotion as decisive evidence in favor of the Tomkins-Ekman approach to the emotions.[54] Yet in the last few years the study has been called into question.[55] In particular, Alan Fridlund—Ekman's former student—in a powerful critique published in 1994 demonstrated convincingly that the account given by Ekman and Friesen over the years of their Japanese-American experiment was inaccurate, and that their interpretation of the results in terms of the opposition between genuine emotional expressions versus culturally coded display rules was unsupportable. Fridlund made a number of methodological-technical criticisms of Ekman's experiment. Although a thorough discussion of Fridlund's critique lies outside the scope of this chapter, I want to emphasize that central to Fridlund's damning assessment was his rejection of Ekman's fundamental assumption that the faces people make when they are alone are readouts, or authentic signs, of the truth of their inner emotional states. Ross Buck has put Ekman's position this way: "When a sender is alone . . . he or she should feel little pressure to present a proper image to others, and any emotion expression under such circumstances should be more likely to reflect an actual motivational/emotional state."[56] As Fridlund has observed, Ekman made this same assumption in his crucial experiment on the differences between Japanese and American facial displays. Thus Ekman stated of the results of that investigation: "In this experiment we had shown how facial expressions are both universal and cultural. In private, when no display rules to mask expression were operative, we saw the biologically based, evolved, universal facial expressions of emotion. In a social situation, we had shown how different rules about the management of expression led to culturally different facial expressions."[57] Or as Ekman declared, "expressions do occur when people are alone . . . and contradict the theoretical proposals of those who view expressions solely as social signals."[58]

Ekman's assumption that the truth shows itself on the face when someone believes he or she is alone is the same assumption that, as I earlier remarked, motivated Lavater's physiognomic project. It is an assumption that depends on the claim that a distinction can be strictly maintained between authentic and artificial signs, between nature and culture. But Fridlund rejects that claim, offering instead a "Behavioral Ecology View" of faces that stresses the implicit sociality of even so-called solitary facial movements. He treats the differences observed between the facial displays of the Japanese and American students in Ekman's well-known experiment as cultural differences in the management of facial behavior. He points out in this connection that "the experimenter himself is always an implicit audience, and his or her laboratory is always the stage for the directorial effort known as an 'experiment.' Thus the 'alone' phase of the study was implicitly social, and the . . . interview phases were simply more explicitly social. Thus contrasting the facial behavior in the 'alone' versus the interview phase as authentic versus managed [or cultural] is over-statement at a minimum." In short, Fridlund regards Ekman's Japanese-American experiment as a study of "audience effects," arguing that "just because a viewer is alone *physically* does not mean that he is alone *psychologically*."[59]

The same year, in a masterly assessment of the cross-cultural facial judgment or recognition experiments reported by Ekman and his colleagues, James A. Russell demonstrated that the results were artifactual, depending on forced-choice response formats and other problematic methods, such as within-subject experimental design, lack of variability in the order or stimulus presentation, and the use of posed expressions, which begged the questions to be proved in ways that fundamentally undermined Ekman's claims for the universal nature of the emotions.[60] The net result of Fridlund's and Russell's analyses has been to dramatically challenge the empirical and theoretical validity of the Tomkins-Ekman research program. Fridlund has gone on to propose instead that facial movements or displays should be viewed, not as expressions of hardwired, discrete internal emotional states leaking out into the external world but as meaningful behaviors that have evolved in order to communicate motives in an ongoing interpersonal or interindividual context or transaction. As Fridlund has put it: "Displays are specific to intent and context, rather than derivatives or blends of a small set of fundamental emotion displays. . . . Instead of there being six or seven displays of 'fundamental emotions' (e.g., anger), there may be one dozen or one hundred 'about to aggress' displays appropriate to the identities and relationships of the interactants, and the contexts in which the interaction occurs."[61] From this perspective, facial behaviors are relational or communicative signals that take other (real or imagined) organisms into account.[62]

Recently, building on the work of Fridlund, Russell, and others, Lisa Feldman Barrett has published an impressive series of reviews of the growing empirical evidence that is inconsistent with the idea that there are six or seven or eight basic emotions in nature. She has come to the conclusion that "fear" and the other emotional categories posited by Ekman do not have an ontological status that can support induction and scientific generalization or allow for the accumulation of knowledge.[63] The consensus among this group of formidably well-informed critics is that a new scientific paradigm for research on the emotions is needed. All the indications are that, whatever model or paradigm gains acceptance— *if* it ever gains acceptance (more on this in a moment)—it will be based on the same general intentionalist assumptions embraced by Freud in the sense that it will make the question of the affective meaning to the organism (or subject) of the objects in its world a central issue and concern.

As I have already begun to suggest, a constant motif in recent critiques of Ekman's work has been the question of posing. It is sometimes said in this connection that because the expressions on the faces of people who have posed for the camera are artificial or exaggerated and don't appear in real life the results of experiments based on such pictures lack "ecological relevance" or "ecological validity." The argument is that such posed expressions are caricatures that, unlike "prototypical" expressions that are close to the average set of features for a naturally occurring emotion, are exaggerated expressions designed to maximally distinguish each hypothesized emotion category from the other. Evidence indicates that such caricaturized expressions are easier to categorize than prototypical ones when the categories in question are otherwise hard to distinguish.[64] The ways in which these posed expressions are produced has also come under scrutiny. Fridlund has offered a dramaturgical analysis of experiments involving the use of posed expressions, suggesting that those experiments are social scenarios in which the investigator implicitly functions as a director and the subject as a Stanislavski actor who "slips into role."[65] In a somewhat similar fashion, Russell has observed that Ekman's universality thesis is not, or at least is not directly, about posed faces and states: "Posed faces do not express the emotion of the poser, but what the posed chooses to pretend and in a manner most likely to be understood by the observer."[66] Russell here puts an emphasis on deliberate feigning that may be somewhat misplaced, for he implies that actors or posers are never caught up in the emotional feelings they are trying to represent on their faces. The philosopher Ian Hacking may have come nearer to the truth about this matter when he recently suggested that what is often involved in posing is a subtle form of unconscious compliance. In a review of Ekman's edition of Darwin's *The Expression of the Emotions in Man and Animals*, he remarks of Darwin's and many of Ekman's choices of illustrative faces that they are "quite extraordinary social documents. I am not sure I have seen anyone in real life looking like any of these people. One can wonder if all three groups, the American students, the wild men of New Guinea, and the investigators, were not collaborating to generate the phenomena. These experiments may serve as instances of another human need, namely, wanting to please, wanting to get along. This is not simulation: if you are an experimental subject, you do not behave as you do because the scientist is boss but because you are in a situation where you feel good about accommodating to his wishes, just as he feels good about accommodating to yours."[67]

In spite of these incisive criticisms—others could be cited—Ekman's approach to the emotions continues to thrive. Why this should be so raises interesting questions about scientific influence, authority, and power that cannot be addressed here. Instead I will turn in closing to the case described by Damasio and Adolphs of the patient with the damaged amygdala who cannot experience fear in order to raise some final questions about the way the Tomkins-Ekman paradigm is being used today to underwrite the scientific investigation of the emotions.

"HAVE NO FEAR"

In 1976, in *Pictures of Facial Affect*, Ekman and Friesen made available in slide form a set of black-and-white photographs of posed facial expressions. Confident that emotions are universally recognizable, they presented these pictures as prototypical expressions of six discrete affect categories. Two years later they published a new coding system called the Facial Action Coding System (FACS) for measuring and analyzing facial movements. This coding system, which replaced the earlier FAST coding system, was designed to provide an atheoretical, anatomically based, standardized scoring system of the movements of the face that researchers could use to test their hypotheses about the relationship between emotion and facial expression. Ekman's pictures and FACS have since been used in hundreds of research studies.[68] One scientist who has deployed Ekman's work to great effect is Antonio Damasio, arguably the best-known neuroscientist in the emotion field today.[69] Damasio accepts the Tomkins-Ekman paradigm, at least for the basic emotions. He regards affective responses as biologically determined, adaptive processes that depend on innately set devices with a long evolutionary history. According to him, although culture and learning introduce individual variations, emotions are fundamentally stereotyped and automatic responses of the body and face that can occur automatically, without conscious deliberation. That is why, he explains, Darwin was able to catalog emotional expressions in humans and animals, and that is why, in different parts of the world and across different cultures, emotions are so easily recognized. "The thing to marvel at, as you fly high above the planet," he says, "is the similarity, not the difference" in facial expression among people, a view he sees as having been given "immeasurable support" by the work of Ekman. The biological function of emotions is thus to produce specific reactions to specific events in a fast and exquisitely reliable, automatic way. "For certain classes of clearly dangerous or clearly valuable stimuli in the internal or external environment," Damasio writes in this connection, "evolution has assembled a matching answer in the form of emotion. This is why, in spite of the infinite variations to be found across cultures, among individuals, and over the course of a life span, we can predict with some success that certain stimuli will produce certain emotions. (This is why you can say to a colleague, 'Go tell her that; she will be so happy to hear it.')"[70] One might be tempted to protest that a colleague won't be happy unless she understands what she has been told, and if she understands it, she's doing cognition. Damasio seems to think, however, that her feeling of happiness will automatically follow from the "stimulus."

In 1994 Damasio teamed up with Ralph Adolphs to study the case of a young woman, SM, whose brain scan revealed that she suffered from an extremely rare genetic disease, producing in her case complete, bilateral damage to the amygdala. Since the work of Joseph LeDoux and others, the amygdala has been implicated in rapid emotional responses, especially the emotion of fear.[71] Adolphs and his colleagues reported that SM was normal in every way except for one strange symptom: she was unusually—that is, inappropriately, even excessively—forthcoming with people. Indeed, she so lacked normal reserve and reticence that she had often been taken advantage of by those she trusted. When tested on her ability to judge prototypical facial expressions of six basic emotions in pictures taken from Ekman and Friesen's *Pictures of Facial Affect*, SM was unable to identify the expression of fear, as was demonstrated by the fact that her ratings intensity for fearful faces was low compared to those of normal subjects, although she had no difficulty identifying familiar faces.[72] In a subsequent study Adolphs and his colleagues showed that SM was unable to draw a face representing fear; she complained that *"she did not know what an afraid face would look like,* and that she was unable to draw any depiction of it," even though she could depict other emotions. Moreover, tests also showed that, although SM did not lack the *concept* of fear, she seemed to lack the capacity to *experience* fear in a normal way, since she did not appear to feel frightened given the appropriate stimulus.[73] Damasio stated in his commentary on the case that SM's fearlessness, the result of bilateral damage to her amygdalae, had prevented her from learning "the significance of unpleasant situations that all of us have lived through. As a result she has not learned the telltale signs that announce possible danger, especially as they show up in the face of another person or in a situation."[74]

That this was true appeared to be demonstrated in yet another study. The experiment called for SM and two other patients with complete bilateral amygdala damage to rate one hundred slides of facial expressions, again selected from Ekman and Friesen's collection of such posed expressions, slides that had previously been rated by a group of normal individuals as indicating various degrees of "trustworthiness" and "approachability." As Damasio reported, these normal subjects had been asked an apparently simple question: "How would you rate this face on a scale of one to five, relative to the trustworthiness and approachability that the owner of the face inspires? Or, in other words, how eager would you be to approach the person with this particular face if you needed help?"[75] Fifty faces that were judged by normal individuals as inspiring trust and fifty faces that were judged untrustworthy were then shown to SM and the two other patients. The experiment demonstrated that although the latter were quite capable of judging trustworthy faces normally, they were severely impaired in their ability to judge untrustworthy or dangerous faces.[76] As Damasio reported, they "looked at faces that you or I would consider trustworthy and classified them, quite correctly, as you and I would, as faces that one might approach in case of need. But when they looked at faces of which you and I would be suspicious, faces of persons that we would try to avoid, they judged them as equally trustworthy. . . . Immersed in a secure Pollyanna world, these individuals cannot protect themselves against simple and not-so-simple social risks and are thus more vulnerable and less independent than we are."[77]

Several comments are in order. The first point to notice is that in Damasio's narrative of the case the concepts of "trustworthiness" and "untrustworthiness" have been stripped of all context in order to treat these traits as objective, identifiable features of persons that are immediately, universally, and unambiguously readable in the human face. The aim of Damasio's and his colleagues' experiment was not to assess the meaning certain facial expressions might have had for SM but to establish the difference between abnormal and normal subjects on the basis of an ostensibly objective standard. The posed facial expressions drawn from Ekman's *Pictures of Facial Affect*, with which SM was tested, were taken to provide that objective standard because they came with a predetermined "correct" estimation of danger. The assumption underlying the research project was that dangerousness or what is frightening inheres unambiguously in certain facial expressions that everyone has the competence to decipher, because that competence is an evolved skill shared by everyone with normal brain function.[78] Russell has shown that when forced-choice response formats and other problematic methods advocated by Ekman are abandoned, the results obtained fail to support the Tomkins-Ekman position on the universal recognition of facial expressions of emotion. Ignoring such criticisms, Damasio employed the Tomkins-Ekman paradigm in order to argue that SM can't feel fear because she has an abnormal amygdala and therefore makes errors when judging the dangerous faces she encounters. Her emotional deficit is that she cannot conform to a fixed standard or norm.

What interests me here is the kind of scientific object fear is imagined to be when analyzed in these terms. The issue is not whether the amygdala plays a role in the fear response—it clearly does—but what kind of role it plays and how that role is to be conceptualized. Among the questions that arise are: Did Damasio and Adolphs make unwarranted assumptions in their analysis of the case? To what extent did their commitment to Ekman's taxonomic approach to the emotions and their use of the latter's pictures of emotional expression predetermine their findings? How specific is the amygdala's role in the fear response? Does other work on the amygdala show that its part in fear processing is somewhat different from what Damasio and Adolphs first proposed?

The answer to the last question now appears to be yes. Subsequent studies of SM by Adolphs in collaboration with Russell (the same investigator who has queried the validity of Ekman's cross-cultural judgment studies) and others now suggest that the amygdala is involved not in making categorical fear judgments but in something different, a judgment of arousal levels based on attention to features such as wide-open eyes.[79] Tests have shown that SM fails to look normally at the eyes in *all* facial expressions and that if she is explicitly instructed to look at the eye region when performing an emotion detection task her recognition of fear is normal. Her selective impairment in identifying fear thus appears to be due to the fact that her defective amygdala is unable to direct her attention to the wide-open eyes that are thought to characterize the expression of fear. Furthermore, neuroimaging studies have revealed that humans presented with pictures of fearful faces do not report feeling "afraid," yet amygdala activity is nevertheless altered, suggesting that reported emotion and amygdala activation should not be equated. The strong inference from these and related experiments is that, rather than functioning as the site for the production of discrete emotional states, such as fear, the amygdala modulates the vigilance and arousal levels required to attend to especially ambiguous stimuli of relevance to the organism (for example, fearful faces that provide information about the presence of a threat but not the source of that threat). At the very least these experiments suggest that the amygdala is not the locus of a discrete fear "entity" but that both vigilance and emotions are *processes* set in motion by amygdala activation.[80]

On the basis of these newer findings, some scientists involved in research on the human amygdala have begun to question the general taxonomic-categorical approach to the emotions associated with the Tomkins-Ekman paradigm.[81] But this is not a direction Damasio and Adolphs seem to want to pursue. In line with the newer findings about SM they have revised their understanding of the mechanism by which bilateral amygdala damage compromises the recognition of fear. But they do not appear to have altered their general commitment to the Tomkins-Ekman paradigm.[82] I can think of several reasons for the continued success of that paradigm. Its ostensibly objective approach to the affects; its solidarity with evolutionary theories of the mind; the agreement between its assumptions about the independence of the affect system and cognition and contemporary presuppositions about the modularity and encapsulation of brain functions; the congruence between its image-based approach to the emotions and neuroimaging technologies such as positron emission tomography (PET) and functional magnetic resonance imaging (fMRI); the promise it holds for surveillance experts keen to find ways of detecting liars as easily as a blood test can detect DNA—all these and other factors help explain why the "basic emotions" view is so entrenched in contemporary thinking.[83]

Especially important in this connection is the convenience of Ekman's methods in facilitating research. His photographs of posed expressions are so easy to use that even his critics continue to employ them in their own experiments—an extraordinary fact, when you think about it. Moreover, I sense that Ekman's critics face another difficulty, which is that the moment one abandons the basic emotions approach in favor of some kind of intentionalist interpretation of the kind associated with Freud and appraisal theorists, one finds oneself forced to provide thick descriptions of life experiences of the kind that are familiar to anthropologists and indeed novelists but are widely held to be inimical to science.[84] At the same time, one is obliged to engage with an array of tremendously difficult questions about the nature of intentionality, including the intentionality of nonhuman animals, which have traditionally belonged to the domain of philosophy. Quite apart from those considerations, however, it is precisely Ekman's *non-* or *anti-intentionalism* that makes his work particularly attractive at the present time, at any rate in certain quarters. For, once you imagine that emotions are nonintentional states that are simply triggered by various stimuli, and once you imagine that, as inherited patterns of response, under the right conditions they will inevitably express themselves on the face—which is what it means for them to be universal—you are likely to conclude that the inner truth about a person will be detectable by properly trained observers, which is to say, you will conclude that there is an important sense in which the body cannot lie. That is why since 9/11 Ekman's research program has been of interest to American intelligence and security agencies. Whereas for critics of Ekman's approach to the emotions such as Fridlund, it is not true that what is hidden in deception is destined to "leak out" from unmanaged behavior. Rather, humans and nonhuman animals produce facial behaviors or displays when it is strategically advantageous for them to do so and not at other times, because displays are dynamic and often highly plastic social and communicative signals. Deception is thus omnipresent in nature and potentially highly advantageous for the displayer, not something that covers over the hidden truth of authentic feelings.[85] But this way of thinking introduces a degree of complexity and uncertainty that contrasts, to its disadvantage, with the reassuring idea that the truth of our emotions is bound to reveal itself.

4

SOLDIERS AND EMOTION IN EARLY TWENTIETH-CENTURY RUSSIAN MILITARY PSYCHOLOGY

Jan Plamper

The main feature of the Suvorov school of drill was the eradication from the heart and banishment from the human head, not just of *the emotion of fear* but of the very idea of this feeling, which is so disgraceful for the soldier.

> [V. P.?] Prasalov, "Neskol'ko slov k stat'e V. Polianskogo —'Moral'nyi element v oblasti fortifikatsii'"

Just as I cannot imagine a plesiosaurus on Nevskii Prospekt, I cannot imagine that anyone does not know what fear is and how it affects the organism.

> A. [M.] Dmitrevskii, "Vospitanie voina mozhet byt' tol'ko v styde nakazaniia, a ne v strakhe nakazaniia"

LOOKING FOR THE emotion of soldierly fear in first-person accounts of the War of 1812 resembles the proverbial search for a needle in the haystack. One is more likely to discover overt absences that sound like this comment made by officer Mikhail Petrov: "Yet the Russian soldiers looked at the huge enemy hordes with an unflinching spirit. With Faith, Hope, and Love, and with the Great Suvorov implanted in our hearts, our souls were prepared for sacrifices to save the Fatherland."[1] Only the following quote from Petrov offers a deeper glimpse into the soul of the soldier in Alexander I's times: in the Battle of Borodino, Petrov's men were ordered to destroy two bridges, which they did "under heavy enemy fire at close quarters; the enemy shot at us with eight cannons from the hills of the village and with guns from the outermost houses and fences.

But I executed this order successfully thanks to my officers' special striving for honor [chrez osobennoe sorevnovanie k chesti moikh ofitserov]."[2]

A hundred years later descriptions of fear were legion. Consider this Russian First World War memoir:

> "What kind of fear is that supposed to be?" a bearded guy in rags
> interrupted Semenych. "You don't croak from that kind of fear. In the
> trenches—that is where the real fear is! It creeps under your very skin.
> I once crawled out of my trench. Boom! Shells are exploding with ter-
> rible noise. Around me there is lots of groaning. I want to walk away,
> but can't lift my leg; it's as if someone grabbed my ankle. I can't look
> left, can't look right—I'm afraid. Fear of death has taken hold of me,
> has overwhelmed my heart, and no fear is more brutal than this kind
> of fear. It's as though someone poured cold snow under your skin; your
> jaw starts chattering, and your blood stops flowing in your veins: it
> has frozen. I wanted to aim with my rifle, but it was so damn' heavy,
> like a pud; I wanted to scream, but I could only rattle like an animal, I
> wanted to pull the trigger, but I couldn't."[3]

Clearly, something changed between 1812 and 1914. Either soldiers at some point began to experience more fear, and in different ways, or the boundaries of what could be and actually was said about soldierly fear in personal documents profoundly shifted or a new and real experience of fear came together with a discursive shift.[4] One thing is certain: constituting fear as a legitimate object of scientific inquiry was crucial in this change. Here the disciplines of neuropathology, psychiatry, psychology, psychoanalysis, and pedagogy, which for purposes of simplicity I will collectively call "military psychology," played a pivotal role. These fields formed in the late nineteenth century and underwent complex processes of cultural transfer, entanglement, and professionalization. Just how the practitioners of these fields wrote about fear is my main emphasis, but I will also ask why it became possible to speak of fear in the first place and provide short answers.

The chief sources for this chapter are publications (journal articles and books) by military psychiatrists and psychologists.[5] Since the historical and cultural specificity of emotional expression becomes visible in sharper relief when compared with other cultures and over the *longue durée*, there will be several side-glances at Germany, France, Britain, and the United States as well as a look back to the early nineteenth century. The chronological focus, however, is the first two decades of the twentieth century, when Russia fought two major wars—the Russo-Japanese

War (1904–1905) and the First World War (1914–1918). In these years it became the first nation in history to deploy frontline military psychiatrists to treat the fear-induced symptoms of soldiers that would later come to figure as "military contusion" or "traumatic neurosis" (*voennaia kontuziia, travmaticheskii nevroz*) in Russia, "shell shock" in Britain, "war commotion" or "war emotion" (*commotion de la guerre, émotion de la guerre*) in France, and "war neurosis" (*Kriegsneurose*) in Germany and Austro-Hungary.[6]

HOW SOLDIERS LEARNED TO ARTICULATE FEAR: SIX CAUSES

What accounts for the striking fin-de-siècle expansion of fear in soldiers' textual artifacts? I believe there are six explanations, which I will sketch briefly. Most important, since this expansion coincided with the modernization of warfare, it was connected with an increase in the real psychological stress that modern war produces. Modern war exposes soldiers to drastically longer periods of rifle and machine gun shooting, shelling, and air bombardment. It makes the source of the attack difficult to locate. Trench warfare, a major feature of the First World War, immobilizes soldiers, thus incapacitating the reflex to flee from the source of danger; by contrast, a premodern open battlefield and one-on-one bayonet combat offered the—shame-free—option of forward attack as an outlet for fight-or-flight reactions. And modern war is fought by national, mass-conscripted armies, whose soldiers serve for comparatively short periods of time, can hope for a return to civilian life, and lack much of the esprit de corps that united standing armies.[7] All of these factors amount to a real and significant increase in psychological stress that had to spill over into the ways soldiers felt—and sometimes wrote—about what they endured.

Also connected with the onset of modernity was the emergence of an image of man as a creature who fashions his world and ultimately himself, an image of, in short, an autonomous self. The possibility of destruction of self—for example, by death in a war—then produces much greater anxiety than if the potential for death remained in the realm of transcendent forces that control man and his world; it is no longer the will of a god, just as a business success or horse-riding accident is no longer the will of a god, but a threat to the autonomy of selfhood, the very foundation upon which man rests in the modern world.[8]

Another explanation, a Foucauldian explanation, points to the interiorization of feelings that was a hallmark of modernity. As soon as soldiers became autonomous subjects and ceased to think of themselves as caught in webs of dependence, intent on saving their honor in front of fellow human beings, feelings moved from the body surface to the body interior. Linked with this shift was the invention of "sciences" of the interior, psychology and psychiatry. The psychological sciences, in this explanation, not only furnished some of the language in which emotions could be expressed but their own emergence legitimized, if not invented, the public communicability of soldierly fear.[9]

It can further be argued that the Russian case differs from the Western European case in that it imported the change in speaking about fear related to modernity. Russia, in other words, widened the limits of the sayable, not because it entered modernity itself but rather because it aped an entrance into modernity—a variant of mimicry. By producing texts about soldierly fear, Russia proved to itself and the outside world that it had arrived in modernity.

There was also the expansion of literacy and the new mass media, which produced not only more soldiers who could write about fear but also genres like crime novels and a scandal-hungry yellow press with unheard-of possibilities to evoke fear in readers.[10] Static media such as broadsheets, paintings, and photography are less apt to *evoke* (as opposed to depicting) fear; moving media such as narrative text and especially film are ideal for the creation of suspense and fear. This explanation hinges on the very characteristics of a genre or medium. The argument goes like this: because new genres like crime novels that allowed for the production of fear in readers (whose numbers were increasing due to the spread of literacy) appeared, a new permissibility of fear took hold. This permissibility eventually affected medicine, which began turning fear into an object of inquiry, as well as soldiers' first-person accounts.

Finally, and second in importance only to the onset of modern warfare, Russian belles lettres played a large part in widening the boundaries of what soldiers could publicly say about fear. Leo Tolstoy's *Sevastopol'skie rasskazy* (Sevastopol' sketches; first published in 1855) are crucial here. In these stories, which build on Stendhal's *Chartreuse de Parme* (1839), Tolstoy provides three snapshots from different phases of the siege of Sevastopol' until its fall in September 1855.[11]

The twenty-seven-year-old Tolstoy experienced the siege of Sevastopol' at a close distance as an observer. A veteran himself (he was almost killed by a shell in the Caucasian wars), Tolstoy sets his readers on a long road to fear, the central emotion in these stories, suggesting that one of his aims was to elicit fear in his readers. He starts with a description of the whole gamut of sensory impressions that overwhelm the soldier, including the howling of bombs, the pinging of bullets, and the booming of bursting shells: "Suddenly you realize, in an entirely new way, the true significance of those sounds of gunfire you heard from the town. . . . You start thinking more about yourself and less about what you observe around you, and are suddenly gripped by an unpleasant sense of indecision. The sight of a soldier glissading downhill over the wet mud, waving his arms and laughing, silences this cowardly voice that has begun to speak within you at the prospect of danger, however, and you find yourself straightening your chest, lifting your head a little higher." In what follows, Tolstoy creates a sense of mounting danger. Fear in Tolstoy arrives excruciatingly slowly; it is as though the narrative strategy of evoking fear overpowers his photographic realism, as though a war between two narrative strategies is taking place, with realism losing out to emotionally conditioning readers. The first utterance of the fear word "terror" (*uzhas*) is climactic (and mirrored by the narrator's arrival at the apex of one of Sevastopol''s defensive hills): "You think you hear a cannonball land not far from you; all around you seem to hear the various sounds that bullets make—from the ones that hum like bees to the ones that whistle rapidly by or twang with a noise like a plucked string; you hear the terrible boom of an artillery discharge: it shakes you to the core and inspires you with a profound sense of dread. 'So this is it, the 4th bastion, that dreadful, truly dreadful place,' you think to yourself, experiencing a slight feeling of pride, and an anything-but-slight feeling of suppressed terror."[12]

From now on Tolstoy maps that vast and multifarious terrain he calls "a whole world of feelings." He describes the corporeal aspects of soldiers' fear—the heart-pounding, sweating, breathing difficulties, pallor, and cold blood. He describes the phenomenon of thrill—"a strange blend of fear and enjoyment."[13] He describes how both soldiers and officers feign bravery. He describes cowardice and the fear of appearing a coward to others. For Tolstoy there is only one hope: religion—its practices (prayer, icons) and its promise (life after death). At the very end of his second story, "Sevastopol' in May," Tolstoy legitimizes his realism in religious terms:

> It might be supposed that when these men—Christians, recognizing
> the same great law of love—see what they have done, they will instantly
> fall to their knees in order to repent before Him who, when he gave
> them life, placed in the soul of each, together with the fear of death,

a love of the good and the beautiful, and that they will embrace one another with tears of joy and happiness, like brothers. Not a bit of it! . . . No, the hero of my story, whom I love with all my heart and soul, whom I have attempted to portray in his beauty and who has always been, is now and will always be supremely magnificent, is truth.[14]

With a love for truth, grounded in the Christian virtue of charity, Tolstoy proffered officers—and indirectly soldiers—a strong argument to break the silence of their fear. Thus an idiosyncratic realism with Christian-Tolstoyan undertones contributed to a significant expansion of the boundaries of what could be said about soldierly fear in nineteenth-century Russia.

THE PLACE OF FEAR IN RUSSIAN MILITARY PSYCHOLOGY BEFORE THE 1860s

In late nineteenth-century North America and Europe (including Russia), the medical fields of psychiatry, neuropathology and neurology, psychology, and psychoanalysis developed and differentiated rapidly. The military had a much greater part in this than histories of psychiatry usually acknowledge.[15] The military looked to the psychological medical sciences to treat—in order to restore to fighting capability—soldiers who suffered from nervous disorders, and medical scientists looked to soldier-patients to observe, classify, and indeed create the symptoms, causes, and treatments of nervous ailments. At the center of it all was fear. How fear moved there only becomes clear by taking a closer look at the institutional, political, and ideational contours of the evolution of the psychomedical sciences.

Until the early 1920s Russia followed the Western and Central European pattern of development, some time lag and differences notwithstanding.[16] As for institutions, insane people were largely left under the purview of their family, local communities, the church, and monasteries until the first insane asylums were established during Peter I's reign. In 1832 an insane asylum opened at St. Petersburg's Hospital of All Mourners under the direction of first I. F. Riul' and later F. I. Gertsog, who both have been termed the "grandfathers" of Russian psychiatry. In the 1830s psychiatry was included in the curriculum of regular medical students but remained a marginal subject. The state university statute of 1835 advanced psychiatry, but it was the Crimean War—and Russia's 1856 defeat in it—that gave the greatest boost to psychiatry. The military

defeat not only spawned the Great Reforms and thus the educational professionalization of psychiatry but it also—and this is often overlooked—
made clear to military officials that in future wars the psychological sciences would play a crucial role in restoring soldiers to full fighting power,
which would become ever more necessary given the elements of modern
warfare foreshadowed in the Crimean War.

In the greater tree of medical knowledge and institutionally (university departments, hospitals, state licensing), a combined psychiatric-neu-
rological branch began growing out of internal medicine from the 1850s
onward.[17] In the 1890s psychiatry and neurology began to separate, and
later psychoanalysis grew out of psychiatry. By 1900 Russian psychiatry
could be said to have "come of age."[18] It is impossible to disentangle the
military and civilian sides of these developments. Suffice it to say that the
"father" of Russian psychiatry, I. M. Balinskii, was a military physician
by training; that St. Petersburg was the undisputed center of medical
learning in large measure due to the presence of capital-city state institutions, first of all the War Ministry; and that the best-funded institution of
medical education was the Military-Medical Academy in St. Petersburg
(later Leningrad), which only ceded this position to civilian universities
in the 1940s under Joseph Stalin. The Russo-Japanese War, the First Bal-
kan War of 1912, and the First World War gave a great boost to military
psychiatry; the Russo-Japanese War, which produced an estimated 6,225
total Russian cases of "hysteria and nervous exhaustion" and is often
considered the first modern war or World War Zero, was watched closely
by the outside world because, as the American military psychiatrist Cap-
tain R. L. Richards observed in 1910, "for the first time in the history of
the world mental diseases were separately cared for by specialists from
the firing line back to the home country."[19] By the second decade of the
twentieth century, Russia had become the leader in global military psychiatry.

Russian psychiatrists themselves frequently turned to the past of
their own discipline.[20] Their histories and periodizations—religious care,
Peter I, the establishment of the Medical-Surgical Academy in 1798, and
the influence of Western psychiatry—resembled each other greatly, but
the locus of fear in these shifted markedly. In A. L. Shcheglov's 1899
historical overview of Russian psychiatry, fear surfaced only twice, and
one of these times, almost, but not quite, as a psychological cause for
mental disorders. This emerges in his recounting of German psychiatrist
Werner Nasse's writing on the Austro-Prussian War of 1866 and once in
an account of German psychiatrist Rudolf Arndt's work on the Franco-

Prussian War of 1870–1871, where fear was clearly portrayed as pathogenic. A mere eight years later, M. O. Shaikevich squarely placed fear at the center of pathogeny for mental disorders and eventually even elevated fear to a cipher for a multitude of pathogenic factors in wartime.[21] The proliferation of fear, now both pathogen and symptom, was spawned and sped up by the Russo-Japanese War on the one hand and by the Russian Revolution of 1905 on the other. While the Russo-Japanese War had made it patently obvious that soldiers broke down with nervous disorders in modern war, and that fear was critical in this, the revolution of 1905 definitively opened the discursive floodgates: widespread talk of fear in society—fear of revolution and chaos—made it possible to talk of soldierly fear as well and to insert fear retroactively in the Russian psychiatric profession's version of its own history.[22] Psychiatrists were now able to write self-confidently that while "the leaders of the medical institutions could claim that there were no soldiers suffering from nervous disorders" in the Crimean and Russo-Turkish Wars, in truth "of course there were nervous disorders; . . . it is only because the doctors at the time had an inadequate knowledge of nervous disease that these disorders were not recognized and filed under other diagnoses."[23]

Psychiatrists' historicizing insider writings on the place of fear in psychiatry are one thing, but what does fear's trajectory in the psychiatric sciences look like from the outside? *Opyt voenno-meditsinskoi politsii, ili pravila k sokhraneniiu zdorov'ia russkikh soldat v sukhoputnoi sluzhbe* (The experience of the military-medical police, or: Rules for the healthcare of the Russian soldiers of the land forces; published in 1834) explicitly mentioned fear only once; when discussing the advantages of the Russians, Ukrainians, and Cossacks over other ethnic groups of the empire, the book stresses the idea that these three particular peoples tend to be "brought up in fear of God."[24] True, the book encouraged officers to shape the will of their soldiers so that they can "overcome all needs, difficulties, and dangers in order to defeat the enemy, without kindling depressing passions in them or weakening their mental powers."[25] But on the whole the categories in which fear could be discussed or almost discussed were still in the realm of morality and religion rather than medicine and psychology, and the strong ethnic component in the description of soldiers deduced national character from climate and religion rather than genes or individual personality types. Insofar as diseases surface, these are epidemics caused by a lack of hygiene, and insofar as feelings surface, these are primarily religious and patriotic feelings caused by national character ("v strakhe Bozhiem, liubvi i pokornosti k GOSUDARIU").[26]

The emotionalization ("feelingization" would be a better term because feelings and passions had yet to turn into scientific "emotions") of religion, the tsar cult, and patriotism had gotten underway, which, together with such existing physiological feeling categories in Russian as *organy chuvstv* (sensory organs) and *obman chuvstv* (hallucination), was crucial in preparing the linguistic ground for the later medicalization of soldierly fear.[27] This language of emotions is also evident in A. Kislov's *Voennaia nravstvennost'* (Military morality; 1838), in which fear of God and love for tsar and motherland are considered inborn qualities; heroism is depicted as a natural outgrowth of these qualities and hence independent of any kind of remuneration, material (money), symbolic (medals), or otherwise; officer and soldier are said to be bound by feelings of love and gratitude.[28]

Despite introducing a language of feelings, then, these works of the 1830s still belong to a universe of honor and the duel, a universe in which the negation *neustrashimost'* was sayable but *strakh* was not and in which Kutuzov showed tears not of fear but of grief—and only once, namely, when he was forced to condemn two of his soldiers to death.[29] This did not change overnight. The Crimean War, Tolstoy's *Sevastopol'skie rasskazy*, and the military reform during the Great Reforms accelerated this continuum of change. Part of the military reform was intended to give soldiers better training and one result was a new doctrine and a manual of training. Here the work of General Mikhail Dragomirov deserves to be singled out.[30]

GENERAL DRAGOMIROV AND THE DOCTRINE OF CONTROLLED BERSERKERDOM

Mikhail Dragomirov (1830–1905) quickly rose through the military ranks and was sent to Western Europe in the late 1850s to study tactics and the training of recruits. After his return to reform-era Russia, not only was he instrumental in revising basic military training but he also served as a private tutor to several tsareviches. His active military duty included the suppression of the Polish uprising in 1863, his participation in the Second Prussian Army during the War of 1866, and especially his command over the Fourth Division in the victorious Russo-Turkish War. He was wounded in that war and henceforth directed the Military Academy in St. Petersburg, where he excelled as Russia's most productive— and widely read, both at home and abroad—military theoretician.[31]

The fear problem was at the heart of Dragomirov's influential military theoretical writings. Dragomirov started from an axiomatic assumption about human nature: "the willingness to suffer and to die, that is, self-sacrifice," was universal.[32] According to Dragomirov, the Russian variant of self-sacrifice was marked by the soldier's special loyalty toward his motherland, embodied in the tsar. The Russian soldier was character-ized by "a feeling of duty toward tsar and motherland, a feeling that goes as far as self-denial."[33] Self-denial in Dragomirov's scheme constituted the antipode to self-preservation.[34] The key to the victory of self-denial over self-preservation was drilling, especially the training of obedience. The most effective antidote to fear, in other words, was practice and routine. It was only logical that maneuvers in peacetime ought to be as realistic—as fear inducing—as possible.[35]

A crucial part of the Dragomirov theory was the doctrine of con-trolled berserkerdom. Dragomirov believed the Russian Army differed from Western armies in its emphasis on morale instead of military tech-nology, and the Russian soldier differed from the Western soldier in his ability to unleash and reign in his aggressions without using modern fire weapons and in a manner that was fundamentally superior to that of the Western soldier, who had become weak and decadent because of mod-ern life.[36] This doctrine is often expressed in the short formula "bayo-nets before bullets" (*pulia dura—shtyk molodets*).[37] At bottom, we have an attempt to resuscitate the premodern immediacy of face-to-face warfare. Paradoxically, Dragomirov's doctrine was based on an image of self that stemmed from the Enlightenment and modernity: only an autonomous, rational subject can, on command, start and stop himself from going berserk. Put differently, in order to conceive of the subject's planned retreat from reason, this subject first has to be endowed with reason.

The Dragomirov doctrine was turned into normative documents (for example, via the first new infantry regulation since 1831, the *Ustav stro-evoi pekhotnoi sluzhby,* published in 1866), and Russian soldiers received their training on its basis until the First World War. With this doctrine Russia developed an "emotional regime" that openly revolved around fear surprisingly early—with the express goal, of course, of channeling, managing, and ultimately overcoming this fear.[38] Thus, Tolstoy's realist fiction and Dragomirov's military theorizing were the first stages in a wider rhetoric of soldierly fear. They prepared the ground for early public talk about fear by high-ranking officers in the aftermath of the Russo-Turkish War (1877–1878). General Mikhail Skobelev, for example, wrote, "There is no one who does not fear death; and if someone tells you that he does not fear death—spit in his eye; he is lying. I myself fear death no less than everyone else. But there are people who have enough willpower not to show this, while others cannot restrain themselves and flee out of fear of death. I have the willpower not to show that I am afraid; but the battle inside me is terrifying, and this has a constant effect on my heart."[39]

THE PLACE OF FEAR IN RUSSIAN MILITARY PSYCHOLOGY AFTER THE 1860s

As for the psychomedical sciences proper, Russia first imported the idea that fear caused nervous disorders in soldiers from Germany in 1873, that is, in the immediate aftermath of the Franco-Prussian War.[40] The next milestone was A. I. Ozeretskovskii's 1891 dissertation "Ob isterii v voiskakh" (On hysteria in the army).[41] One of the first Russian commentators to factor fear into the equation, Ozeretskovskii denied that fear caused hysteria. The etiology of "male hysteria," which he found occurred mostly in young soldiers, boiled down to a notion of psychological trauma stemming from causes understood in exclusively physiological terms—"dropping off the gymnastic ladder or trapeze, infelicitous jumps, and similar downfalls or injuries" as well as light and sound impressions, in one case "caused by continuous work in an electric light factory, where the factory light itself was electrical."[42] Ozeretskovskii's uncoupling of fear from mental disease dominated the discussion for about a decade until this uncoupling gave way to an understanding of fear as the primary cause of mental illness, an understanding that, as we have seen, was around before the Russo-Japanese War but became more common and more highly charged because it was intertwined with the massive social crisis of the 1905 revolution. This shift was not a sudden but a gradual move that included such spurts as a physical trauma-cum-"fright" (ispug) pathogen that saw fear as a symptom of illness ("after fright from some loud thunder") and a patient's identification of fear as a cause of his illness while the doctor denied this causal link.[43]

As for the image of human nature that lay at the bottom of first Ozeretskovskii's, then others', etiology, there were, in essence, two options: either fear was a component of human nature, or fear was unnatural. This binary opposition received a highly influential label in 1911, when *Voennyi sbornik* published an article that identified two "doctrines" regarding the fear of soldiers—a "romantic doctrine" and a "realistic doctrine." As the author M. V. Enval'd explicated it, the romantic doctrine saw fear as an aberration from the norm of brave, fearless soldiers, while the realistic doctrine assumed that all soldiers experience fear before, during, and often after battle.[44] This binary of a romantic versus a realistic doctrine provided a language for an existing opposition and, after it began to circulate in the military-scientific community, was cited again and again. Thus fear in military psychiatry was a discursive field demarcated by two poles—on the one hand an image of soldiers who were constitutionally fearless (the "romantic doctrine"); on the other hand an image of soldiers who were constitutionally fearful (the "realistic doctrine"). Over time the latter came to dominate, though this was not a linear development and requires qualification depending on the group one is speaking about (generals, officers, soldiers, or military psychiatrists). Unsurprisingly, military psychiatrists always tended toward this latter pole; after all, they owed their jobs—treating soldiers for fear-induced disorders— to the existence of soldierly fear.

There were other reasons why Russian military psychiatrists were likely to believe that their patients' symptoms resulted not from personality (the "cowardly" type), innate mental disorders merely triggered by an eerie moment in war, or mental-cum-moral retardation (the female-coded "prissy" or biological "degenerate") but from war-related events too traumatic to be managed by the coping mechanisms soldiers had at their disposal. Russian military psychiatrists by and large belonged to the liberal intelligentsia, and the chasm that separated them from the autocracy was wider than that between military psychiatrists and the state in Western Europe. Consequently their empathetic hearts and social consciences sided with the common soldier. Of consequence too is the fact that Russia never produced the kind of veteran pension debate that took place in Germany, where breakdown in battle was aggressively essentialized and depicted as the phenotypical expression of a preexisting genetic disposition—in order to absolve the state from having to pay the follow-up costs, namely veteran pensions, as Paul Lerner has convincingly argued.[45]

The dominant realistic approach to fear provided plenty of room for definition, differentiation, and discussion. Scientists customarily began with a description of the symptoms and then moved to the definitions of different kinds of fear (for this they used the Russian terms *strakh*, *ispug*, *trepet*, *boiazn'*, *trevoga*, *panika*, and others). In an article for the general reading public, Grigorii Shumkov, the head of the psychiatric ward at the military hospital in Harbin during the Russo-Japanese War and the preeminent military psychiatrist during the first two decades of the twentieth century, summarized the panorama of feelings a soldier experienced: "Soldiers go through a lot; they fear, they get angry, they rejoice, sometimes they despair, they hope, they believe in victory, are disappointed and start to believe again. Life in a war is a striking kaleidoscope of different feelings, feelings that people experience in time of peace as well, but that get expressed more clearly and vividly in war."[46] From this followed a distinct set of tasks for the military psychiatrist, which Shumkov also summarized: "Followers of the second, realistic school [pace Enval'd] . . . attempt to study man, the psychophysical nature of the soldier, they try to penetrate into the realm of psychological phenomena; they try to explore the laws of soldiers' psyches in armed conflicts, and having analyzed these laws, they explain to future soldiers the nature of these phenomena and recommend means of fighting these undesirable phenomena." Eager to elevate nervous disorders to the status that respectable, bacteriological diseases enjoyed and to indicate that nervous disorders could be studied in a comparable rational manner, Shumkov drew parallels between the fear of soldiers and cholera: "In order to fight cholera it is essential to study cholera. . . . In order to fight fear of death in war, the followers of the second, realistic school study the manifestations of this fear; in order to avoid panic, they strive to analyze its nature, genesis, manifestation, dissemination, etc."[47] Shumkov's final conclusion was that "the science of military psychology is indispensable."[48]

As time went by, psychiatrists' descriptions of the symptoms of fear grew more complex and multifaceted.[49] Grigorii Shumkov's study of the "mental state of soldiers" before, during, and after combat is unsurpassed in this regard. Drawing upon his own practice and a wealth of other sources, Shumkov construed an ideal-typical soldier and followed his psychological state through a battle. At least one of his thick descriptions deserves closer scrutiny; the precombat stage is particularly apt, since if we are to believe Shumkov, it exceeds combat and postcombat on the anxiety scale. The "psycho-physiological" picture of the soldier before combat starts with preparations for battle and the background noise of artillery; everybody is waiting for the order to go: "The soldiers all start digging in their notebooks, purses, and bags, they pull out the letters and read them. Most of them get burned after having been quickly reread. They hand each other notes and verbal requests: 'If I die, send this home and let them know that I thought of them.' . . . Many religious soldiers take their sacred icons out, *cross themselves zealously,* kiss the icons, and hang them on their chest." After the "last" tasks of existential significance have been completed, soldiers turn to fixing their uniforms, their equipment, and especially their weapon. Because soldiers are so nervous, "boots and belt hurt more noticeably than in peacetime." Throughout it is impossible to concentrate on a single thought, "Thoughts are cascading as rapidly as the pictures in a movie." The atmosphere is characterized by general silence and tense nervousness: "Many run off to relieve themselves, and this several times." Everyone tries to quench their thirst and fill their water bottles: "The rifle gets examined many times . . . The bag for bullets is also there, and hands go into it more often than necessary."[50]

Finally the unit starts moving and part of the tension disappears. The increasing proximity of artillery fire makes all soldiers feel "that they are about to die. 'But death is better than waiting for death.' Everybody pushes forward and hopes to reach the destination and some kind of end, any kind of end." A few hundred steps in front of the firing zone the order comes to stop and wait: "It is precisely this situation—'stop and wait' for combat—that is the most unbearable of all in war." "Not only did I pace back and forth from all the anxiety," recounted one officer, "I think I rather ran and leaped . . . I couldn't sit still in any place. . . . In my soul . . . my heart aches so bad, hurt so much, as never before. . . . You start talking and jump to the next topic, without finishing the previous sentence. . . . When you ask a comrade about something, you don't hear his answer, and at the same moment it is as though you are intoxicated by your own thoughts. As soon as he stops talking, you wake up and ask: 'What? What did you just say?'" During this worst waiting period the receptiveness for rumors, half-truths, and lies grows strongest. A propaganda newspaper item can become the truth: "Suggestibility more than anything else is responsible for upswings and downswings in the mood of the troops."[51] If there is bad news, everyone falls silent, the mood deteriorates, and soldiers go into battle in a depressed state. Good news has the contrary effect, Shumkov concluded.

The symptoms that doctors observed in the Russo-Japanese War were one source of information. Another method of gathering data was to interview soldiers after their return from the war. In 1909–1910 at the behest of the military psychology section of the Society of the Devotees to Military Science (Obshchestvo revnitelei voennykh znanii) K. Druzhinin distributed a questionnaire to veterans, which included such questions as "How did you feel (sad, happy, angry, did you experience fear, were you terrified [ispytyval li strakh, bylo li zhutko])" and "Were you aware of danger, to what extent and when exactly" (fig. 4.1). The rubric "How did you feel physically" asked about body temperature, perspiration, heartbeat, breathing, appetite, sleep, urination, and defeca-

— 4 —

3) Состояніе здоровья до войны, во время войны и послѣ (если есть та или иная хроническая болѣзнь, необходимо указать).

4) Отношеніе къ употребленію спиртныхъ напитковъ (было ли употребленіе алкоголя болѣе значительнымъ, болѣе умѣреннымъ или оставлено).

5) Полученное образованіе.

6) Сколько времени проведено на войнѣ и гдѣ именно.

7) Если случилось бывать нѣсколько разъ въ одинаковой обстановкѣ, то измѣнялись ли ощущенія и какъ именно (первый бой, послѣдующіе).

8) При сообщеніи свѣдѣній крайне желательно всегда отмѣтить: къ какому именно бою (Ляоянъ 20 августа), къ какому моменту боя, или войны, относятся переживаемыя душевныя состоянія, какую должность (ротный командиръ, младшій офицеръ и т. д.) и роль (офицеръ для связи, начальникъ боевой части) исполнялъ авторъ въ описываемое время и т. п.

Затѣмъ, описывая какой либо строго опредѣленный моментъ или событіе, напр. ожиданіе штурма или ночной бой,—желательно указать.

II. Что чувствовалъ самъ и переживалъ по сравненію со спокойнымъ состояніемъ.

1) Какъ текли мысли, скоро или медленно и какія именно (одна навязчивая или нѣсколько быстро смѣняющихся, никакихъ мыслей, касались-ли данной обстановки или нѣтъ и т. д.).

2) Какое было настроеніе (приподнятое, безразличное, подавленное и т. д.).

— 5 —

3) Какъ себя чувствовалъ (грустно, весело, злобно, испытывалъ ли страхъ, было ли жутко).

4) Что дѣлалъ (сидѣлъ, стоялъ, ходилъ, лежалъ) и почему: безсознательно или сознательно. Вліяніе примѣра другихъ. Вліяніе получаемыхъ извѣстій или слуховъ.

5) Не было ли невольныхъ движеній, схватыванія за голову, за сердце, за шею, за животъ, за ноги и т. п.

6) Сознавалась ли опасность, въ какой мѣрѣ и когда именно.

III. Какъ чувствовалъ себя физически.

1) Чувствовалъ ли себя тепло или холодно (какая была погода и во что былъ одѣтъ).

2) Потѣлъ или нѣтъ.

3) Сердце было ли спокойно, усиленно билось, или казалось, что оно горитъ, ноетъ, давитъ, готово выскочить и т. п.

4) Какъ дышалось — спокойно полной грудью или тяжело съ недостачей воздуха.

5) Сохло ли во рту. Часто ли пилъ и по сколько.

6) Отправленіе мочевого пузыря и кишечника.

7) Аппетитъ и сонъ во время переживаемаго и послѣ пережитаго.

IV. Что замѣтилъ у другихъ въ то же время.

1) Какіе ведутся разговоры и о чемъ говорятъ.

2) Какимъ ведутся голосомъ (звучнымъ, сиплымъ, шепотомъ и т. п.).

Figure 4.1. Druzhinin's questionnaire, from K. M. Druzhinin, *Issledovanie dushevnogo sostoianiia voinov v raznykh sluchaiakh boevoi obstanovki po opytu russko-iaponskoi voiny 1904–05 gg.* (St. Petersburg: Russkaia Skoropechatnia, 1910), 4–5

tion. Another rubric, "What did you notice in others at the same time," inquired about the kinds of things fellow soldiers were talking about and in what tone of voice, about "the expression on and color of the faces of those surrounding you (calm, agitated, sad, pale, cyanotic-pale, etc.)" and "did you notice any awkwardness or trembling hands (when lighting matches, rolling cigarettes, loading the rifle, etc.)."[52]

Druzhinin summarized the results of this questionnaire and interspersed accounts of his own experience as a reconnaissance officer in the Russo-Japanese War. Immediately before the beginning of a battle and especially "when cannon and, most important, rifle shots can be heard, the anxiety . . . and fear of the unknown, the consciousness of a possible close death or injury, becomes maddeningly palpable in soldiers who are not being shot at." There was, to be sure, a learning curve or at least some kind of adaptation, which meant that "before the first battle, the mood was more nervous; before further battles, calmer." The soldiers' ability to overcome their fear rested largely on the prospect of victory. As long as victory was on the horizon, soldiers were able to endure incredible hardship; logically, therefore, a principal task of the successful officer was to make soldiers believe that victory was certain, even if things were hopeless. A command to retreat is always dangerous, since retreat runs the risk of dissolving into chaos and panic. During the Russo-Japanese War, Mukden was emblematic of everything gone awry: "To delay the main battle, as was the case in Mukden, and then to admit a loss and to order the soldiers to turn their backs on the enemy is too dangerous, in fact, it is totally impossible."[53]

Druzhinin's own experience already pointed in the direction of distinguishing between different kinds of fear. Here is how he differentiated between two types of fear that he himself felt before his first-ever battle:

> In late March 1904 around noon I was lying on my bed in the dark. A dragoon who had been sent from the sea coast appeared at the door and reported: "Your Honor, the Japanese have started to disembark!" I didn't have to worry about hiding my excitement [*volnenie*], because, though I was able to see the dragoon standing in the light of the room next door, the dragoon could not see me. This message from the dragoon—never mind that it turned out to be a false alarm—had special meaning to me: for the first time in my army life I heard that I was about to engage in combat. I remember clearly that I didn't get scared, but I did experience a highly uneasy feeling [*trevozhnoe chuvstvo*], perhaps palpitation.[54]

The term "trevozhnoe chuvstvo" would resurface three years later, when a number of specialists, above all Shumkov, A. S. Rezanov, and Antonii Dmitrevskii, the influential editor of *Voennyi sbornik* and an amateur military psychologist himself, plunged into a long discussion about the types of fear.[55] This discussion with its obvious philosophical overtones (concerning Søren Kierkegaard) revolved around Shumkov's thesis that "anxiety" (*trevoga*) was not goal oriented—it was impossible to be anxious of some object—and ought to be separated from "fear" (*strakh*), which always had an object.[56]

A related set of issues that occupied military scientists concerned questions of heroism, valor (*khrabrost'*), cowardice, and medals.[57] While some argued that constitutionally fearless soldiers were abnormal and potential sociopaths, unsuited to and even dangerous in civilian life, others, such as Shumkov, actively tried to reinterpret the meaning of heroism and to forge an image of a soldier who was fearful and heroic at the same time.[58] After reviewing "heroes of bravery [*khrabrosti*]," "heroes of audacity [*smelosti*]," "heroes of decisiveness," and "heroes of cold-bloodedness," Shumkov introduced a quiet, "unnoticeable" hero, a "hero of patience," as the title of his article announced (based, most certainly, on a medical history from his Harbin psychiatric ward in the Russo-Japanese War). Veteran Iushchenko recounted: "I am thirty years old and a peasant . . . and married, I have children. . . . I was always healthy and went to this war with pleasure. I didn't know cowardice and was never afraid, as sometimes happens with others. I knew no fear, not when getting shot at, not when fighting with a bayonet. What was there to fear! If they kill me, I will die for the tsar and the faith; perhaps God will forgive my sins; and if I stay alive, thank God!"[59]

Iushchenko was then caught by the Japanese, which he described as a great dishonor. After several attempts, he managed to escape. He wandered through the heat for eighteen to twenty days and probably only survived because he drank his own urine. Eventually he was rescued by a Cossack reconnaissance troop who described this event as follows: "Suddenly we see a stark-naked man running down from a hilltop toward us and screaming something incomprehensible. He stumbled, fell down, and couldn't get up again. Emaciated, covered with scratches, with bulging eyes, he lay there mumbling something. Our little Russian soldier has gone mad, we thought. . . . He was constantly talking nonsense about the Japanese: 'The Japanese . . . ,' 'the Japanese are whistling.'" Thanks to the Cossacks who picked him up in this state, Iushchenko came to Shumkov in Harbin. Shumkov summarized his diagnosis and treatment as follows: "On 14 August 1904 Iushchenko was declared nervously feeble [*nervno-slabym*] and emaciated and sent home for recuperation." Shumkov concluded this article, a collage of his own, medical-diagnostic voice, his liberal-political voice, the Cossacks' voice, and Iushchenko's voice (extracted from his medical history): "He, yes he, Private Iushchenko, is a true hero!"[60]

What about the etiology of a collective version of soldier trauma that went beyond individual bodies and psyches? Softline liberal doctors were fond of locating the larger cause of the epidemic of Russian shell shock in the sociopolitical sphere. They reasoned that the Russo-Japanese War was unpopular, hence the breakdowns of soldiers. According to these softliners, a comparison between the Russo-Turkish War and the Russo-Japanese War clearly showed the difference: if the *narod* was motivated by the "touching idea" of the Russo-Turkish War to "stand up for their slain Slavic brothers," the "baselessness" of the Russo-Japanese War turned "society" against this war or at least led to "indifference, which had an extremely detrimental impact on the morale of the troops."[61]

But this was just a minor strand in the psychiatric community's discussion about the larger causes of the breakdowns. Like their Western colleagues, Russian psychiatrists were most likely to attribute this increase to the development of modern warfare and technology. One doctor argued that, although technology had made huge strides, "man's soul, his inner 'I,' remains unchanged."[62] With the old training, soldiers "could be victorious at the beginning, perhaps the middle of the bygone [nineteenth] century, relying on the Suvorov bayonet and a feeling of unconditional self-sacrifice, which is characteristic of the Russian soldier, but nowadays it would be too hard for them to bear the demoralizing impact of modern warfare with its new, destructive factors."[63] The modern soldier was almost as atomized and lonely in the battlefield as modern man in the city: "the battlefield is empty, you can see neither your own soldiers nor the enemy, you don't feel any support" and, to make things worse, neither auditory nor visual diversion is available ("the banners don't fly, the music doesn't play").[64]

This is not to say that the so-called romantic, hardline doctrine ever completely disappeared. In fact, this doctrine's denial of the existence of soldierly fear led to a greater silence on this subject, as did something else, namely the argument that an open discussion of soldierly fear in the mass media would prove infectious and produce more fearful soldiers. Both factors skew our view of fear's place within military psychiatry, factors that are amplified by our own liberal bias, which makes us more likely to side with the liberal psychiatrists.[65] There were, in short, plenty of observers who plainly denied the idea that all soldiers experienced fear.[66] The hardliners argued that the best antidote to fear was fear—of punishment and shame and, more concretely, of reintroduced military colonies and corporeal punishment.[67]

The liberals in turn were quick to point out that army training in its then-current state, with its reliance on drill and the drill masters (*diad'ki*), contained enough brutality and fear, which only worsened preexisting mental conditions; as N. Butovskii put it in 1888: "Strictness and coarseness are synonyms for such a commander. . . . He experiences his greatest pleasure when the new recruit stands in front of him at attention and shakes under his terrifying stare. He thinks of military service as something that is based on the fear that the officer exerts over his subordinate."[68] As the liberal Shumkov demanded, "means of frightening and intimidation should be eliminated from military pedagogy."[69] Dmitrevskii concurred in an article that bore the programmatic title "Vospitanie voina mozhet byt' tol'ko v styde nakazaniia, a ne v strakhe nakazaniia" (The education of the soldier can only rest on shame of punishment, never on fear of punishment): "Just as I cannot imagine a plesiosaurus on Nevskii Prospekt, neither can I imagine that anyone does not know what fear is and how it affects the organism. But I guess I have to reiterate. Fear is the *expectation* of evil, misfortune, trouble, pain, and so forth."[70]

In the late 1890s the theories of French crowd theorist Gustave Le Bon began to infiltrate the arguments of both hardliners and softliners. Army units at all levels were thought to act like Le Bon's hyperemotional, "hysterical," feminized crowds and show a high susceptibility to external stimuli. Only a male officer could shape them and direct their functioning.[71] From here it was a small step to the outright pathologizing of the act of desertion, panic, and the lack of military discipline and the likening of rumors to contagious viruses.[72] And while Russian specialists continued to be less likely than their French or German colleagues to make a connection between lower-class background and pathological heredity, liberals such as Dmitrevskii still thought that smarter, better-educated soldiers were less prone to fear. "Indeed," he claimed, "the higher the intellectual level, the fewer superstition-based fears, the fewer fears you will generally find. . . . The intellect only . . . tolerates fear in certain situations, and a fear that has been tailored to these situations, that is, rational fear: caution and circumspection."[73]

This exploration of fear in Russian military psychological thought leaves us on the verge of the cataclysm that is often regarded as the proper beginning of the twentieth century. As the First World War drew closer, many Russians—and not just Russians—felt that they lived in "an era of nerves, nervousness, neurasthenia, that is, of mental imbalance."[74] The centrality of soldierly fear in the psychological military sciences was both a symptom and a product of this era. A century earlier there was hardly any military psychology, but there was also hardly any mentioning of soldierly fear in first-person sources. The beginnings of modern warfare in the Crimean War and the introduction of a modern, mass-conscripted army in its aftermath; the channeling through fiction in general and Tolstoy in particular, a variant of the well-known "art imitates life imitates art" pattern; the invention of the autonomous self; the interiorization thesis; modernity as mimicry; and the birth of soldierly fear from the spirit of the crime novel—these are, in descending order of significance, six explanations of why soldiers' fear entered different kinds of Russian texts in the late nineteenth century.

By 1914 fear could look back on a remarkable, if willful, career with distinct way stations: its emancipation in the writings, first of Tolstoy, then of military theorist Dragomirov, was followed by a migration (via the analyses of German colleagues) into military psychiatry, which, confronted with traumatized soldiers from the Franco-Prussian War, had begun to ponder the pathogenic nature of fear. At first Russian military psychiatry mostly saw fear as a symptom of combat-induced mental illness, but the Russo-Japanese War and the revolution of 1905 moved fear to the top of the list of causes of mental illness.

Where does this exploration, then, leave a Russian history of emotions? While future research in this young field might delve into the history of concepts of emotion (*Begriffsgeschichte*), the analysis of emotional norms, or the causal role of emotion in explaining human action, I have attempted to trace across time the locus of fear in military writings, especially military psychology. In other words, I have tried to unearth scientific emotion talk and have hinted at the causes of this talk's appearance—a departure from much of discourse analysis with its disregard for causality.[75] The current attention paid to the history of emotions itself is due, in part, to a renewed interest in causality in history writing. Life science approaches to emotion hold the greatest potential for the establishment of clear causal connections.[76] This is a potential I have chosen not to tap into for general methodological reasons that I expound upon elsewhere.[77]

This exploration of soldiers and fear, finally, leaves us with swaths to be mapped out in the future and prospective paths to be taken. One could move beyond 1914–1918 and discuss the reincarnation of Enval'd's "romantic" fear paradigm in penal battalions and blocking detachments (*zagraditel'nye otriady*) formed after Stalin's "no step backward" order no. 227 in July 1942: their task was to shoot panicked, deserting soldiers, that is, to place these soldiers in a kind of Catch-22.[78] Or one could look at the rehabilitation of military psychiatry and the "realistic" school under Khrushchev.[79] One could also move beyond Russia and point to the signs of a Cold War entanglement of 1970s Soviet psychopharmacological fear research and the development of modern Western anxiety drugs. There may well be a Soviet genealogy of Prozac waiting to be researched and written.[80] Or it would be possible to examine the return of legal prosecution for cowardice in the American military, which had been dormant since the Vietnam War because of the inroads psychoanalysis was making in military psychiatry: because of the curative promise anxiety drugs hold, the tolerance of behavior that might be deemed cowardly has diminished, so that in November 2003 during the Iraq War the U.S. Army initiated its first cowardice prosecution since 1968, charging Sergeant Georg Anderas Pogany, thirty-three years old, with "cowardly conduct as a result of fear."[81] The likelihood of an uncoupling of soldiers from the emotion of fear—anywhere and anytime soon—is about as high as the appearance of a Plesiosaurus on Nevskii Prospekt.

5   FEAR OF A SAFE PLACE

Jan Mieszkowski

IN HER 1973 *On Photography*, Susan Sontag describes the West as "a society which makes it normative to aspire never to experience privation, failure, misery, pain, [or] dread disease, and in which death itself is regarded not as natural and inevitable but as a cruel, unmerited disaster." The suggestion that human beings have difficulty acknowledging their own mortality is hardly novel, but Sontag draws an unusual inference from the observation, suggesting that "the feeling of being exempt from calamity stimulates interest in looking at painful pictures, and looking at them suggests and strengthens the feeling that one is exempt."[1] Her claim is that spectacles of death exert a profound influence over us not because in pondering them we tacitly acknowledge our own finitude but for precisely the opposite reason, that is, because such images help sustain our fantasies of indestructibility. Far from trying to hide from the harsh realities of mortality, we want to view them as regularly as possible. Beyond the psychological dynamics that may inform an individual's acknowledged or unacknowledged conviction that he or she cannot

99

die, a variety of different issues about information media and the powers and limits of representation are raised by the obsessive spectatorial loop Sontag outlines whereby voyeuristic impulses and feelings of exemption mutually reinforce one another in an ever-intensifying circle.

Perhaps the most important thing to say about Sontag's argument is that recent experience would appear to contradict the assumption that people are compulsively interested in scenes of others' misery. In the twenty-first century, anyone with access to a television, computer, or cell phone has an unprecedented number of opportunities to engage with the detailed documentation of privation and death twenty-four hours a day. Nonetheless, there is little evidence that people's efforts to confirm their sense of being exempt from suffering drive them to view it more and more. Statistical studies of the media's coverage of violence in the Middle East since the 2003 U.S. invasion of Iraq, for example, suggest that the American consumer does not treat reports of war casualties with greater interest than reports of bloodless election frauds or the comical antics of foreign leaders on vacation.[2] Popular taste would seem to demand not that the news be comprised of fearful spectacles of gloom and doom but that it change regularly and be presented in neatly packaged narratives with well-defined beginnings, middles, and ends.

Sontag herself anticipates this state of affairs when she argues that if photographs initially make an event "more real," repeated exposure to them ultimately has the opposite effect.[3] Since the Vietnam War, when color images of severely injured and dying U.S. servicemen first became widely available on the evening news, the public's blasé attitude toward its daily dose of horrors on tap has often been explained by the observation that an excess of information about the suffering of others desensitizes an audience, which becomes so familiar with scenes of atrocity that it no longer finds them terrifying. Repetition breeds complacency and, finally, indifference. Sontag's version of this argument is striking for the way in which it divides it into two distinct models of repetition that have divergent effects: on the one hand, she offers a circular schema in which we look with ever-increasing frequency at pictures of other people's woes because they somehow confirm the "reality" that these privations will not visit us; on the other hand, she offers a model of accumulation whereby the collection of endless scenes of misery deadens us to their poignancy, rendering them surreal and eventually unremarkable.[4]

One might suspect that the problem with Sontag's argument is that it lacks a comprehensive account of the representational modalities peculiar to visual media such as photography or film. Art historians and media scholars have long asked whether the reproducible images made possible by technological innovations in the nineteenth and twentieth centuries are organized by figures of deferral and belatedness, if not by irreducibly traumatic temporal paradigms. In the latter case, the viewing audience necessarily has an alienated relationship to its experience of these horror shows since that experience is defined by noncomprehension or by what one misses rather than by what one consciously registers. In this chapter, I argue that such discussions can be considerably enriched if we look more closely at the concepts of fear that are formulated in late Enlightenment aesthetics and that continue to shape our ideas about what it means to take pleasure in scenes of others' demise. To understand the contemporary Western viewer and his or her interest, or lack thereof, in ostensibly terrifying spectacles of death and destruction, we must consider the Napoleonic era as the moment at which the modern mass audience first emerges and the idea of observing horrific events from a "safe place" becomes an essential feature of daily life as the populace learns how to watch war for fun. Charting the rise and decline of a paradigm of sublime shock, I propose that recent theories of modern media spectatorship have failed to explain why sights of terror are invariably shows in which what we see is not cause and effect or the machinations of destiny but a curious indistinction between chance and determination.

The Old English root of "fear" names "a sudden and terrible event."[5] In subsequent centuries, as fear acquires the more familiar connotations of dread, disquiet, or negative feelings brought on by the anticipation of danger, the meaning of the word is effectively inverted: if originally it referred to a horrible occurrence, it comes to describe the uncertainty that arises in the gap between what is the case and what may not come to pass (and may not be as bad as one worries if it does). It is as a figure of anticipation, delay, and above all uncertainty that fear plays an important role in Enlightenment accounts of intense aesthetic experiences. In *A Philosophical Enquiry into the Origin of our Ideas of the Sublime and Beautiful* (1757), Edmund Burke maintains that "no passion so effectually robs the mind of all its powers of acting and reasoning as fear. For fear being an apprehension of pain or death, it operates in a manner that resembles actual pain."[6] Burke's "apprehension" denotes not just feeling or grasping something in the present but the now more archaic sense of representing to oneself what is still in the future. For Burke, fear is not the experience of pain or death but a "near-pain" or "near-death" experience. Fear apes physical discomfort; it is less an affect per se than an intimation of one, pre-affective. Insofar as it is a passion that mimes a sensation that may never fully exist, fear is always potentially misleading. The more confident we are that we feel it, the less sure we can be that we know what we are feeling, which is to say that fear divides us into a present self and an uncertain future self, and it does so in the very arena, self-affection, in which we presume to have our most immediate relation to self. For this reason, fear never entirely loses its original connotation of an event: it casts a dynamic of simulation—pain and "something like it"—as a relationship between an emotional "now" and a future occurrence that may or may not take place and of which "now" is, paradoxically, only a poor anticipation.

For Burke, this state of apprehensiveness generates not a dynamic of oscillation or some sort of give and take between prospection and retrospection but petrification. He argues that fear or terror is "the ruling principle of the sublime" because the sublime is at its core a state of astonishment, "in which all [the soul's] motions are suspended, with some degree of horror."[7] Fear effects a paralysis whereby "the mind is so entirely filled with its object that it cannot entertain any other, nor by consequence reason on that object which employs it." Unable to redirect his attention or to cognize the object that is in focus, the viewer is frozen. It is not entirely clear how to reconcile Burke's understanding of fear as an anticipatory passion, a promise of adversity to follow, with his understanding of fear as a force that arrests the mind, an a-motional emotion beyond emotion. On this point, it is important to realize that Burke is interested in sublime experiences not because, medusa-like, they turn us to stone, but because we enjoy them. In a qualification that will be crucial for the generation of thinkers that will follow him, he writes that "terror is a passion which always produces delight when it does not press too close." It is not by chance that this statement sounds as if it could have been lifted from a contemporary analysis of reality television. Burke's primary figure of a terror that is not too terrible is a show that allows us to view other people's troubles: "there is no spectacle we so eagerly pursue as that of some uncommon and grievous calamity." In taking this position, Burke is not proposing that human beings are unfeeling monsters constantly reveling in *Schadenfreude*. On the contrary, he is convinced that people invariably feel sympathy for their fellow species beings, based in their innate tendencies toward love and affection, but where others' terror is concerned, this sympathy, "antecedent to any reasoning," is always a mixture of pity and pleasure, of pain and delight.[8]

Fear is championed as "the strongest emotion of which the mind is capable of feeling" less because of the directness of the affective dynamic to which it gives rise than because it is experienced in a thoroughly mediated fashion: "Whatever is fitted in any sort to excite the ideas of pain, and danger, that is to say, whatever is in any sort terrible, or is conversant about terrible objects, or operates in a manner analogous to terror, is a source of the sublime."[9] This string of qualifications—"to excite the ideas of," "in any sort," "conversant with," "in a manner analogous to"— reveals that in enjoying watching the sufferings of others we are doubly buffered from the petrifying horrors on display. If fear itself is only "like" pain, we are happiest when we are dealing with something that is in turn only "like" fear. In this regard, we have to realize that Burke is not simply arguing that we enjoy experiencing other people's fear vicariously. For him, fear *is* the experience of the vicarious, that is, fear divides us against ourselves as we recognize that what we feel so strongly in our encounter with the sublime is at best only "conversant with" the "strongest emotion of which the mind is capable of feeling." Sublime encounters with fearful visions are always derivative experiences that may not produce feelings as such but poor copies thereof that can at most excite "ideas of pain" or operate "in a manner analogous to terror." In offering us a view of others' woes, fear threatens us not because we imagine ourselves undergoing the same trials and tribulations but because in treating fear as an object of aesthetic reflection we are required to treat a thoroughly non–self-affective affect as the standard of our most poignant passions.

The question of exactly what happens when we try to take stock of our feelings about other people's feelings of fear becomes central to late eighteenth-century aesthetics, and in this context, Burke's most famous inheritor is Immanuel Kant. Kant's analysis of the sublime in the *Critique of Judgment* has been extensively discussed in terms of its potential incompatibility with the doctrine of aesthetic judgment that he sets forth in his discussion of the beautiful, and it has been identified as the impetus for a host of different conceptions of modern art that emerge in the ensuing centuries. Curiously, however, these canonical passages have rarely been studied as a theory of fear. For Kant, a judgment of sublimity, in contrast to a judgment of beauty, is predicated not on a harmony of the mental faculties but on the agitation that arises when the imagination realizes that it cannot offer a sensible presentation of the intelligible idea. In a strange recuperation, this failure prompts the mind to recognize that the might of reason outstrips the limited character of the phenomenal realm and that it is the mind itself that is incomparably powerful and not the external phenomena looming over it. With the mathematical sublime, this complex process occurs when we confront a magnitude that highlights the incommensurability of the finite and the infinite; with the dynamic sublime, this experience is prompted by the shock that arises when we encounter the awesome force of nature. In the latter case, Kant is adamant that we can only judge nature as sublime if we present it to ourselves as fearful. In facilitating a posture of resistance in virtue of which we stand over and against nature as a power that may overwhelm our physical being, fear is first and foremost the articulation of a relationship between subject and object, an affirmation that there is something beyond the self. At the same time, this sketch of a boundary between self and other is only a short-lived pretext for an entirely self-involved process. Confronted with nature's violence in the form of rushing water or flowing lava, we do not run and hide but instead grasp that "property, health, and life" are small matters in comparison to the supreme authority of reason, hence "the sight of [such terrors] becomes all the more attractive the more fearful it is, *provided we are in a safe place*" when we watch them.[10]

Compared to the power of reason, argues Kant, everything in nature is small. This transformation of the physical realm from strong and grand to weak and miniscule occurs, however, only because the fear inspired by phenomena such as volcanoes, earthquakes, or hurricanes is not "actual fear [*wirkliche Furcht*]" but "merely our attempt to incur it with our imagination, in order that we may feel that very power's might and connect the mental agitation this arouses with the mind's state of rest." In pretending that we are in jeopardy, in allowing that we are in a situation in which we *should* feel afraid, although we are not, what the mind ultimately feels is "its own sublimity, which lies in its vocation and elevates it even above nature."[11]

It has often been noted that numerous elements of Burke's vocabulary pop up in Kant's argument, at times almost as if he were simply borrowing his predecessor's terminology wholesale and translating it into German. If anything, however, Kant is even more explicit than Burke about the peculiar nature of the affective brinkmanship at work in the sublime and about the need for precise distinctions between "actual" fear and its facsimiles. This is evident when Kant describes the way in which one "beholds massive mountains climbing skyward, deep gorges with raging streams in them, wastelands lying in deep shadow and inviting melancholy meditation, and . . . is indeed seized by an amazement [*Verwunderung*] bordering on terror [*Schrecken*], by horror [*Grausen*] and a sacred thrill [*Schauer*]." Walking the tightrope between terror on the one hand and horror and thrill on the other may seem like a precarious operation, but Kant stresses that "it is impossible to like terror (*Schrecken*) that we take seriously (*der ernstlich gemeint wäre*)," so it is essential that the viewer of sublime spectacles of astonishing power be able to watch these remarkable events without taking them too much to heart.[12] Precisely what, however, prevents our fear that must not be "actual fear" from shading into the real thing, particularly given Kant's own examples of encounters with earthquakes, erupting volcanoes, and hurricanes, where not to be afraid would seem comical, not to mention foolhardy? Exactly where is the late eighteenth-century spectator, unable to avail herself or himself of a helicopter or a speedboat, going to find a "safe place" from which to watch all of this unfold? Moreover, if we constantly need to put ourselves in a safe place in order to win the insight that our physical well-being is trivial compared to the might of intelligible ideas, how can we be sure that we are gaining knowledge of "actual" reason rather than its bastard copy? In other words, is it possible that the artificiality of these pseudo-affective dynamics, the fact that in experiencing the shock and awe of the sublime we are not really afraid, will ultimately reflect back on the glory of the mind's self-aggrandizement?

Acknowledging these worries, Kant goes out of his way to stress that the mind's self-estimation "loses nothing from the fact that we must find ourselves safe in order to feel this exciting liking, so that (as it might seem), since the danger is not genuine, the sublimity of our intellectual ability might also not be genuine." As proof for this assertion, he cites the fact that we hold in high esteem warriors who are brave and "cannot be subdued by danger," adding that a people is sublime "in proportion to the number of dangers in the face of which it courageously stood its ground." If Kant's discussion began with the claim that sublime experiences will be prompted by phenomena that threaten to overwhelm or destroy us, he now turns the argument around and suggests that we value strong minds as sublime precisely because they are not motivated by fear. In an effort to clarify this last point, he invokes the fantasy of a war "carried on in an orderly way," as if even soldiers engaged in battle were not really afraid of being killed.[13] The "safe place" from which the viewer is to observe the might of nature has thus been expanded to encompass virtually the entire human condition. But is this real courage or mock courage? Indeed, in this context one has to ask whether the very triumph of the mind in rendering "health and life" trivial compared to the authority of intelligible ideas reveals that all feelings are something more or less than merely genuine.

The problem may be that in viewing sublime sights "in a safe place" we are too safe and that we require at least some suggestion that the boundary between security and insecurity, between fear and faux-fear, is porous. Otherwise, we may become so complacent in our sanctuary that we can no longer register the power of sublime spectacles at all. Alternatively, what if we have good reasons for leaving our sheltered vantage point and venturing out into the tsunami or onto the field of combat *without taking our sense of security with us,* that is, can we find our way back to a situation in which it is possible to be afraid? Kant's figure of a "safe place" proves to be influential for subsequent efforts to explain the standpoint of the modern spectator and the relative stability of the ground on which he or she stands in order to view shocking events. This influence, however, is as much a product of the fear inspired by safety as a factor of security's comforting buffers.

Several years before the publication of the third *Critique,* Burke offered his famous account of the pleasurable yet painful experience of watching the fall of the House of Bourbon: "As to us here our thoughts of everything at home are suspended, by our astonishment at the wonderful Spectacle which is exhibited in a Neighboring and rival Country— what Spectators, and what Actors! England gazing with astonishment at a French struggle for Liberty and not knowing whether to blame or to applaud!"[14] This image of looking across the English Channel at the grand shows on the Continent became a defining figure of the era. During the French Revolutionary and Napoleonic Wars, the inhabitants of the British Isles were spared the sight of conflict on their own soil as their battles were fought abroad, in other countries or in the colonies. In a time of permanent war, a war that one could follow on a daily basis in regular news reports, vast clashes of men and arms, upheavals of sublime power and proportion, were routinely happening to someone else somewhere else.

Not everyone was happy with this new model of spectatorship in which one could experience a semi-thrilling mixture of pleasure and faux-fear from the security of one's home. Almost a decade after the publication of the third *Critique,* William Wordsworth used the 1800 preface to his *Lyric Ballads* to inveigh against the "craving for extraordinary incident" that was condemning the minds of his fellow citizens to a "savage torpor." With the increasing uniformity of city life, Wordsworth saw his countrymen seeking diversion in sensationalism, a desire for "outrageous stimulation" that went beyond the cheap shocks of the press to infect literary letters as "the invaluable works of our elder writers

. . . [were] driven into neglect by frantic novels, sickly and stupid German Tragedies, and deluges of idle and extravagant stories in verse."[15] In this early critique of mass culture, the sublime shows of Burke and Kant have devolved into cut-rate entertainment that leads not to a discriminating engagement with the ideas of reason but to a far less flashy paralysis than the petrification in which Burke worried that fear might suspend us. In Kant's terms, Wordsworth is arguing that consuming shocking spectacles from the security of one's armchair causes the imagination to stall rather than prompting it to recognize its own limitations and thereby win insight into the greater powers of the intelligible realm.

The notion that the "safe" place that was Britain might not be the ideal environment for the stimulation of the mind was also explored by Wordsworth's friend Samuel Taylor Coleridge. His 1798 poem "Fears in Solitude" was produced, as its subtitle explains, "during the alarm of an invasion [by the French]"—an invasion that may have been a real threat or may have just been a chimerical fear inspired by government rumors designed to fuel popular resentment of the neighbors across the English Channel.[16] Not Coleridge's greatest artistic triumph—he would refer to it as more a sermon than a lyric—the uncertainty about whether the text is a poem or a rant hints that it is far from clear if "Fears in Solitude" is diagnosing the problem of savage torpor Wordsworth describes or if it is itself an example of precisely the sort of sensationalism Wordsworth deplores.

Coleridge plays with the mixture of apprehension and desire that his countrymen could bring to the prospect of the war coming to their shores, asking whether those who watch from a safe place would secretly enjoy the opportunity to become part of the action. In the first instance, the poem presents the people of Britain as consumers of spectacle. While their armies have played a part in many military clashes abroad, the populace has been content to sit back and take in the trials and tribulations of others: "We, this whole people, have been clamorous / For war and bloodshed; animating sports, / To which we pay for as a thing to talk of, / Spectators and not combatants!" (lines 93–96). More specifically, Coleridge describes Britain as a nation of newspaper readers eagerly devouring stories about fighting taking place elsewhere: "Boys and girls, / And women, that would groan to see a child / Pull off an insect's leg, all read of war, / The best amusement for our morning meal!" (lines 104–7). In the emerging mass media, Coleridge believes that a mediated relation to fear, which for Burke or Smith would still allow sympathy to emerge, has been stretched to the breaking point. As the growing consumption of newspapers has made everyone fluent in the terminology required to characterize military atrocities, the discussion of war has come to function as a way of denying the reality of death. We speak, Coleridge writes, "as if the wretch, / Who fell in battle, doing bloody deeds, / Passed off to Heaven, translated and not killed" (lines 119–21). One of the central points of "Fears in Solitude" is that collective spectatorship does not generate a productive communal discourse in which ideas and ideologies, hopes and dreams, can be inspected and debated, rationally and democratically. Instead, we find a public sphere in which Britons have become "too indolent" to care about the difference between truth and lie or between heartfelt proclamations and empty performances (line 68). This new forum about war is always at risk of becoming either a series of "empty sounds" and "dainty terms," expressions of sentiment with no transformative value of their own, or else an abstract "speech-mouthing" of oaths and promises, a self-congratulatory exercise of crass nationalism that is entirely indifferent to its own status as true or false (lines 113–15, 57).

And what of fear? At one point, Coleridge calls upon his countrymen to repel the invaders but to return "Not with a drunken triumph, but with fear, / Repenting of the wrongs with which we stung / So fierce a foe to frenzy!" (lines 151–53). In these terms, fear is to be a kind of clarity-inducing force, a corrective to a prior state of oblivion in which one could fight by proxy, experiencing the world's struggles without actually participating. At the same time, as in Kant this fear emerges only within a simulated medium: the injunction to experience it is a moment in a fantasy about repelling a hypothetical invasion, not part of a call to arms in the face of a real attack. In other words, the fear with which one is enjoined to return to the real world is to serve as proof that one is not content to live in a fantasy world of mediated pseudo-terror, but this can happen only because this real world, the home front become a war front, does not exist. To an extent, the poem collapses on this contradiction, culminating in the hope that the fears of invasion are themselves unfounded, in the hope, that is, that fear can be *just* fear and nothing more: "May my fears, / My filial fears, be vain! and may the vaunts / And menace of the vengeful enemy / Pass like the gust, that roared and died away / In the distant tree" (lines 197–201). The fear of fear effectively prompts Coleridge to call for the dissolution of the sublime spectacle itself. Rather than seeing the enemy hoards devour the fields of England, he hopes that any prospective show of power will evaporate like a gust of wind. The only response to the sensationalism one has manufactured for oneself is to concede that one's presentation of world history is merely a spectral display.

At the same time, Coleridge is well aware that in calling for the dissolution of the fear that the French will invade he is potentially condemning his culture to the stasis of hyper-security. The real fear of "Fears in Solitude" is ultimately solitude itself, and in fact, in the June 8, 1809 edition of the *Friend* Coleridge mistakenly referred to his poem as "Fears *of* Solitude," thereby betraying the worry that one's safe place may become a prison from which one cannot emerge—a place, in Kant's terms, in which the imagination is so well insulated that it never confronts its own limits and remains oblivious to the powers of reason that transcend the empirical connections of the phenomenal world.[17] How to fear the French thus becomes a solipsistic exercise in how to fear not being fearful enough.

Framed by the artificial shock described by Burke and Kant on the one hand and by the sensationalism deplored by Wordsworth on the other, nineteenth-century letters is populated with curious efforts to explore the different forms of pseudo-sublimity that emerge when one's "safe" place starts to seem a little too safe. In his *Memoirs*, François-René de Chateaubriand offers an exemplary instance of such an encounter:

On 18 June 1815, I left Ghent about noon by the Brussels gate; I was going to finish my walk alone along the highroad. I had taken Caesar's *Commentaries* with me and I strolled along, immersed in my reading. I was over two miles from the town when I thought I heard a dull rumbling: I stopped and looked up at the sky, which was fairly cloudy, wondering whether I should walk on or turn back towards Ghent for fear of a storm. I listened; I heard nothing more but the cry of a moorhen in the rushes and the sound of a village clock. I continued on my way: I had not taken thirty steps before the rumbling began again, now short, now drawn out at irregular intervals; sometimes it was perceptible only through trembling of the air, which was so far away that it communicated itself to the ground as it passed over those vast plains. The detonations, less prolonged, less undulating, less interrelated than those of thunder, gave rise in my mind to the idea of a battle. I found myself opposite a poplar planted at the corner of a hop-field. I crossed the road and leant against the trunk of the tree, with my face turned in the direction of Brussels. A southerly wind sprang up and brought me more distinctly the sound of artillery. That great battle, nameless as yet, whose echoes I was listening to at the foot of a poplar, and for whose unknown obsequies a village clock had just struck, was the Battle of Waterloo![18]

Chateaubriand presents his experience as a traditional philosophical exercise in which he attempts to coordinate his sensory perceptions and his cognitive faculties and answer the seemingly straightforward question: What am I hearing? The impetus for these ruminations is ostensibly the most trivial of concerns: Should I abandon my walk and head home because it might rain? Not only are we far from the shock of Kant's hurricane but Chateaubriand's inferential progression moves in the other direction, from the natural to the manmade, for in the sounds of detonation, he detects connections "less interrelated than those of thunder." The key insight is the leap from auditory data to "the idea of a battle," but it is important to recognize that this step in his reflections does not entirely remove him from the pastoral setting in which he begins, complete with a moorhen in the rushes. As our narrator leans against a tree, a wind springs up and brings him "more distinctly the sound of artillery." In addition to its possible status as a cause of the sensory phenomena with which he is engaged, the natural world thereby acquires a second role as the medium that imparts data that may resolve the uncertainty about the sounds he hears, helping to answer the question of whether what his ears discern is a product of human hands.

These calm musings are interrupted by the final sentence of the above passage in which Chateaubriand triumphantly declares that what he was hearing was the as-yet-nameless Waterloo. The closing formulation calls attention to the planned quality of the entire narrative, which, having ostensibly moved from local detail to local detail, now takes a huge leap, a step thoroughly conditioned by the vantage of hindsight and an awareness of just how monumental an event the incident unfolding that day would prove to be. In this regard, it is notable that Chateaubriand declares that the clock rings *for* the battle. As his emphasis on the "unknown" ("for whose unknown obsequies a village clock had just struck") suggests, to juxtapose the noise of the clock with the first set of noises is, even after the fact, an entirely arbitrary alignment, and it is doubly so when considered from the perspective of his immediate perception of the events of June 18, 1815. It is as if the entire experience were so fragile that pushing slightly at the connections holding it together might cause it to unravel. Responding to precisely this concern, Chateaubriand insists that although he cannot see what is going on, he is situated in exactly the right spot to be moved by the event: "A silent and solitary hearer of the solemn judgment of the fates, I would have been less moved if I had found myself in the fray: the danger, the firing, the press of death would have left me no time for meditation; but, alone under a tree, in the countryside near Ghent, like the shepherd of the flocks grazing around me, I was overwhelmed by the weight of my reflections. What was this battle? Was it going to be decisive? Was Napoleon there in person? Were lots being cast for the world, as for Christ's garments?"[19]

With this section, the passage starts to invoke the Kantian sublime explicitly, then inverts it. The idea of being situated at just the right distance from the spectacle in order to appreciate its monumentality most fully recalls Kant's discussion of the mathematical sublime, where he cites a French general's claim that "in order to get the full emotional effect from the magnitude of the pyramids, one must neither get too close to them nor stay too far away."[20] As if to underscore this reference, Chateaubriand goes on to liken his relationship with the unfolding battle to an experience he had in Egypt: "A few miles from an immense catastrophe, I did not see it; I could not touch the huge funeral monument growing minute by minute at Waterloo, just as from the shores of Bulak, on the banks of the Nile, I had stretched out my hands in vain towards the Pyramids."[21] Having arrived in Egypt in flood season, Chateaubriand could not get close to the famed monuments and had to commission a friend to carve his name on the pyramids in his stead. In Belgium, however, Chateaubriand declares that his failure to be near the scene is an advantage, so that although his experience would appear to be the opposite of a confrontation with a rushing waterfall, a towering cliff, or an erupting volcano, he is nonetheless profoundly impacted by it. Initiated by the most minimal of fears—a minor concern about a storm—this antishock experience somehow moves him such that he realizes a meditative depth that would not have been possible if he had been in the "press of death." Radicalizing the logic of Kant's "safe place," Chateaubriand offers a kind of sublime anti-sublime: there was a catastrophe, but I did not see it, and for this reason, I could be moved by my profound thoughts about it.

Of course, it may be erroneous to assume that Chateaubriand's thoughts about Waterloo are primarily about Waterloo. His ensuing gestures of self-aggrandizement do not follow the path of the Kantian sublime and culminate in insights into the power of the mind, although the process is similar in that Chateaubriand's own act of reflection becomes more important than the world-historical events that occasioned it. This is first legible in the shift from impersonal questions about the fate of the world to a Christ simile ("as for Christ's garments") that feels uncomfortably hubristic given that in an earlier simile Chateaubriand casts himself as a shepherd tending his flock. As he goes on to consider his experiences in the twenty-four hours after Waterloo, before he has learned the outcome of the battle, his ruminations become almost childish as he wonders whether it would be better for him if Napoleon or Wellington won, weighing the trade-offs of glory versus liberty, his own inconvenience versus the state's honor, and so on. At this point, any sublime pathos that may have resonated in the triumphant declaration that this was Waterloo has become bathetic.

If Chateaubriand's account of his walk is not simply an instance of the sensationalism Wordsworth deplores and can still be distinguished from Coleridge's "empty sounds" and "dainty terms," it is on the basis of the improbable quality that chance is said to play in the experience. Chateaubriand's readers are asked to believe that if the wind had been blowing in a slightly different direction or if the author had taken a slightly different route on his stroll, his brief pseudo-encounter with the battle of battles would never have come to pass. Yet however casual the opening description of the mysterious thunder-like sounds may appear, in retrospect it can only seem completely overdetermined. Surely he did not just happen to be wandering by that exact spot on that exact day such that he could almost, but not quite, espy what was going on at Waterloo. His claim that the battle noises rouse him from an ambulatory engagement with Caesar's *Commentaries* about the Gallic Wars, as if his subject matter had suddenly come to life in a modern form, is similarly too good to be true: we are invited to accept a fairy tale in which a man reading about famous generals and their exploits sees them—or almost sees them—appear right before his eyes! Fear has been completely banished from the experience of the sublime, leaving in its wake only the imaginative artifice of Burke and Kant's staged terror—faux-fear without the fear. Chateaubriand's story gives credence to Kant's worry, echoed by Coleridge, that the imagination may linger in its empirical connections and never facilitate an engagement with reason.

Still, the joke may be on us, as it were, for one of the central concerns for the inheritors of Kant's figure of the safe spectator is whether any narrative can successfully represent the power of chance encounters. Throughout nineteenth-century reflections on the sublimity of Napoleonic warfare, in novels such as Victor Hugo's *Les Misérables* and

Leo Tolstoy's *War and Peace*, accounts of the battlefield as a scene to be viewed with a mixture of pleasure and terror are invariably organized by sustained reflections on the contrast between events with definite causes and events that are no more than random products of happenstance. To understand what this means for Kant's legacy, we can turn to Sigmund Freud's 1915 "Thoughts for the Times on War and Death." Freud wrote the essay in an effort to come to terms with the profound disillusionment that he assumed must be plaguing all reasonable people as a terrible conflict gripped Europe. "We cannot but feel," he declared, "that no event has ever destroyed so much that is precious in the common possessions of humanity." Five years later, Freud developed his theory of the death drive, but his suspicion that the aggressivity that propels people to slaughter one another cannot be fully explained by libidinal dynamics predated the struggle of 1914–1918. Already in 1915, then, he took some care to consider our views on the killing of others, and one of his central claims was that it "is . . . impossible to imagine our own death [der eigene Tod ist ja auch unvorstellbar]" and that "whenever we attempt to do so we can perceive that we are in fact still present as spectators." Because "in the unconscious every one of us is convinced of his own immortality," any representation we might hazard of our own demise is fundamentally a ruse; scrutiny will always reveal that what we are really depicting is someone else's fall rather than our own, and that we are still there, as implicit bystanders, looking on.[22] In other words, the problem with war is that we can never fear it enough. Freud noted that this dynamic applied not just to civilians on the home front but to those who were actually fighting as well—in the heat of battle, they still partly treated themselves as onlookers rather than as participants. Extending Burke's claim that fear is at its heart "an apprehension of pain or death," Freud reminds us—in fine Kantian fashion—that this *apprehension* of death never becomes the *comprehension* of death. In this sense, the sublime of Burke or Kant reveals not that the mind is more powerful than nature but that all fear is a product of a staged scenario in which there is no need to offer a qualifying "providing we are in a safe place" because, emotionally speaking, we invariably feel that we already are.

Under normal circumstances, even the most oblivious among us cannot help but notice that people die, but Freud says that we tend to emphasize the fortuitous quality of death, its status as an accident, that is, we transform death from a necessity to a contingency. Is it possible, however, that in the blizzard of violence that was the mechanized slaughter of the First World War death had begun to lose its grip on its own haphazardness? Does modern combat give rise to a new form of Kantian shock or does it counter the traditional notion of sublimity with a different kind of spectacle of power? Freud writes: "It is clear that the war is bound to sweep away this conventional treatment of death. Death will no longer be denied; one must believe in it. People really die; and no longer one by one, but many, often tens of thousands in a single day. Death is also no longer a chance event. To be sure, it does still seem a matter of chance whether a particular bullet hits this man or that; but a second bullet may well hit the survivor; and the accumulation of deaths puts an end to the impression of chance."[23]

Thanks to the democratization of assembly-line death, there is more than enough random mishap and misfortune to go around. With so many bullets in the air, chance, *Zufall*, becomes the general case, *der allgemeine Fall*—and these accidents are no longer merely accidents. By a strange arithmetic, the accumulation of mishaps retroactively negates the accidental quality of the events in the aggregate, although considered individually each one remains a product of Fortuna's whim. Somehow quantity unsettles, if not entirely undoes, the qualitative distinction between chance and determination.

This uncertain dynamic is further complicated by Freud's claim that the accumulation of bullets that find their marks ends the *impression* of chance. The comment is ambiguous, for it is unclear if it indicates that what is being amassed are semblances of randomness or semblances of determined connections. In other words, while the very universality of chance events seems to herald the retreat of chance, this retreat is itself predicated on what *seems* to be the case, so all we "see" is that any appearance of cause and effect may always in fact be a manifestation of contingency. This is why Freud must acknowledge that things could be otherwise: "a second bullet may well hit the survivor"—*or not*. Suspended between an old idea of death we have now begun to challenge and a new notion of death we cannot entirely embrace, we find that the negation of the semblance of death's contingency only confirms the underlying commitment of our unconscious to contingency over determination. The unconscious—a discourse, in Freud's notorious formulation, without negation (*Verneinung*)—is the language of could-be-otherwise. Accordingly, allows Freud, even soldiers on the battlefield in the midst of slaughter, their comrades falling all around them, will regard themselves as bystanders rather than as participants in a carnage that may very well spell their demise at any second.

Among contemporary scholars, the relations between war and technological media have been most extensively explored by Paul Virilio, who is perhaps best known for his lapidary formulation: "War is cinema, and cinema is war." In his discussions of combat and spectacle, Virilio has maintained that military campaigns consist of efforts to convince an adversary of his own mortality before doing him in: "To fell the enemy is not so much to capture as to 'captivate' him, to instill the fear of death before he actually die."[24] Following Freud, the show one puts on is fated to be misinterpreted by one's audience, the opponent on the battlefield, because no matter how convincingly one menaces one's foe, he or she will always understand one's threats as a representation of an Other's death, not his or her own. On a physical level, war is the most gruesome paradigm of human "interaction"—bodies and arms clash and demolish one another in the most horrifically intimate ways imaginable. On the level of viewership, however, war is an elaborate noncollision of menacing postures, a shadow conflict between sights that no audience member will take seriously, a series of failed efforts to fan the fires of a fear that can never ignite. War should be the ultimate scene of force, an ideal object for the Kantian subject to fear from afar and thereby win insight into the greater powers of his or her mind, but somehow the faux-terror required to jump start the process never emerges or rather fear fails to function in such a way that we can grasp the spectacles of military conflict as a force for which our physical being is no match.

In the late 1930s, Walter Benjamin characterized this strange state of affairs as self-alienation: "'Fiat ars—pereat mundus,' says fascism, expecting from war, as Marinetti admits, the artistic gratification of a sense perception altered by technology. This is evidently the consummation of *l'art pour l'art*. Humankind, which once, in Homer, was an object of contemplation for the Olympian gods, has now become one for itself. Its self-alienation has reached the power where it can experience its own annihilation as a supreme aesthetic pleasure."[25] Focusing on the militaristic maxims of futurism, Benjamin treats war as an object of beauty rather than sublimity.[26] There is no reason, however, that the Burkean or Kantian sublime should not prompt us to anticipate with eagerness the mixture of pleasure and pain with which we could watch the self-destruction of our species, providing we could do so from a safe place. This would be the grimmest lesson of "Fears in Solitude," the absolute coincidence of sanctuary and security with decimation and extinction.

Burdened with these gloomy pronouncements, it is tempting to respond that from Burke and Kant to Benjamin we have been looking at an *aesthetic* tradition and that it is still possible for human beings to fear, and abhor, the prospect of their own destruction. After all, Kant himself is the first to acknowledge that in discussing the sublime he is dealing with something other than real fear. Unfortunately, our analysis has suggested that the opposition between fear and faux-fear is far from stable. Perhaps more troublingly, Freud's account of our inability to conceive of our own death unsettles the distinction between an interested and a disinterested relationship to a spectacle, the distinction on the basis of which Kant differentiates between judgments of taste and judgments based on the interests of sense or reason. The fact that where the misery of others is concerned we will never be able to convince ourselves that what we are watching has anything to do with us may mean that by default we can only relate to such scenes as objects to be deemed sublime or beautiful even as we keep trying to prove that we are reacting to them in nonaesthetic terms.

Despite the technological advances that provide us with unimaginably precise audio-visual feeds in the comfort of our homes, offices, and other safe places, we can never be afraid enough when we watch other people die. Discussing the U.S. invasion of Iraq in 2003, Nicholas Mirzoeff argued: "In the second Gulf War, more images were created to less effect than at any other period in human history. . . . What was in retrospect remarkable about this mass of material was the lack of any truly memorable images. For all the constant circulation of images, there was still nothing to see." Mirzoeff invokes part of Sontag's argument as he tries to explain this state of affairs by "media saturation," adding, "to adapt a phrase from Hannah Arendt, the war marked the emergence of the banality of images. There is no longer anything spectacular about this updated society of the spectacle."[27] This "banality" is not, however, simply a product of the modern audience's overexposure to visions of death and destruction; it is also a factor of what is or is not there to be grasped in any given image. If Freud is right that no scene of war can provide us with convincing evidence that things might not have been different, then both the indirection that is the essence of Burke's fear and the inherent security that organizes Kant's scenes of terror inform our modern shock experiences at every stage. Through its countless opportunities to follow the trials and tribulations of the battlefield, the modern war audience has learned to fear what it sees, but only in the sense in which Burke would have us be "conversant with terrible objects" and not because such shows make us anxious that we are about to die. In the end, Sontag's account of a media public suspended between a hyperreality and a surreality, between images that are too real and images that are never real enough, may be the most apt description of how we watch the suffering of others as something that could, after all, always be otherwise.

6

THE LANGUAGE OF FEAR

SECURITY AND MODERN POLITICS

Corey Robin

My TOPIC HERE is the political language of fear and one language in particular: security. There are other languages of fear: racism, religion, risk assessment, to name a few. But security, both national and domestic, is the most potent and pervasive. Security is the one good, theorists agree, that the state must provide.[1] It has the ability, like no other language, to mobilize the resources and attention of the state and its citizens. It has arguably inspired—and, in the case of nuclear deterrence, certainly threatened—more devastation and destruction than any other language of the modern era.[2] It has also provided the single most effective and enduring justification for the suppression of rights. Why that is so—why security has furnished what appears to be the strongest reason for eliminating or otherwise limiting rights—is the specific topic I address here.

At first glance, this seems like a question that answers itself. When people are afraid for their lives, they will do anything to protect themselves and their families. And when the safety of the nation or the state is threatened, it too will do whatever it takes to defend itself. Limiting the rights of its citizens is the least of it. That is the theory, at any rate, and it is commonly associated with Thomas Hobbes, whose name is often invoked as the guiding intelligence of our times. But if we look closely at what Hobbes said, we find a more interesting and revealing argument about how fear works to abridge rights and limit freedom.

Contrary to popular understanding and some scholarly accounts, Hobbes does not argue that the state of nature is a condition where people are naturally driven by their instinct for self-preservation to submit to an all-powerful sovereign.[3] What he does argue is that the state of nature is a condition where people cannot agree upon the basics of morality—about what is just and unjust, good and evil, and so on—and that this disagreement about morality is a leading source of conflict. The one thing—the only thing—that people can agree upon is that each person has the right to preserve his own life and to do whatever he believes is necessary to preserve his life. To repeat: Hobbes's point is not that each person naturally fears for his own life or that each person actually seeks to preserve his own life; it is that no one, whatever his beliefs, can condemn another person for fearing for his life and trying to preserve it. Acts of self-preservation are blameless and thus are acts we have a right to do.

But as soon as we acknowledge this right, we confront a problem: not only do we have the right to preserve ourselves, but we also have the right to do whatever we think is necessary to preserve ourselves.[4] In the state of nature, each individual is the judge of his own situation, the judge of whether or not he is in danger and of what he must do to protect himself from danger. "Every man by right of nature," Hobbes writes in *The Elements of Law*, "is judge himself of the means, and of the greatness of the danger."[5] But when each of us is the judge of whether or not we are in danger, and when each of us is the judge of what we must do to protect ourselves, we inevitably find ourselves, for reasons unnecessary to explore here, in a state of war. Thus, what seemed initially to offer the basis for agreement and the resolution of conflict—that is, the right of each person to seek his own preservation—turns out, in the state of nature, to generate more conflict, more instability, and less self-preservation.

The only solution to this problem, Hobbes concludes, is to create an all-powerful sovereign to whom we cede this basic right—not the right to defend ourselves from certain and immediate danger (that is a right no one can rationally cede) but the right to be the judge of what *might* threaten us and of what actions we will take to protect ourselves from what might threaten us. When we submit to sovereign power, Hobbes says in *The Elements of Law*, we are forbidden "to be our own judges" of our security, for the sovereign, Hobbes adds in *Leviathan,* is he "to whom in all doubtfull cases, wee have submitted our private judgments."[6]

Returning to the language of fear, we can say that in the state of nature, a generalized fear of death or bodily destruction entitles us to do anything we think might protect us from real or sincerely perceived dangers. Under the sovereign, however, that generalized fear does not so entitle us—unless, again, we, as individuals, are immediately and incontrovertibly threatened. Once we agree to submit, the sovereign becomes, to use the language of former U.S. president George W. Bush, the decider of our fears: the sovereign determines whether or not we have reason to be afraid and what must be done to protect us from the objects of our fear.

Hobbes's argument has three implications. The first is that it is not necessarily a popular, widespread fear of foreign or domestic threats—real or imagined—that compels the state to abridge civil liberties. When the government takes measures for the sake of security, it is not simply translating the people's fear of danger into a repressive act of state. Instead, the government makes a choice: to focus on some threats and not others and to take certain actions (but not others) to counter those threats.

Even though this power to define the objects of public fear suggests that danger is whatever the state says it is, Hobbes did believe that there were real dangers that threatened a people: the sovereign had every reason to make the proper determination of what truly threatened the people and to act only upon those determinations. The sovereign's interest in his own security dovetailed with the people's interest in theirs: so long as the people were, or at least felt, secure, they would obey the sovereign; so long as they obeyed the sovereign, he would be secure. Hobbes also assumed that the sovereign would be so removed from powerful constituencies in society—in his time, the church and the aristocracy—that the sovereign would be able to act on behalf of an impartial, disinterested, and neutral calculation of what truly threatened the people as a whole and of what measures would protect them.[7] Because the sovereign's power depended upon getting these calculations right, he had every incentive not to get them wrong.

The reality of modern state power, however, is that we have inherited some of the worst aspects of Hobbesian politics with none of its saving graces. Governments today have a great deal of freedom to define what threatens a people and how they will respond to those threats, but far from being removed from the interests of and ideologies of the powerful, they are often constrained, even defined and constituted, by those interests and ideologies.

To cite just one example: it is a well-known fact that African Americans have suffered as much from the United States' unwillingness to protect them from basic threats to their lives and liberties as they have from the willingness of white Americans to threaten those lives and liberties. Throughout much of U.S. history, as the Harvard scholar Randall Kennedy has shown, the state has deemed the threat to the physical safety of African Americans to be an unremarkable danger and the protection of African Americans an unworthy focus of its attentions.[8] In the Hobbesian account, this constitutes a grievous failure; in America, it has been a semi-permanent boundary of state action. At the worst moment of white-on-black violence in U.S. history, in fact, the national government deemed the threat to African Americans a relatively minor item of public safety, unworthy of federal military protection; by contrast, it deemed the threat to employers from striking workers an overwhelming item of public safety, worthy of federal military protection.[9]

Or consider the U.S. government's response to the threat of terrorism. According to the two official commissions appointed to examine what led to the terrorist attacks of 9/11, one of the major reasons U.S. intelligence agencies did not anticipate 9/11 was that turf wars and government infighting prevented them from sharing information. The "obstacles to information sharing were more bureaucratic than legal," write David Cole and James Dempsey in *Terrorism and the Constitution*, and had little to do "with the constitutional principles of due process, accountability, or checks and balances."[10] But while the government has run roughshod over constitutional principles since 9/11, it has done little to remove these bureaucratic obstacles. Even the Department of Homeland Security, which was supposed to unite competing agencies under one aegis, "is bogged down by bureaucracy" and a "lack of strategic planning," according to a 2006 wire report.[11]

In the counterterrorism community, to cite another example, it is widely acknowledged that the preemptive arrest and preventive detention of suspected terrorists frustrates the gathering of intelligence. Yet since 9/11, the U. S. government consistently has relied on such policies. In the two years following 9/11, federal authorities preemptively rounded up more than five thousand foreign nationals. As of 2006, write Cole and Dempsey, not a single one of those individuals stood "convicted of any terrorist crime."[12]

In each of these cases, the particular actions the government has

taken to counter terrorism seem to be inspired by a conservative ideology that views the civil rights movement of the 1960s as a source of
decadence and decline and a contributing factor to American weakness
and insecurity. Constitutional rights, former attorney general John Ashcroft has declared, are "weapons with which to kill Americans." Terrorists "exploit our openness." According to Utah Republican Orrin Hatch,
former chair of the Senate Judiciary Committee, terrorists "would like
nothing more than the opportunity to use all of our traditional due process protections to drag out the proceedings." Immediately after 9/11,
Bush promised that there would be "No yielding. No equivocation. No
lawyering this thing to death."[13] It's almost as if 9/11 was caused, in this
view, not by al-Qaeda but by reading criminals their Miranda rights.

Thus, it is not just threats to the well-being of citizens—or even
the citizenry's fears of those threats—that compel governments to take
action against those threats and certainly not the rights-abridging actions
government officials so often do take. It is threats that the government
deems worthy of public attention that will be acted upon. Louisiana Senator Mary Landrieu gave us a sense of this when, in the course of condemning the Bush administration's slow response to Hurricane Katrina,
she said, "I often think we would have been better off if the terrorists had
blown up our levees. Maybe we'd have gotten more attention."[14] In acting
upon threats, government officials will be inspired by a range of considerations—ideological, political, economic, and so on—that have much
less to do with the threats themselves than with the specific constituencies and interests for which the government speaks. The problem is not
that we live in a world of Hobbesian states; it is that we live in a world of
failed Hobbesian states.

The second implication of the Hobbesian argument is that if security is the foundation of political legitimacy, people will only believe
themselves obliged to obey if they think that their security is imperiled
or potentially at risk. Once people stop worrying about their security,
they may forget the reasons why they should obey. "The end of obedience is protection," Hobbes writes in *Leviathan*, but if people don't feel
themselves in need of protection, they won't sense the need for obedience.[15] That is why, late in life, Hobbes decided to write an account of
the English Civil War. It had been nearly three decades since its conclusion, but Hobbes thought it critical to record and recall its evils, there
being "nothing more instructive towards loyalty and justice than . . .
the memory, while it lasts, of that war."[16] Relying upon a simple fear of
danger to underwrite obedience, in other words, is not enough because

dangers can slip from view, and when they do, obligation is thrown into question. Hobbes was quite attuned to this problem and hoped that it could be solved by the sovereign supplying the people with "prospective glasses" by which they could "see a farre off the miseries that hang over" them but which they did not immediately perceive.[17]

But how does a state make a particular danger or disaster that lies far off appear up close? How does it turn hypothetical dangers into immediate threats? By developing an intellectual apparatus that dispenses with the ordinary requirements of evidence and proof, by articulating a set of arguments that enables the state to take extraordinary measures against postulated perils.

At the dawn of the modern state system, Cardinal Richelieu declared, "in normal affairs, the administration of justice requires authentic proofs; but it is not the same in affairs of state. . . . There urgent conjecture must sometimes take the place of proof; the loss of the particular is not comparable with the salvation of the state."[18] As we ascend the ladder of threats, in other words, from petty crime to the destruction or loss of the state, we require less and less proof that those threats are real. The consequences of underestimating serious threats are so great, Richilieu suggests, that we may have no choice but to overestimate them. Three centuries later, the liberal American jurist Learned Hand invoked a version of this rule: in the course of deciding whether or not to suppress rights, Hand wrote, officials must assess "the gravity of the 'evil'" but make sure that that gravity is "discounted by its improbability."[19] The graver the evil, the higher degree of improbability we demand in order not to worry about it. Or, to put it another way, if an evil is truly terrible but not very likely to occur, we may still take preemptive action against it.

These statements from Richelieu and Hand reveal an inverse relationship between the magnitude of a danger and the requirements of facticity. Once a leader starts pondering the nation's moral and physical extinction, he enters a world where the fantastic need not give way to the factual, where present benignity can seem like the merest prelude to future malignance.

As the run-up to the Iraq War shows, these are by no means ancient or academic formulations. While liberal critics have claimed that the Bush administration lied about or deliberately exaggerated the threat posed by Iraq, the fact is that the administration and its allies often were disarmingly honest in their assessment of the threat or at least honest about how they were assessing the threat.

In his 2003 State of the Union address, one of his most important statements before the war, Bush declared, "Some have said we must not act until the threat is imminent. Since when have terrorists and tyrants announced their intentions, politely putting us on notice before they strike? If this threat is permitted to fully and suddenly emerge, all actions, all words, and all recriminations would come too late."[20]

Notice that Bush does not affirm the imminence of the threat. In fact, he implicitly disavows it by ducking behind the past, darting to the hypothetical, and arriving at a nightmarish, though entirely conjectured, future. He does not speak of "is" but of "what if" and "could be." These words belong to the realm of neither fact nor fiction (which is why Bush's critics, insisting that he take his stand in one realm or the other, never could get a fix on him) but the conditional. And the conditional is a mood where evidence and intuition, reason and speculation, combine to make the worst-case scenario seem as real as the realest fact.

After the war had begun, the television journalist Diane Sawyer pressed Bush on the difference between the assumption "stated as a hard fact, that there were weapons of mass destruction" and the hypothetical "possibility that [Saddam] could move to acquire those weapons." Bush replied, "So what's the difference?"[21] No offhand comment, this was Bush's most articulate statement of the entire war, an artful parsing of a distinction that has little meaning in the context of national security.

Probably no one near or around the administration better understood how national security blurs the line between the possible and the actual than Richard Perle. Here is what Perle said on one occasion: "How far he's [Saddam] gone on the nuclear-weapons side I don't think we really know. My guess is it's further than we think. It's always further than we think, because we limit ourselves, as we think about this, to what we're able to prove and demonstrate. . . . And, unless you believe that we have uncovered everything, you have to assume there is more than we're able to report."[22]

Like Bush, Perle neither lies nor exaggerates. Instead, he imagines and projects and in the process reverses the normal rules of forensic responsibility. For when someone recommends a difficult course of action on behalf of a better future, he invariably must defend himself against the skeptic, who insists that he provide proof that his recommendation will produce the outcome he foresees. But if someone recommends an equally difficult course of action to avert a *hypothetical disaster*, the burden of proof shifts to the skeptic. Suddenly the skeptic must defend their doubt against this belief. And that, I suspect, is why the Bush administration's prewar mantra "the absence of evidence is not evidence of absence"—

laughable in the context of an argument for, say, world peace—could seem surprisingly cogent in the context of an argument for world war.

The language of security, and the discourse of imminence, provides the state with the means to exaggerate threats and to take preemptive action, including the abridgment of vital rights, to avert those threats. It is not the people's simple, unmediated fear of danger that compels this exaggeration and the turn away from evidence and proof. It is a highly elaborated political argument, which is based on the principle, in the words of Burke, that it is "better to be despised for too anxious apprehensions than ruined by too confident a security."[23] Or, as George Eliot put it in *Daniel Deronda*: "The driest argument has its hallucinations. . . . Men may dream in demonstrations, and cut out an illusory world in the shape of axioms, definitions and propositions, with a final exclusion of fact signed Q. E. D."[24]

The third and final implication of Hobbes's argument is that the sovereign can be the judge of our fears and of how we are to respond to those fears only if it possesses a unity of will and judgment.[25] If the sovereign is to be the decider, it must be able to decide; if it is to decide, it must come to a determinative judgment and a single, unified will. There can be no division or conflict; the sovereign must think and act as one.

As much as people try to resist this authoritarian dimension of Hobbes's argument, many politicians and scholars accept some version of it. It's often said that a people hoping to protect themselves from fundamental threats must agree that they are in fact threatened and agree as to how they will meet that threat. According to Cass Sunstein, citizens must "have a degree of solidarity and . . . believe that everyone is involved in a common endeavor" in order to convince "the enemy that it faces a unified adversary."[26]

Throughout the first five years of the Iraq War, to cite another example, Connecticut Senator Joseph Lieberman argued that any disagreement—not only about whether the war should be fought but also about how it should be fought—emboldens the enemy and should be avoided. In December 2005, he declared, "it's time for Democrats who distrust President Bush to acknowledge that he will be the commander in chief for three more critical years and that in matters of war we undermine presidential credibility at our nation's peril."[27] Invoking the language of treason, he wondered aloud during a congressional hearing whether a nonbinding Senate resolution opposing Bush's proposed escalation of American troops in Iraq "would give the enemy some comfort."[28] On *Fox News Sunday*, Lieberman declared again that the resolution would "encourage the enemy" and that "war is a test of wills, and you don't want your enemy to be given any hope."[29]

When it comes to matters of security, then, we are good Hobbesians, at least rhetorically. I say "at least rhetorically" because the fact remains that all states, even the most authoritarian, suffer from a fundamental lack of unity regarding their assessments of danger and of how to respond to danger; they also lack sufficient coercive power to enforce those assessments. Many states, particularly liberal democracies, are divided at the center—with different elements of their war-making powers parceled out to a legislature and an executive and sometimes even a judiciary—and federalist states are divided between the center and the periphery. It is not likely that such states will reach a consensus about what threatens them, and even if they do, it's not likely that the state's various and often fractious officials will agree on how to respond to threats. Even regimes that come closest to a vision of unified state power—one thinks of Hitler's Germany or Stalin's Russia—seldom exhibit that unity. Think only of the bitter arguments that divided the SS from other sectors of the Nazi regime about whether Germany's interests during the Second World War were better served by using the Jews as slave labor or by exterminating them.[30]

Nor do fundamental threats to the survival or integrity of the state necessarily furnish that unity. Consider the War of 1812, when British troops threatened the American state with the greatest challenge to its existential survival it had ever faced—and arguably would ever face—from abroad. As of September 1814, the British had taken control of Washington, DC, burned the Capitol and the White House to the ground, and sent the federal government into exile. They also had massed a terrifying army on Lake Champlain, blocked ports up and down the North Atlantic seaboard, seized a good chunk of Maine, and seemed ready for an invasion of Boston. Desertions from the army were spreading, and many states were left to defend themselves.

At that very moment, leading citizens in New England, who had opposed the war, proposed to meet in Hartford, Connecticut, to discuss measures the region might take to extricate itself from the war. That fall, antiwar candidates were elected to Congress; secession was favored by at least half of the population of Massachusetts, and influential citizens and newspapers throughout New England argued for nonpayment of federal taxes, declarations of regional neutrality, and refusals to cooperate with any federal conscription bill should one be passed. The governor of Massachusetts even sent an emissary to the British to secretly negotiate a separate peace, in which the British would promise to help the New Englanders defend themselves against any federal effort to suppress the rebellion.[31]

Even when there is agreement that the nation is threatened and that it must resist rather than surrender to the threat, there will still be disagreement about how best to defend the nation, and these disagreements can be as divisive and threatening as disagreements about whether the nation is threatened or should resist. As John C. Calhoun wrote of the divisive effects of war, which he ascribed to struggles over the distribution of material resources that accompanies any national mobilization: "The whole united must necessarily place under the control of government an amount of honors and emoluments, sufficient to excite profoundly the ambition of the aspiring and the cupidity of the avaricious; and to lead to the formation of hostile parties, and violent party conflicts and struggles to obtain the control of the government."[32]

The United States' involvement in the First World War offers an instructive example of just how divisive these disagreements about means rather than ends can be. Just after the United States entered the war in April 1917, an official from the War Department testified before Congress about what the military would need to fight the war. When he announced, almost as an afterthought, that "we may have to have an army in France," the chair of the Senate Finance Committee declared, "Good Lord! You're not going to send soldiers over there, are you?" Many in Congress and the public had believed that America's participation in the war would require little more than sending arms to Europe. But what began as an almost charming display of naiveté rapidly became the subject of bitter dispute. When President Wilson finally proposed a draft, the Speaker of the House declared that "there is precious little difference between a conscript and a convict." Though the conscription bill eventually passed, opposition to military service remained widespread. Roughly three million men evaded the draft, and as many as 60 percent of the men who registered may have requested exemptions from fighting.[33]

In addition to conscription, Americans argued about the mobilization of public resources. Conflicts within the military were particularly intense. Despite pressure from Wilson and other officials, the army resisted changes to its outmoded procurement systems, making for inefficiencies, redundancies, and obsolescent weaponry. So chaotic were the army's procedures that its top administrator wound up hoarding twelve thousand typewriters in various government basements. "There is going to be the greatest competition for typewriters around here," he explained, "and I have them all." Businessmen consistently opposed wartime regulations of the economy, arguing that private initiative and the free market were sufficient to fight and win the war. Financing the war was also contentious. While progressives persuaded Wilson of the need to tax wealthy interests in order to fund the war, their efforts were thwarted by industrialists and corporations, leading California Senator Hiram Johnson to complain, "Our endeavors to impose heavy war profit taxes have brought into sharp relief the skin-deep dollar patriotism of some of those who have been loudest in declamations on war and in their demands for blood." Forced to fall back on war bonds, the Wilson administration tried to turn the war into a genuine "people's war." But the government's "Liberty Loan" drives met with lethargy and opposition, leading the Treasury Secretary to declare, "A man who can't lend his government $1.25 per week at the rate of 4 percent interest is not entitled to be an American citizen."[34] Hoping to overcome this popular resistance, Congress inserted a provision into the Sedition Act of 1918 that made it illegal to "say or do anything" with intent to impede the sale of war bonds—though the legislature exempted from prosecution investment advisers who urged their clients not to buy war bonds for "bona fide and not disloyal" reasons, that is, because war bonds were a bad investment.[35]

On the one hand, then, we have an ideological imperative toward unity and solidarity. On the other hand, the modern state lacks that unity and solidarity. It seldom agrees upon the threats it faces, and even when it does, it can dissolve over arguments about how to meet those threats.

What do these three implications—that states have a great deal of freedom to determine what threatens a people and how to respond to those threats, and that in making those determinations, they are influenced by the interests and ideologies of their primary constituencies; that states have strong incentives and have been given strong justifications for exaggerating threats; and that while states aspire, rhetorically, to a unity of will and judgment, they seldom achieve it in practice—tell us about the relationship between security and freedom, of why security is such a potent argument for the suppression of rights and liberties?

Security is an ideal language for suppressing rights because it combines a universality and neutrality in rhetoric with a particularity and partiality in practice. Security is a good that everyone needs and, we assume, that everyone needs in the same way and to the same degree. It is "the most vital of all interests," John Stuart Mill wrote, which no one can "possibly do without."[36] Unlike other values—say justice or equality—the need for and definition of security is not supposed to be dependent upon our beliefs or other interests and it is not supposed to favor any one set of beliefs or interests. It is the necessary condition for the pursuit of any belief or interest, regardless of who holds that belief or has that interest. It is a good, as I've said, that is universal and neutral. That's the theory.

The reality, as we have seen, is altogether different. The practice of security involves a state that is rife with diverse and competing ideologies and interests, and these ideologies and interests fundamentally help determine whether threats become a focus of attention, and how they are perceived and mobilized against. The provision of security requires resources, which are not limitless. They must be distributed according to some calculus, which, like the distribution calculus of any other resource (say income or education), will reflect controversial and contested assumptions about justice and will be the subject of debate.[37] National security, it turns out, is as political as social security, and just as we argue about the latter, so do we argue about the former.

Even when it comes to the existential survival of the state, diverse constituencies will respond to that threat in diverse ways, depending upon their proximity to physical danger, their identification with the state, the level of sacrifice that might be expected of them, and so on. And while we might think that a threat to the existential survival of a people—say from a genocidal regime—would provide an instance of a neutral, universal definition of security around which a people could unify, such threats seldom inspire that unity of will and judgment. Instead, genocidal threats usually prompt a return to the Hobbesian state of nature, wherein individuals and families act upon their own definitions of danger and take whatever actions they deem necessary to secure their own survival.[38]

Because the rhetoric of security is one of universality and neutrality while the reality is one of conflict and division, state officials and elites have every motivation, and justification, to suppress heterodox and dissenting definitions of security. And so they have, as Hobbes predicted they could and would. But because a neutral, universal definition of security is impossible to achieve in practice, repression for the sake of security must be necessarily selective: only certain groups or certain kinds of dissent will be targeted. The question then becomes: which groups, which dissent?

Because government officials are themselves connected with particular constituencies in society—often the most powerful—they will seldom suppress challenges to security that come from the powerful; instead they will target the powerless and the marginal. So the U.S. government during the First World War made it illegal to urge people, like the Socialists, not to buy war bonds—but it did allow a Wall Street adviser to counsel his client not to make a bad investment. Or, when Congress passed the Sedition Act in 1918, which made it illegal to "willfully utter, print, write, or publish any disloyal, profane, scurrilous, or abusive language" about the U.S. government or the military or to bring these institutions "into contempt, scorn, contumely, or disrepute," the Republicans attempted to insert an amendment that would have protected themselves and their constituencies, who were aggressively criticizing Woodrow Wilson and the Democratic leadership of the U.S. government. "Nothing in this act shall be construed," the amendment read, "as limiting the liberty or impairing the right of an individual to publish or speak what is true, with good motives and for justifiable ends."[39] Suppressing dissident Socialists or activists against the draft was fine; suppressing dissenting Republicans was not.

But there is a second reason why security has proven the most potent justification for the suppression of rights. And that has to do with the liberal tradition. While liberalism has given us excellent reasons to oppose the use of coercive state power on behalf of religious or moral orthodoxy, it has given us far fewer reasons to oppose the use of that power on behalf of security. In fact, if we look at three touchstones of liberal discourse—Locke, Mill, and Oliver Wendell Holmes—we find that each of them actually provides excellent justifications for the use of coercive state power on behalf of security.

Each of these writers tried, in his way, to prevent the state from using its coercive power on behalf of some controversial question of ideology or belief: for Locke, it was religion; for Mill, it was morality; for Holmes, it was politics. And each of them formulated a test or condition for when the use of such power was legitimate: for Locke, it was "the security and safety of the commonwealth"; for Mill, it was harm; for Holmes, it was the "clear and present danger."[40]

The assumption behind the proscription against using coercive power in the first set of cases—religion, morality, and politics—and the endorsement of it in the second set of cases—the security and safety of the commonwealth, harm, or a clear and present danger—was not only that the first set was a source of controversy and division while the second set was not. It was that the first set was by its very nature a source of controversy, while the second set was, by its very nature, a source of unity. Unlike religion, morality, and politics, in other words, security offered the basis for an uncontroversial exercise of coercive state power.

As we have seen, this assumption has not been borne out by reality. But that failure has not stopped liberals from arguing, as the saying goes, that politics stops at the water's edge. And so when they have tried to confront conservatives for using security for political ends, they have found themselves hopelessly outgunned. Having endorsed—indeed, invented—the idea that security is not, properly speaking, a subject of and for the political arena, they cannot possibly hope to beat their opponents at a game that they claim does not even exist.

7 THE NEW YORK STOCK MARKET CRASH OF 1929

Harold James

THE U.S. STOCK market crash of October 1929 is indisputably history's most famous financial collapse. It is evoked wherever and whenever financial sentiment becomes nervous. And policy recommendations for the following eighty years have consistently been made on the basis of analyses or presumptions of what went wrong in 1929.

In particular, John Maynard Keynes's *General Theory of Employment, Interest, and Money* (1936) has at the heart of its diagnosis a critique not of the general operation of the stock exchange but specifically of the American market and its peculiar experience: its propensity to destabilizing and irrational speculation, which followed from the obsession of market participants with psychological rather than economic dynamics and expectations. The problem for Keynes lay fundamentally in a system of valuation in which values had no necessary or direct correspondence to long-term productivity. As a result, the American market became a casino with an inherently destabilizing quality. It was uniquely volatile because of the extent of popular participation, while more exclusive or "aristocratic" markets were less vulnerable:

> A conventional valuation which is established as the outcome of the mass psychology of a large number of ignorant individuals is liable to change violently as the result of a sudden fluctuation of opinion due to factors which do not really make much difference to the prospective yield; since there will be no strong roots of conviction to hold it steady.
> . . . The actual, private object of the most skilled investment today is "to beat the gun," as the Americans so well express it, to outwit the crowd, and to pass the bad, or depreciating, half-crown to the other fellow.
> . . . Even outside the field of finance, Americans are apt to be unduly interested in discovering what average opinion believes average opinion to be; and this national weakness finds its nemesis in the stock market.[1]

Extreme financial turmoil was, in other words, a specifically American malaise.

Keynes's analysis became the most influential policy prescription for the middle of the twentieth century: it required government action (on fiscal policy) to stabilize overall expectations and in this way establish a predictable or, as Keynes would have called it, "conventional" framework for the valuation of economic activity and thus for the functioning of a market economy. In the 1960s, President Johnson's advisers repeatedly justified the combination of tax cuts and expansion of social spending as necessary in order to avoid a repetition of the disaster of 1929. In the mid-1970s, in the aftermath of stagnation and the first oil price shock, the world again relearned a Keynesian lesson from the experience of the Great Depression.

In 1987 a seemingly exact replication of the stock market panic led to a different lesson, but again one that was historically derived: that a massive liquidity injection was needed to stop a stock market crash from becoming a generalized business depression because of the danger of a destabilization of financial institutions and of credit intermediation. This was the monetarist or Friedmanite conclusion. Again, like Keynes's analysis, it was derived from a very detailed empirical historical study of what Milton Friedman and Anna Schwartz, in their monumental *Monetary History of the United States*, termed the Great Contraction.[2] Their emphasis was on how a stable monetary framework created the sole basis on which expectations could be reliably and predictably formulated. The Chicago or monetarist interpretation played down the significance of

the October 1929 panic and explained the Great Depression in terms of
the Federal Reserve's mistaken policy after 1930 in not reacting to bank
failures, which produced a colossal monetary contraction (deflation).[3]
The year 1929 has, in short, become a standard part of the (theoretically
contradictory) justifications offered by central banks for stabilizing monetary policy and by governments for stabilizing fiscal policy.

More recently, the volatility of financial markets has increased due to
the globalization of markets. The memory of 1929 is now invoked with
each financial crisis (whatever the origin) as part of a call for a fundamental rethinking of policies aimed at financial liberalization. Helmut
Schmidt, for instance, who as German chancellor in the 1970s had been
obsessed by the possibility of a repeat of the Great Depression, in 1997,
after the East Asia crisis, stated that "the main parallel lies in the helplessness of many governments, which had not noticed in time that they had
been locked in a financial trap, and now have no idea of how they might
escape."[4] The financial speculator George Soros at the same time warned
of "the imminent disintegration of the global capitalist system," which
would "succumb to its defects."[5] The aftermath of the subprime crisis of
2007 has produced similar reactions. Again, George Soros opined that
"this is not a normal crisis but the end of an era."[6] Marcel Ospel, the
chairman of the Swiss bank UBS, while defending himself from criticism
after an $18 billion write-down, noted that the world was experiencing
the "most difficult financial circumstances since 1929."[7] The statement is
quite typical of much market sentiment in the midst of bad times, but it is
also curiously erroneous. Most of the world, and particularly European
countries, still had considerable financial stability in 1920, and the really
severe jolt, the annus terribilis, came in 1931.

THE MYSTERY OF 1929

The crash of 1929 is a substantial curiosity in that it is a very major
event, with really world-historical consequences (the Great Depression,
even perhaps the Second World War), but no very obvious causes. Above
all, the supposed causes can only be very poorly fitted (if at all) into the
still prevailing paradigm of social-science explanations in the efficient
markets hypothesis. According to the efficient markets view, stock prices
accurately reflect all the publicly available information about a security;
they will not change without the availability of new information.[8] Panics
in which prices change very abruptly cannot easily be conceptualized

in the terms of this hypothesis, especially if there appears to be little in the way of new information driving the panic. In consequence, financial crises have become a major rhetorical resource for critics of efficient markets.[9]

Belief in the rationality or nonrationality of the crash of 1929 can thus be a proxy for the extent to which there is popular acceptance of a theory about market behavior. There exists a continued fascination for 1929 and for books that tell its story, notably Frederick Lewis Allen's *Only Yesterday*, John Kenneth Galbraith's *The Great Crash*, John Brooks's *Once in Golconda*, and Charles Kindleberger's *Manias, Panics, and Crashes*.[10] All are frequently republished and seem to be widely consulted as guides to contemporary financial panics. It might be plausible to think that this is one area where historical study has a really formative impact on the behavior of a very large number of market participants.

The U.S. experience is quite unique in this regard, and this is one of the reasons why 1929 is exemplary and why it plays such a large part in Keynes's story. There were equivalent financial disasters in other large industrial countries, which in each case contributed to a worsening of economic fundamentals and to the severity of the Great Depression. In April 1927, Japan was shaken by a series of bank panics after the Bank of Taiwan suspended operations. Germany was brought down by the failure, on July 13, 1931, of the Darmstädter und Nationalbank. Britain was pushed off the gold standard on September 21, 1931. But in each case, it is possible to give a relatively clear account of what caused the panic. The Japanese failures were the result of a political controversy over the "earthquake bills" held by the Bank of Taiwan that had been given special treatment after the Great Kanto Earthquake of 1923. The German banking crisis followed from a coincidence of a political crisis following the announcement of plans for the Austro-German Customs Union and the difficulties of a major textile producer, Nordwolle. Britain was propelled into a crisis by a deep split within the government over fiscal policy and unemployment benefits and by an unprecedented naval mutiny that nervous commentators saw as the beginning of a British Bolshevik revolution.

The unique feature of the American panic is that no one has ever been able convincingly to explain what caused it or even what the specific trigger for the panic might have been. There are two potential "rational" explanations, but they do not look very satisfying.

One is that investors were able somehow to guess that there would be a Great Depression.[11] There were certainly some signs of slowing down in the U.S. economy, and construction had peaked several years before, in 1926, and had fallen off (in part perhaps because of declining flows of immigrants). But there was no evidence of a general downturn. For this time, there exist no direct measures of consumer confidence. Up to the last quarter of 1930, when there was a distinct change of tone, most surveys of business confidence were relatively upbeat. Periodicals such as *Business Week* were talking about an upturn in the summer of 1930. Peter Temin has identified as the most significant business indicator the change of classifications by bond rating agencies (Moody's and Standard and Poor's) and shown that in 1929, and even in 1930, a smaller proportion of corporate bonds were downgraded than either before, in 1921, or after, in 1937.[12] In other words, there is no hard evidence that anyone in 1929 could or should have expected a significant fall in American output or employment.

Perhaps, however, people experienced in political economy might have seen the likely effects of a big policy mistake: the Tariff Act of 1930 that became known as the Smoot-Hawley Tariff?[13] It had its origins in an election promise of Herbert Hoover's in October 1928 to address the plight of the farming population. In the course of congressional debate, first in committee and then in the full House, large numbers of nonagricultural tariffs were added, so that the eventual act included some twenty-one thousand tariff items. In the course of October 1929, the likelihood that Congress would pass the bill increased significantly. Financial prophets would then have had to think about the possible or likely forms of trade retaliation by other countries. But there is no real sign of such discussion of the probable path of world trade. The consequences of the new tariff may, however, have been reflected in some market responses, and the immediate outside price signal given to the financial markets on October 24 was a sharp drop in some commodity prices.[14]

The inability to find a precise cause of the panic of 1929 is baffling and intriguing. Paul Krugman has asked: "Could a small cause have large effects? Yes, it could. After all, the Great Depression had no obvious cause at all."[15] Ben Bernanke has put the point even more vigorously, stating that "to understand the Great Depression is the Holy Grail of macroeconomics."[16] Social scientists (and maybe also policy makers) are thus on an endless quest. Is it—like the Grail quest—fundamentally a futile one? Are the participants simply buffeted by wildly unpredictable psychic upheavals?

THE DEVELOPMENT OF STOCK PRICES

Between early 1926 and the spring of 1929, the Dow Jones Industrial Average (DJIA) index almost doubled, from 158.54 at the beginning of 1926 to 308.85 at the end of March; then it moved ahead even faster during the summer, with a peak of 386.1 on September 3.

The first signs of weakness in the market appeared on September 3, but small drops tempted many new investors into the market, so that volatility and trading quantities rose. On September 20, in England, the conglomerate built up by Clarence Hatry collapsed, and the New York market responded with a 2.14 percent drop. In the week of October 14, the decline in stock prices accelerated, with dramatic drops on October 16 (3.20 percent), October 18 (2.51 percent), and October 19 (2.83 percent), though punctuated by a rise on October 17 (1.70 percent). But the first day of real panic was Thursday, October 24, when the market fell very abruptly from an opening of 305.85 to a low of 272.32. Major New York bankers assembled at the offices of J. P. Morgan, as they had on a famous occasion in the panic of 1907, and a senior Morgan banker, Thomas W. Lamont, told the press that "due to a technical condition of the market," there "had been a little distress selling on the Stock Exchange."[17] The public outcome of the meeting was that the vice president of the New York Stock Exchange, Richard Whitney, whose brother was a Morgan partner, went onto the floor of the exchange and made a series of bids aimed at stabilizing the market. The first of these, a bid at a price of $205 per share for 10,000 for U.S. Steel, became one of the central collective memories of the New York market. The market indeed went up again, although in the afternoon selling orders from across the country continued to stream in, and the DJIA index closed at 299.47—in other words, down only 1.78 percent on the day. The volume of share transactions, which earlier in the year had been in the 1 to 2 million range, was 12,895,000.

An initial press comment for Thursday, October 24, emphasized the irrationality of imagination. The *New York Times* wrote: "At the climax of such a movement, the speculative imagination runs as wild as it does on the crest of an excited rise. Whereas it pictured impossible achievement in prosperity and dividends last August and last February, it now looks for equally impossible disasters."[18] The impossible? Sometime it becomes possible.

Over the weekend, there was a brief pause for reflection, as commentators commented and moralizers moralized. The result was an

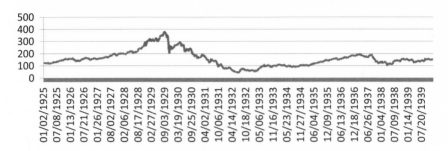

Figure 7.1. Dow Jones Industrial Average close, January 1925–July 1939

even more extreme panic on the following Monday (October 29) that continued on Tuesday, with very high trading volumes (9,213,000 and 16,410,000 shares respectively; see fig. 7.1).

On Monday, there was no repeat of Richard Whitney's appearance and his stabilizing bid for U.S. Steel. Instead, rumors about the continued bankers' meetings suggested that they had agreed to a concerted *selling* of stock, and Thomas Lamont was obliged to issue a formal rebuttal. In fact, New York banks did increase their lending to brokers dramatically at a time when out-of-town banks were calling in loans and foreign institutions were undertaking massive withdrawals.

But on Wednesday, October 30, there was a dramatic bounce, with a gain of 12.34 percent and again exceptionally high trading volumes (10,727,000 shares). After that, however, bad news continued. On November 2, the failure was announced of the Foshay utilities company of Minneapolis, which owned companies in twelve states. Again, the weekend was filled with rumors of the bankers' committee liquidating stocks. The market slid down until on November 13 the DJIA close was 198.69. This was followed by a quite spectacular (but incomplete) recovery to 294.07 on April 17, 1930. After this, there was a long slide, with fewer bounces, until the trough of July 1932, with a low of 40.56 on July 8.

The panic of October 1929 was immediately exacerbated by the interruptions to communications caused by the extent of the panic. Phone lines were swamped; in addition, the technical mischance of escaping steam in the Equitable Life Building at 120 Broadway put phones out of action. Lines between New York and Boston, Montreal, Chicago, Detroit, Cleveland, and Toledo were overwhelmed; the transatlantic phone lines had twice their normal business.[19] The high volume of orders meant that some were simply overlooked. Clerical workers continued to process orders until after midnight; downtown restaurants remained open, with every table occupied until early in the morning.

In the longer term, policy failures also exacerbated the impact of the stock market crisis. The first reaction of the New York banks had been to replace the credits that had been called by out-of-town banks, but this left them with an increasing vulnerability as lenders worried about the quality of loans. The Federal Reserve Bank of New York immediately stepped in to provide liquidity to the market by open market operations (purchases of government securities) that increased bank liquidity, and the Federal Reserve System also bought securities in the last three months of 1929. But New York's operations had not been approved by the Washington Board or its Open Market Investment Committee, and they became the subject of increasing criticism in Washington, which eventually succeeded in suspending the New York actions.

Why did the Washington federal institutions behave in this damaging way? Its actions were based on an erroneous theory, in which it had the responsibility to respond to the needs of the economy by discounting bills, but only "sound" bills that related to actual physical sales of goods, not to financial or speculative transactions. This "real bills doctrine" produced catastrophic monetary destabilizations in the early twentieth century: inflation in Germany and central Europe, where the central banks insisted that they were just responding to an exceptional but real business demand, and deflation generally in the early 1930s, when real transactions simply seemed to dry up.

Some explanations go further, and suggest that the U.S. central bank was gripped by the liquidationist doctrine that was memorably formulated by Treasury Secretary Andrew Mellon, "liquidate labor, liquidate stocks, liquidate the farmers, liquidate real estate, . . . purge the rottenness out of the system."[20] This was certainly the view of some influential economists of the time, who saw, as did Lionel Robbins, the problems of the 1920s as lying in an inflationary overextension of credit. It is striking that Robbins's sharpest formulation of the view actually directly draws on Keynes, whose apparent retraction of his earlier (and later) views in the *Treatise on Money* Robbins cites: "For my part I [Keynes] took the view at the time that there was no inflation in the sense in which I use this term. Looking back in the light of fuller statistical information than was then available, I believe that whilst there was probably no material inflation up to the end of 1927, a genuine profit inflation developed some time between that date and the summer of 1929."[21] The idea of purging the ills out of the system that was at the heart of the outlook of Robbins, and of Mellon and the Federal Reserve policy makers, depended on an extensive moral and psychological theory of what had gone wrong with the American economy.

THE MACROECONOMIC EFFECTS OF THE STOCK MARKET CRASH

From 1929 to 1932, U.S. gross domestic product (GDP) fell by a third, from $103.1 billion to $58 billion. How much of the collapse was the result of the stock market collapse? The Dow reached its low (40.56 points) in July 1932. The result of the long decline was a substantial loss of wealth, which had an immediate impact on consumption. Investors (sometimes described as six hundred thousand widows and orphans) lost more than $20 billion as a result of the stock exchange collapse.[22] This is a vast amount of wealth, but it still does not account for the extent of the collapse of GDP. In a detailed investigation, Peter Temin showed how, at the beginning of the slide into depression in 1930, only $1.3 billion of the $3 billion drop in consumption could be explained.[23]

Another transmission channel was probably more important. The reduced wealth as a consequence of the stock market panic reduced the collateral on which individuals and corporations could borrow and thus pushed the process of credit disintermediation that characterized the Great Depression.[24] The effects of wealth reduction were thus magnified and augmented through their impact on the structure of credit.

Clearly, the Great Depression was the result of more than one chain of causation, and other independent influences made the crisis more intense and spread it across national boundaries, making it hard to isolate the impact of the stock price move on its own. Such autonomous causes included the long slide in commodity prices since the mid-1920s, the political disputes over war reparations and Inter-Allied debts, the beggar-thy-neighbor trade policy that ricocheted across the world after the Smoot-Hawley Tariff, and the fixed-exchange-rate regime of the international gold standard, which proved to be a ready mechanism for the transmission of monetary deflation from one country to another. But of course, in one sense, all these provided information that might be expected to inform the action of the multitude of market participants.

THE EFFECTS OF THE PANIC ON WELL-BEING

A great deal of the early fascination with the stock market crisis focused on its psychological effects. Newspaper comments immediately picked up on suicides as a result of the market, such as John G. Schwitzgebel of Kansas City, who had shot himself in the chest at the Kansas City Club on October 29. Crowds formed expecting to see distraught investors and brokers jumping from the Wall Street skyscrapers. Every popular history of 1929 picks up this focus. John Kenneth Galbraith tells us how "two men jumped hand-in-hand from a high window in the Ritz. They had a joint account."[25] But he goes on to show that there were actually fewer suicides nationwide in October and November than in the summer months, when the market "was doing beautifully."

The press also reported incidents of heart attacks, such as that suffered by David Korn while watching the stock ticker in his broker's office in Providence.[26] It is easy to imagine how exposure to intense stress and fear would be reflected in temporarily increased blood pressure. Research published in 2008 has tried to link coronary disease and bank failures in a more rigorous and systematic way. A study at Cambridge University used historical data to show how a systemwide financial crisis increases deaths from heart disease by an average 6.4 percent in wealthy nations and more in developing countries. The lead author of the survey, David Stickler, told the press: "Our findings show that financial crises aren't just about money—they also impact on people's health. This report shows that containing hysteria and preventing widespread panic is important not only to stop these incidents leading to a systemic bank crisis but also to prevent potentially thousands of heart disease deaths."[27]

In this regard, there is a significant difference between financial and political crises. The unhealthy effects of financial crisis do not usually appear in moments of political stress. It is tempting to think that political upheavals are indicative of increased levels of hope about a better future. The result is a general decrease in levels of mortality related to physical stress and distress: thus, in Poland during the Solidarność crisis of 1980–1981, deaths from heart disease and cancers (as well as from violence) fell, as they did in 1989–1990 when the Communist system collapsed.[28] In each case, a plausible working assumption is that political turmoil was accompanied by a sense of optimism and the possibility of change for the better. By contrast, the rise in fatal cases of heart disease and cancers in New York City during the Great Depression is much more striking than

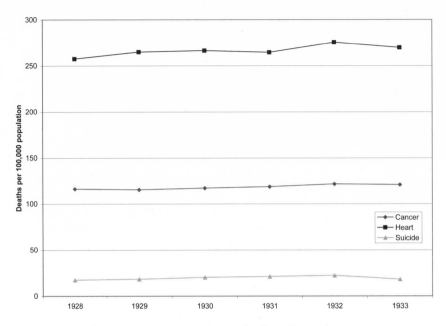

Figure 7.2. Death rates in New York City in the Great Depression

the much more often commented on suicide statistics, with deaths from heart disease per 100,000 rising from 257.4 in 1928 to 264.9 in 1929 and then to 275.5 in 1932 and then falling from 1933 (fig. 7.2). It is clear that the financial panic was accompanied by a rise in physiological stress, which was a reaction to the sense that the future consisted literally and psychically of loss and renunciation.

INTERPRETING THE CRASH

The newspapers on October 24 emphasized simply the abnormality of the market responses over the past days, especially the Monday and Wednesday, with their massive trade volumes: "It was very manifest on both occasions, to experienced Wall Street watchers, that the market was not acting as it had usually done when causes of special weakness had been eliminated."[29]

A striking feature of the reporting on the crisis was how much reference was made to the past history of crises as the only guide to current experience. The day after the October 24 collapse, the *New York Times* carried on page three an article entitled "Breaks of the Past Recalled on

Street": "Many reminiscent comparisons were made yesterday with other periods of critical readjustment on the stock market. It was generally agreed that no previous decline this year and in 1928 compared in either scope or violence with the break of this month. . . . Comparisons most frequently made by older members of the Stock Exchange yesterday were with 1920, 1907 (the 'panic years'), 1903 and 1901."[30] In other words, history was the major reason why individuals suddenly felt that there might be a broad range of alternative, much lower, valuations of stock. History actually induced the sense of crisis.

Exactly the same historical parallels, but this time to 1929, have been the stock-in-trade of commentary in every subsequent stock market panic. The most obvious parallel to October 1929 was the global stock market collapse of October 1987, with very similar percentage declines (22.61 percent in the DJIA on October 19) but a significantly different outcome: there was no world great depression of the interwar type. Again, market weakness in the preceding week was followed by a weekend replete with doom-laden journalistic prophecies. Again, as in 1929, there was no obvious trigger or news item, with the possible exception of the news that the United States had attacked an Iranian oil station (announced in the early morning of October 19).

In the immediate aftermath of the October 1987 crash, surveys of individual investors and institutional agents were conducted to attempt to judge whether their motivation could be explained by reference to economic fundamentals or rather to an endogenous determination because of some psychological theory of panic based on historical comparisons. On the basis of surveys, Robert Shiller concluded that "investors had expectations before the 1987 crash that something like a 1929 crash was a possibility, and comparisons with 1929 were an integral part of the phenomenon. It would be wrong to think that the crash could be understood without reference to the expectations engendered by this historical comparison. In a sense many people were playing out an event again that they knew well."[31] The historical reference is, in other words, a continuous and necessary driver of financial crises: in euphoric states, people are prepared to imagine futures that they can paint in utopian terms; when the euphoria collapses, they pick up memories of past disasters (that they may never have personally witnessed).

One point repeated very early in commentaries on the panic—whether in 1929 or 1987—was that there were historical precedents to the speculative boom. Past experience seems to contradict the repeated claims made during the period of market euphoria that there existed some entirely novel phenomenon that transformed business relations and hence was likely to bring a permanent prosperity. The following report, from 1929, is thus a perfectly characteristic postcrisis diagnosis, with its strong dependence on historical reminiscence: "Indeed, the favorite principle that times have so far changed that nothing of pre-war finance could nowadays be repeated, ignored rather singularly the fact that all these eccentric notions were recurrently in absolute control of the speculative Wall Street mind as far back as 1901. They were dispelled and discarded then, as they have been on the present occasion, through contradiction of all of them by the emphatic action of the stock market itself."[32] Looking back into a distant past was the way of inducing a giddiness about the heights that had been reached. This was indeed how the increasingly common but erroneous recall of Black Friday came about: it was a reference to the collapse of (Friday) September 24, 1869, that was conflated with (Thursday) October 24, 1929.

In this regard, reassurances from experts or authorities were irrelevant or counterproductive. Government officials—from the president down—and financial institutions emphasized that the markets were fundamentally sound. In a radio address on October 29, the assistant secretary of commerce reminded his audience that President Hoover had said that the "fundamental business of the country is sound." (There were echoes of this in 1987, when President Reagan shouted to reporters, "There is nothing wrong with the economy. . . . All the business indices are up. Maybe some people see a chance to grab a profit.")[33] John D. Rockefeller broke a long public silence to issue a statement: "Believing that fundamental conditions of the country are sound . . . my son and I have for some days been purchasing sound common stock."[34]

On October 30, with further declines in the market, the leading stockbrokers all went out of their way to reassure their clients. Hornblower and Weeks said, "Yesterday's amazing volume would seem to indicate that the process of liquidation was in its final stages." Jackson Brothers, Boesl, and Company concluded that "yesterday's record-breaking market" meant "that forced selling had been practically completed and that the stock market had touched its natural bottom." Clucas and Company was more modest: "We do not expect an immediate turn in the market for quick profits, but do believe that purchase of sound securities around current levels will prove a profitable investment over a period of time."[35]

While the experts tried in vain to sound reassuring, a different sort of opinion was articulated with increasing fervor. Moralistic commentators from outside the financial world attributed the crisis to the wages of sin. The *New York Times* extensively reported Protestant, though not Catholic or Jewish, responses to the stock market turmoil. The Bishop of Winchester (England) was, by coincidence, preaching on the Sunday after the Thursday crash at Grace Episcopal Church on Broadway: "Whatever this financial crisis in Wall Street means, it means distress to many innocent persons. But I shall not be sorry it has come if it has administered a severe blow to that gambling spirit which attempts to get something for nothing, to obtain large profits at the ruin of others." The Reverend Trowbridge of All Angels Episcopal Church tried to express some sympathy: "Though I do not believe it is morally or economically sound to gamble as men and women have been doing with ever increasing fervor, and though I cannot help but feel that they have in a sense received their just deserts, nevertheless one feels desperately sorry that they should have to suffer such humiliation and defeat." The Reverend Overlander of St. John's Evangelical Lutheran Church on Christopher Street called for a more philosophical approach: "True, a lot of money was involved and in some cases, I suppose, some men and women were literally wiped out. Yet I wonder how many of those persons stopped to think, even with that hard blow, how many things they should be thankful for."[36]

The Governor of New York Franklin D. Roosevelt criticized the "fever of speculation."[37] When, in 1933, Germany defaulted on its international debt, he slapped his thigh and said that it "served the bankers right." Roosevelt's treasury secretary, Henry Morgenthau, explained his vision of Bretton Woods agreements as "driving the usurious money lenders out of the temple of international finance." This tone spilled over into the general interpretation of the character of the crisis. Keynes, whose background in prewar Bloomsbury and the philosophical school of G. E. Moore made him unlikely to think in theological terms, concluded in *The General Theory* that "the sins of the London stock exchange are less than those of Wall Street."[38]

The Great Depression was also accompanied by inquiries and court cases aimed at punishing the evildoers. Beginning in April 1932, Ferdinand Pecora pushed the Senate Committee on Banking and Currency into an examination of the actions of the bankers. The chief executive of Chase, Albert Wiggin, was attacked for short selling the stock of his own bank during the panic of 1929. Charles E. Mitchell, the chief executive of National City Bank, was arrested for tax evasion on share deals in March 1933. Richard Whitney, the temporary hero of October 24, 1929, was arrested and imprisoned for embezzlement.

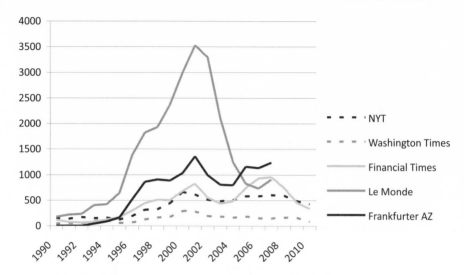

Figure 7.3. Number of references to the term "globalization" in major world news-papers, 1990–2010

There remains today a strong religious tone to comments on the financial crisis in its aftermath. In 1998, the middlebrow London *Daily Mail* thought that "investors are possessed by a demon of self-destruction and, like the Gadarene swine of the New Testament, they rush over the cliff and are dashed to pieces."[39] At the beginning of 2008, the founder and chief promoter of the Davos World Economic Forum, Klaus Schwab, announced, "We have to pay for the sins of the past."[40] And Paul Krugman wanted to discuss the credit crunch in terms of a "crisis of faith."[41]

Theological perspectives can of course be used to derive insights into market behavior. The most striking example is the fear and greed index pioneered in 1986 by the analyst James Montier at Dresdner Kleinwort, in which sentiment is driven entirely by a bipolar opposition of greed as the market moves ahead and fear of loss when it stalls. Greed, measured in this way, reached an all-time peak in early 2007, just on the eve of the most devastating financial crisis since the Great Depression. The insight behind the analysis is that the potential for fear increases with the extent of greed. Fear is the historically determined—or perhaps the moral—answer to greed: the wage of greed and sin. Fear arises when deep historical experience suddenly reemerges and becomes alive as a possible version of the present.

The volatile fluctuations of this index conceal a long-term trend, with a tendency toward optimism in the period 1990–2000, followed by a severe swing to the "end of the world" standpoint with the collapse of the dotcom boom, and a new optimism after 2003. We can find the same from other analyses of prevalent modes of thought. Strikingly, references to "globalization" in the world's major newspapers show the same increase in the 1990s and the same decrease until 2003 (fig. 7.3).

The prominence of fear, and a resurgence of thinking in terms of sin, seem in the modern era to be accompaniments to a turning away from internationalism (or globalization). These sentiments are an integral and causative part of the mechanism by which severe financial crises are propagated. But we should recognize that this is not simply a phenomenon of the twentieth or twenty-first century. The emphasis on fear is part of a broader package, a worldview that has its historical antecedents in figures such as Girolamo Savonarola or Martin Luther at the height of Renaissance euphoria or John Dickinson during the American Revolution. The panic of 1929 remains a major monument to twentieth-century fear, the fear that President Franklin D. Roosevelt tried to exorcise in what is probably still his best-remembered phrase: "The only thing we have to fear is fear itself."

8 LIVING DEAD

FEARFUL ATTRACTIONS OF FILM

Adam Lowenstein

FEAR AND FILM have always been intimate companions. One of cinema's primal scenes testifies to this intimacy and originates from the medium's very beginnings: the famous screening in 1895 of Louis and Auguste Lumière's *L'Arrivée d'un train en gare de La Ciotat* (*Arrival of a Train at La Ciotat*, also known as *Arrival of a Train at the Station*) at the Grand Café in Paris. The spectators in the Grand Café, among cinema's very first public audiences, responded to the image of a train pulling into a station with pure terror. The power of this new technology to grant movement to photography was so overwhelming that viewers turned and fled from the train as if it threatened to crush them. For this audience, the cinematic image of the train became the train itself—something to fear.

At least that's how the story goes. The film historian Tom Gunning points out how the oft-repeated accounts of this incident appear more mythological than truthful after careful study of evidence from the period. Writing in 1989, Gunning observes how "this primal scene at the cinema" lives on nevertheless, how "the terrorized spectator of the

Grand Café still stalks the imagination of film theorists who envision audiences submitting passively to an all-dominating apparatus, hypnotized and transfixed by its illusionist power."[1] Today, this situation in film studies has changed considerably, due in no small part to Gunning's own pathbreaking scholarship.[2] His description of early cinema (1895–1906) as dominated by an aesthetic he calls "the cinema of attractions" has become perhaps the single most influential concept in film studies over the last twenty years.[3]

Gunning's definition of the cinema of attractions is worth quoting at some length, as I will use it to anchor my own discussion of fear and film to key debates within the discipline of cinema and media studies:

> The cinema of attractions directly solicits spectator attention, inciting visual curiosity, and supplying pleasure through an exciting spectacle— a unique event, whether fictional or documentary, that is of interest in itself. The attraction to be displayed may also be of a cinematic nature, such as . . . trick films in which a cinematic manipulation (slow motion, reverse motion, substitution, multiple exposure) provides the film's novelty. Fictional situations tend to be restricted to gags, vaudeville numbers or recreations of shocking or curious incidents (executions, current events). It is the direct address of the audience, in which an attraction is offered to the spectator by a cinema showman, that defines this approach to filmmaking. Theatrical display dominates over narrative absorption, emphasizing the direct stimulation of shock or surprise at the expense of unfolding a story or creating a diegetic universe. The cinema of attractions expends little energy creating characters with psychological motivations or individual personality. Making use of both fictional and non-fictional attractions, its energy moves outward towards an acknowledged spectator rather than inward towards the character-based situations essential to classical narrative.[4]

This initial formulation of the cinema of attractions, revised and expanded by Gunning in a series of linked essays he began publishing in 1986, already suggests a number of reasons why the concept has continued to resonate so powerfully with film scholars within and beyond the subfield of early cinema. A cinema of attractions uncovers an alternative set of film aesthetics and film histories that had been relegated previously to the margins of what was usually assumed to be central: film's evolution as a narrative-based, storytelling medium. Prior to the recognition of a cinema of attractions, film historians routinely proceeded as if it were cinema's destiny to develop the sort of narratives we now associate with the classical Hollywood style—the dominant form of commercial film style in the United States from roughly 1917 to the present, with remarkable worldwide influence.[5] Classical Hollywood style emphasizes psychologically motivated, goal-oriented characters as the active agents who move through cause-effect chains of events. These events are based on a series of temporal deadlines that resolve with a strong degree of closure by the time the film concludes.[6] The result is a film style where "telling a story is the basic formal concern" and conventions of "realism" arise from commitments to concealment of artifice, "comprehensible and unambiguous" storytelling, and a "fundamental emotional appeal that transcends class and nation."[7]

If classical Hollywood style is posited as the norm, then filmmaking practices that deviate from it risk becoming seen as "primitive" (such as early cinema) or "excessive" (such as genres where spectacle often seems to trump narrative, including musicals and horror films). The cinema of attractions has come to stand for an alternative tradition, one that embraces a set of practices and conventions different from those of classical Hollywood style. Through the lens of a cinema of attractions, what once seemed "primitive" or "excessive" now emerges as a tradition in its own right, worthy of engagement on its own terms.[8] Gunning himself has always maintained that a cinema of attractions must be understood as existing alongside and in dialogue with those narrative priorities at the heart of classical Hollywood style, rather than as a mode incommensurable with it or fundamentally opposed to it. According to Gunning, the fate of the cinema of attractions after its dominance during the early cinema period is not disappearance but relocation; it "goes underground, both into certain avant-garde practices and as a component of narrative films, more evident in some genres . . . than in others."[9] If the entire notion of a cinema of attractions springs from the primal encounter—as mythically persistent as it is historically inconsistent—between fearsome film and fearful audiences, then what does the horror film genre in particular have to tell us about the attractions of cinema? Is it possible that this genre, with its multiple and varied investments in shocking, terrifying, disturbing, and haunting its viewers, has more to teach us than perhaps any other about the fearful attractions of film? This chapter attempts to generate some provisional answers to these difficult questions.

Much of my own previous research can be seen as responding to similar questions. I have argued elsewhere that the modern horror film (post-1960), in particular cases tied to specific national contexts, confronts viewers with the traumatic legacies of events such as the Holocaust,

Hiroshima, and the Vietnam War. I have contended that the allegorical method these horror films employ to engage historical trauma results in a more confrontational address of the spectator than is found in those contemporaneous art films that are often more explicit in their references to traumatic historical events (and always more critically praised). My ultimate goal was to trace a series of "allegorical moments" in these horror films that enact "a shocking collision of film, spectator, and history where registers of bodily space and historical time are disrupted, confronted, and intertwined."[10]

The concept of a cinema of attractions helped to inspire my formulation of the allegorical moment in several ways. First, my sense of the horror film's direct, visceral address of the spectator's body was influenced by the aesthetic of attractions described by Gunning. Second, my claim that the "excess" of the horror film could be construed as a strength rather than a weakness when compared with more "legitimate" art films mirrored the dynamics of Gunning's encounter between early cinema and classical Hollywood style. Finally, I wished to extend the logic of a cinema of attractions to areas that seemed absent or marginalized in Gunning's model. For example, Gunning's emphasis on the differences between early cinema's attractions and classical Hollywood style's narrative-driven pleasures often constructs a divide between the bodily, sensational aspects of cinematic spectatorship and its more rational, cognitive dimensions focused on storytelling. Although Gunning devotes considerable care and attention to reminding us that such distinctions must not be perceived as absolute or noninteractive, his interest in elucidating one set of terms rather than the other necessarily highlights attractions more so than narrative. What, then, do we make of the horror film's allegorical representation of historical trauma? Is it rooted in attractions, in the direct address of the spectator at the level of bodily sensation? Or is it the product of cognitive processes such as memory and identification upon which narrative depends? My notion of the allegorical moment in the horror film points toward a both/and response to these questions, rather than an either/or.[11]

In this chapter, I wish to extend my investigation of historical trauma and the horror film by revisiting the cinema of attractions, this time delving more deeply into issues of temporality, particularly deferral, belatedness, and retranscription. This emphasis on temporality aims to illuminate the nature of cinema's fearful attractions—the medium's ability to frighten us in ways that are visceral and cognitive, personal and historical. My case study focuses on a landmark in the history of the modern horror film: writer and director George A. Romero's extraordinarily influential *Dead* series, which began with *Night of the Living Dead* (1968) and now stands at six entries, including the most recent installment *Survival of the Dead* (2010).[12] Given my concerns with belated and retrospective temporalities, I will concentrate especially on two of the more recent entries in a series that now spans over forty years and shows no signs of stopping.

LIVING IN THE *LAND OF THE DEAD*

Surely the distinction of "most deferred" film of 2005 belongs to *Land of the Dead*, Romero's fourth *Dead* film. *Land of the Dead* appears thirty-seven years after *Night of the Living Dead*, twenty-six years after *Dawn of the Dead* (1979), and twenty years after *Day of the Dead* (1985). Of course, there were persuasive commercial factors for why the time seemed right for producers to risk a new entry in a series whose most recent entry dates back two decades; most prominent among these was the considerable financial success of such recent Romero-inspired films as *28 Days Later* (Danny Boyle, 2002) and the remake of *Dawn of the Dead* (Zack Snyder, 2004). *Land of the Dead* performed respectably at the box office but did not replicate the success of those films. I would submit that one reason for this difference in popularity was not the belatedness of *Land of the Dead* but its timeliness.

Indeed, one of *Land of the Dead*'s most remarkable qualities is that its belatedness is precisely what contributes to its unsettling historical timeliness. It is this sense of temporality that makes *Land of the Dead* a more rewarding and important work than those recent films indebted to Romero, but it is also what makes Romero's film much more difficult, demanding, and confrontational to watch, particularly within a contemporary American reception context. I will attempt to uncover the functions of timeliness in *Land of the Dead* with the goal of reflecting upon how cinema represents trauma and inspires fear. In short, I want to examine a "deferred" film to grapple with cinema's relation to the complex temporalities of trauma—temporalities that Sigmund Freud famously characterized as *nachträglich* or "deferred."[13]

Although Freud's concept of *Nachträglichkeit*, or deferred action, was never fully defined within his writings, Jean Laplanche and Jean-Bertrand Pontalis note that the term crops up "repeatedly and constantly . . . from very early on" and that it was "indisputably looked upon by Freud as part of his conceptual equipment." Laplanche and Pontalis define deferred action as an idea "frequently used by Freud in connection with his view of psychical temporality and causality: experiences, impressions and memory-traces may be revised at a later date to fit in with fresh experiences or with the attainment of a new stage of development. They may in that event be endowed not only with a new meaning but also with psychical effectiveness."[14] Freud always conceived of the psyche as a stratified mechanism, where memories are subject to "rearrangement" and "retranscription" according to shifts in time and experience, but he usually reserves deferred action for experiences impossible for the subject to integrate in a meaningful way at the time of their occurrence.[15] As Laplanche and Pontalis note, "the traumatic event is the epitome of such unassimilated experience."[16]

If a memory is deferred or revised or reimagined in possibly fantastic ways commensurate with the affective rather than the veridical truth of traumatic experience, is this memory still "true"? Janet Walker offers the valuable observation that when we enter the realm of what she calls "the vicissitudes of traumatic memory," dichotomies such as true and false, however tempting to enlist in the face of circumstances often accompanied by dire personal and political consequences, are simply not adequate to the complexity of the problems that have surfaced.[17] What we need instead is a more nuanced theoretical approach to traumatic memory that permits us to weigh concerns such as truth and falsehood alongside questions of how exactly trauma and memory interact, with particular sensitivity to the variety of possibilities with which traumatic memory may manifest itself. I believe one promising avenue of research into detailing these possibilities is to study how media deals with the representation of traumatic events and to learn from these representations what the range of responses to trauma may look like. Such research should not simply equate media representations (or our reactions to them) with individual psychological mechanisms but use the media representations as touchstones for generating questions that may or may not illuminate certain psychological or social processes.

I believe that since the horror film is a genre built upon depicting frightening, often traumatic experiences yet rarely considered "serious" enough to portray traumatic history, its engagements with historical trauma are particularly valuable. The horror film's allegorical moments serve to open up debates about what exactly counts as a frightening representation of historical trauma. Why do certain forms of art cinema and national cinema tend to "count" when it comes to representing historical trauma while others do not? Is there any relation between such distinctions and the demarcations used to characterize certain forms of traumatic memory as more "accurate" and "true" than others?

Near the beginning of *Land of the Dead*, we are introduced to a black gas station owner whose uniform announces him as "Big Daddy." This is all we learn of his name, because he does not speak—he is a walking corpse, or zombie, reanimated with millions of other recently deceased bodies when the Earth falls prey to a mysterious plague that causes the dead to rise and eat the living. From the outset, Big Daddy (Eugene Clark) distinguishes himself from his lumbering zombie brethren by demonstrating unusual proficiencies in tool use, problem solving, strategic leadership, and empathic understanding. In fact, as Big Daddy comes to occupy an increasingly central position in the film, he displays a sense of social justice so compelling that his surface attributes as monster fade while his sympathetic qualities as underclass revolutionary grow.[18]

I choose the term "underclass" deliberately, for Romero's dark world in *Land of the Dead* is an America whose class divisions mirror our own in their harsh, often race-bound demarcations. At the top is Kaufman (Dennis Hopper), the rich, white overlord of a high-rise compound called Fiddler's Green where the wealthy can live in hermetically sealed luxury apart from the apocalyptic world below. The middle class includes people who work for Kaufman or subsist on the scraps he tosses, a mixed bag of soldiers, servants, and poor citizens from a variety of ethnic backgrounds that eke out an existence below Fiddler's Green. The middle class is protected from zombie encroachment by natural and military barriers, but they cannot hope to rise to the class status of Fiddler's Green residents. Of course, this means that the underclass is a mass of zombies, whom even most of the middle class refuse to recognize as anything more than dangerous animals. Yes, the zombies present a real threat to the living, but don't the living also threaten the zombies? Do the zombies possess a right to exist as well, especially as they seem to assume increasingly "human" traits? Big Daddy certainly seems to think so, and his leadership of his undead comrades helps convince viewers of the same. When he sets his sights on nothing less than Fiddler's Green itself as the proper inheritance of the zombies, it is difficult not to root for the revolution that will shatter this corrupt and suffocatingly privileged space, even if it means that those we call "the living" must die in the process.

In one of the climactic acts of the zombie siege on Fiddler's Green, Big Daddy corners a fleeing Kaufman in his getaway car. With Kaufman protected behind locked doors, Big Daddy reaches for a nearby gasoline hose and pierces the car's windshield with its nozzle, sending a stream

Figure 8.1. Big Daddy in *Land of the Dead*. George A. Romero, 2005, Universal
Pictures

of gasoline pouring inside (fig. 8.1). Big Daddy then walks away, leaving the underground garage. Kaufman, more irritated than mystified
by Big Daddy's behavior, steps out of the car and removes the spewing
gasoline hose, tossing it on the ground carelessly. As he tends to the duf-
fel bags packed with cash he has brought with him, he is threatened by
the entrance of Cholo (John Leguizamo), a Latino soldier for hire whose
dreams of upward mobility have been crushed by Kaufman. The two
fire weapons at each other, Cholo missing his target and Kaufman hit-
ting his. So Kaufman is surprised when, shortly afterward, Cholo rises
to menace him once again. But of course Cholo is not dead but undead.
As the two struggle, Big Daddy returns to the garage with an explosive
canister that he rolls toward Kaufman's car and the pool of gasoline that
has collected around it. The ensuing blast sends Cholo flying away from
the car while Kaufman is apparently immolated, his flaming dollar bills
sailing in the air like confetti as the car burns and Big Daddy looks on.

This scene is a striking example of how Romero interweaves commentary on class inequities with imagery tied to the contemporary
trauma of the Iraq War. Romero has often said that *Land of the Dead*
is his attempt to explore the post-9/11 American mentality, and that
Kaufman's administration of Fiddler's Green could be seen as analogous to the presidential administration of George W. Bush.[19] Romero
sees Kaufman's establishment of a society that refuses to reckon with the
true nature of the zombie crisis as mirroring the Bush administration's
posture toward terrorism, where the problem is functionally ignored
through what Romero calls "living around it and profiting from it."[20] In
this particular sequence, Kaufman must face what he has denied in the
forms of Cholo and Big Daddy.

Cholo, who has been used by Kaufman for dangerous military missions that serve his own ends but whom Kaufman refuses to recognize as an equal, embodies the tragic position of rank-and-file American soldiers in Iraq. Like Cholo, these soldiers are often nonwhite and working class. They fight and die for an authority that disrespects them through dishonest arguments concerning the reasons for their sacrifices. But in this scene Kaufman must reckon with the fact that he has effectively condemned Cholo to death—and that this death is not the end in terms of Kaufman's responsibility.

When Big Daddy penetrates the façade of Kaufman's insulated world with the gasoline hose nozzle, the gesture carries much symbolic weight. At the level of commentary on the Iraq War, the gesture evokes the popular antiwar slogan of "no blood for oil" as well as the economic reality that the war abroad helped send gas prices soaring at home, resulting in particular hardship for the working class. In terms of class commentary, the gesture asserts Big Daddy's pride in his profession (he remembers what a gasoline hose can do) as well as his defiant determination to "stick it" to Kaufman in a manner that not only makes concrete the very working-class labor that Kaufman strives to ignore but also reminds him that this labor is capable of turning the exploitation that his wealth rests upon against him.

There is also a provocative intertextual dimension to Big Daddy's gesture, one that becomes clearer when Big Daddy returns to the garage with the explosive canister that he uses to detonate Kaufman's car. This automobile explosion beside a gasoline pump in *Land of the Dead* echoes a similar moment in *Night of the Living Dead*, when three members of a besieged farmhouse group attempt to escape the surrounding zombies by filling a truck with gas at a nearby pump (fig. 8.2). The escape attempt goes awry and two of the three are burned to death when spilled gas catches fire and the truck explodes. Only Ben (Duane Jones), the black leader of the farmhouse group, survives this incident.

The similarities between these charged moments in *Night of the Living Dead* and *Land of the Dead*, joined together across nearly four decades, invite us to consider the matter of cinematic deferred action. If *Land of the Dead* encourages allegorical connections with the Iraq War, then this framework for historical allegory must be understood through *Night of the Living Dead*'s relation to the Vietnam War. *Night of the Living Dead*'s status as an allegorical commentary on America eating itself alive through the contemporary trauma of Vietnam and resistance to the civil rights movement—an interpretation articulated persuasively by crit-

Figure 8.2. Ben in *Night of the Living Dead*. George A. Romero, 1968, Image Ten

ics within two years of the film's original release—has only grown more established in the years that have followed.[21] But if *Land of the Dead*'s relation to Iraq must then be filtered through *Night of the Living Dead*'s relation to Vietnam, then how is historical trauma revised and retranscribed in the process?

Let me reply to this question first by turning to one of Freud's own examples of traumatic memory and deferred action. In "Project for a Scientific Psychology" (1895), Freud describes the case of Emma, a woman who suffers from a hysterical compulsion that prevents her from entering a shop alone. Freud traces this compulsion to two linked memories that only become fully comprehensible as traumatic through their deferred distribution across several different temporalities. The more recent memory comes from Emma's experience as a twelve-year-old: she fled a shop after seeing two male clerks laughing together. She believed they were laughing at her clothes, and she recalls that one of the clerks struck her as sexually attractive. The older, more buried memory comes from Emma's experience as an eight-year-old: her genitals were fondled through her clothes by a shopkeeper who grinned at her during the assault. The trauma of this original memory could not be assimilated at the time because of Emma's sexual naiveté, so the trauma was deferred through the temporalities of Emma as a twelve-year-old and Emma as an adult in analysis. Associations between the two memories are conveyed through the shared characteristics of clothing, laughter, shopworkers, and sexual feeling; these associations across several different temporalities combine to produce the compulsion that prevents Emma from being able to enter shops alone as an adult. Freud concludes, "Here we have the case of a memory arousing an affect which it did not arouse as an experience, because in the meantime the change [brought about] in puberty had made possible a different understanding of what was remembered."[22]

Land of the Dead also presents a case where viewers are challenged to arrive at a "different understanding of what was remembered" about *Night of the Living Dead*, to bring the historical trauma of Iraq and Vietnam together. Just as Emma's memories are joined through deferred action and the associative glue of certain shared elements, so too are the similar sequences I have presented from Romero's two films. Both films feature black men as the survivors of, and witnesses to, a deadly automobile explosion caused by fire igniting spilled gas—scenes of destruction that evoke and connect the military violence of wars waged outside America with the social and economic violence within America. Such violence must be endured especially by disadvantaged groups such as racial minorities and the poor. In *Night of the Living Dead*, Ben looks on in horror as two of his comrades are killed in the flames; in *Land of the Dead*, Big Daddy watches Kaufman's demise with the grim satisfaction of a mission accomplished. In both cases, the audience is meant to identify with the affective position of the black character—a daring venture in 1968 and still daring in 2005.

With Ben, Romero asks the audience to empathize with a powerful black male lead—an exceedingly rare figure in commercial American cinema of the time (and still far too unusual today). With Big Daddy, Romero demands an even more uncommon point of empathy—Big Daddy is not just black, he is undead. In *Night of the Living Dead*, Ben's humanity is asserted by contrasting him with the inhuman zombies that he battles, as well as the despicable white father Harry Cooper (Karl Hardman) who repeatedly attempts to undermine his authority. *Land of the Dead* revises this affective map for the spectator by suggesting that "humanity" is not just a matter of putting aside racial differences in the confrontation with the inhuman but that this very distinction between human and inhuman can be transformed into one more layer of racial and economic discrimination turned to the advantage of those with wealth and power. Romero retranscribes Ben as Big Daddy in order to re-remember *Night of the Living Dead*, to revisit the original film's vision of historical trauma with the benefit of experience gained in the interim—experience that includes the Iraq War.

Again, I do not wish to suggest that Romero's films, or our memories of those films, are somehow equivalent to Emma's traumatic memories. Diagnosing films or spectators as if they were patients in therapy is a pursuit doomed to distort the very different ways that clinical and cinematic meaning gets made. Instead, I want to hold open the possibility that there is something to be learned from the structural affinities between the deferred nature of personal trauma in Emma's memories and historical trauma in Romero's films. In short, the processes of psychological retranscription described by Freud offer a valuable framework for interpreting the historical deferrals across Romero's films without becoming themselves clinical instances of Freud's Nachträglichkeit.

One effect of Romero's deferred presentation of historical trauma across these two films is to heighten the stakes of what audiences are willing to incorporate as their own when confronted with those forces conventionally designated as "other."[23] How far are you willing to go for the cause of social justice when its enemies mutate and reorganize? Can you empathize across lines of race, class, and even those divisions that separate the "living" from the "dead"? And is empathy enough? These questions form one major challenge that viewers of Romero's films encounter. Another is the refusal to allow spectators to rest comfortably with any nostalgic imagination of the 1960s, or *Night of the Living Dead* itself, as a utopian moment in progressive political activism immune to critique. The fact that Dennis Hopper, a countercultural icon of the 1960s for his role in *Easy Rider* (Dennis Hopper, 1969), appears in *Land of the Dead* as Kaufman speaks cynical volumes about how counterculture becomes dominant capitalist culture.[24]

But there is also a less cynical, even cautiously optimistic aspect to *Land of the Dead*'s revisions of *Night of the Living Dead* on historical trauma. *Night of the Living Dead* ends on a devastating, nihilistic note when Ben survives the zombie onslaught only to be killed by his rescuers when they mistake him for one of the undead. In the film's closing images, Ben again faces gasoline and flames, only this time he is just one more anonymous corpse added to a bonfire of lifeless bodies. *Land of the Dead* concludes with Big Daddy caught in the gun sights of a retreating truckload of the living as they abandon Fiddler's Green to the conquering zombie masses. It seems as if Big Daddy, like Ben before him, must die as the price of embodying the demands for social change he represents.

But then, at the last minute, the leader of the living spares Big Daddy, explaining that he and his kind are "just looking for a place to go, same as us." This simple but powerful statement of recognition, "same as us," is the closest Romero comes to believing in something resembling the healing potential of Freud's "talking cure" for trauma. That this healing can only exist, in the end, through a series of deferred actions means that any glimmer of hope must be located within cyclical histories of pain.

A NEW (RE)VISION: *DIARY OF THE DEAD*

When *Land of the Dead* retranscribes *Night of the Living Dead* by concluding with Big Daddy's survival rather than Ben's murder, does Big Daddy's status as something to be feared disappear? After all, doesn't Big Daddy's survival, his provisional fulfillment of viewer hopes so cruelly dashed when Ben dies, consolidate his identity as protagonist rather than monster? In other words, are we frightened (if at all) by the same things in *Night of the Living Dead* as in *Land of the Dead*? Romero's *Diary of the Dead* (2008) offers a useful vantage point on these questions.

Diary of the Dead, perhaps even more than *Land of the Dead*, encourages viewers to perform the work of retranscription. While all of the previous *Dead* films proceeded chronologically, depicting the zombie plague at increasingly advanced stages (but always with a different set of characters), *Diary of the Dead* returns to the temporal frame of *Night of the Living Dead*. The zombie plague has just arrived—we return to where we began forty years before.

Of course, it is fair to ask whether most viewers will remember or have even seen a film released four decades earlier. Some doubtlessly will not. But several factors suggest that many viewers will indeed be ready to retranscribe *Diary of the Dead* alongside the previous *Dead* films. First, the nature of horror film fandom in general often inspires unusually loyal, informed devotion to the genre and sometimes extends to forms of identification with horror-oriented subcultural communities (such as goths).[25] Second, the status of the *Dead* series as "cult" cinema, a specialized set of films spread across a wide variety of genres that for any number of reasons (oddness, originality, shock value, unheralded excellence, sublime awfulness, particular kinds of cultural or historical significance) encourages repeated viewings, revival screenings, and avid word-of-mouth promotion sometimes bordering on worship long after the date of original release.[26] Third, the popularity of prerecorded entertainment technologies for the home, from VCRs in the 1970s to today's high-definition DVD players and Internet-based distribution hubs, means that the *Dead* films (like thousands of others) are more accessible to a wider audience than ever before.[27] The flipside of this accessibility is invisibility, with the deluge of film titles easily available potentially drowning each other out. But it is precisely those films like the *Dead* series, with strong name recognition and a pronounced cultural presence grounded in deep, sustained appreciation among critics and fans alike, that stand to thrive in this media-saturated landscape. One obvious sign of the success of Romero's films in this regard is the virtual army of remakes, imitations, offshoots, homages, and parodies that range across decades, nations, and media as varied as cinema, television, novels, comic books, video games, music videos, and web shorts.

So when *Diary of the Dead* returns to the temporal frame of *Night of the Living Dead*, there are compelling reasons to believe that many viewers will respond to this turning back of the narrative clock as an even more emphatic invitation to participate in the work of retranscription I have described in *Land of the Dead*. *Diary of the Dead* follows a University of Pittsburgh film crew (a band of students accompanied by an alcoholic emeritus professor who is also a war veteran) as they drive across the wide state of Pennsylvania, from Pittsburgh to Philadelphia, looking for refuge from the zombie plague. The crew's director, Jason Creed (Joshua Close), insists on chronicling their odyssey on digital video cameras every step of the way. His girlfriend, Debra (Michelle Morgan), voices the most heartfelt opposition to Jason's fixation on filming rather than simply surviving under such deadly circumstances, but it is she who finally completes the editing of Jason's footage into a documentary called *The Death of Death*. It is this documentary that comprises the entirety of *Diary of the Dead*—every scene we watch is drawn from the footage Jason's crew shoots or from the material they access via television and the Internet.

The temporal structure of *Diary of the Dead* mirrors other contemporary films I will refer to as "camera confessionals," such as *The Blair Witch Project* (Daniel Myrick and Eduardo Sánchez, 1999) and *Cloverfield* (Matt Reeves, 2008). We know from the outset that the events depicted through the simulation of raw, first-person footage have already taken place, that the visual record created by these characters remains even if the characters themselves may have died in the interim between their filming and our viewing. The difference in *Diary of the Dead* is that the context provided by the *Dead* series affords a remarkably rich opportunity to embed the camera confessional format with issues of retranscrip-

Figure 8.3. The conclusion of *Diary of the Dead*. George A. Romero, 2008, Artfire
Films

tion. For example, *Diary of the Dead* ends with a harrowing scene that
Jason has downloaded from the Internet, filmed in the style of a YouTube
web short. In other words, the scene is a brief, user-generated document
incorporated into the longer camera confessional that is Jason Creed's
The Death of Death, which in turn doubles as Romero's feature-length
fiction film *Diary of the Dead*. The scene shows a group of redneck hunters shooting at tied and bound zombies for target practice, for fun. They
string up a female zombie by her hair to a high tree branch and then blast
away her body with their guns, leaving only her eyes and forehead swing-
ing from the tree. She stares back at the camera, at us, a trickle of blood
running like a tear from her left eye (fig. 8.3).

At one level, this shot of the mutilated female zombie functions very
much as an attraction in Gunning's sense. The confrontational address
of the audience, the direct look at the camera that acknowledges the
spectator, the shocking image of an execution, the emphasis on pure display rather than narrative development—all are markers of a cinema of
attractions. Even Debra's voiceover that accompanies this image works
similarly to the showman or magician often present either within the
early films analyzed by Gunning or outside them, as speakers in the tradition of carnival barkers who drew attention to the spectacle by performing "the important temporal role of announcing the event to come,
focusing not only the attention but the anticipation of the audience."
Debra's voice fulfills this "announcing gesture" by explaining the source

of the spectacle we are about to witness, as well as how what we will see was deliberately staged by the hunters.[28] She sets us up for the attraction itself.

In other ways, this spectacle of the mutilated zombie operates somewhat differently than an attraction. Debra's voice extends the confrontational address of the attraction by speaking to us directly over the grisly final shot: "Are we worth saving? You tell me." But her voice is a far more developed narrative presence than are those of the magicians and barkers of early cinema. In addition to being a central protagonist, she has contributed voiceover narration from the very beginning of the film; by the film's end, we know that even if authorship of *The Death of Death* is attributed to Jason, it could not have been completed without Debra's editing—Jason himself dies before he can finish this task. So Debra, as editor and narrator, shapes *The Death of Death* (as Romero shapes *Diary of the Dead*) into a narrative film, rather than a disjunctive series of attractions.

But it is not only Debra's editing and narration that transform the temporality of this final scene in *Diary of the Dead* into something other than the temporality Gunning assigns to the attraction. For Gunning, the attraction's temporality "is limited to the pure present tense of its appearance," where a "*now* you see it, *now* you don't" temporal frame departs from narrative temporality's movement "from *now* to *then*, with causality as a frequent means of vectorizing temporal progression."[29] The unmistakable visual markers of lynching in this scene—the hanging from the tree, the redneck hunters, the execution staged as entertainment not only for the hunters themselves but for audiences imagined by the camera operator, the distribution of this lynching via the Internet mimicking earlier distribution of lynching photographs as postcards— collide with retranscription to generate the "now *is* then" temporality of the allegorical moment, where historical trauma infiltrates the shocking spectacle and confrontational viewer address of the attraction.[30] Even though *Diary of the Dead*'s lynching features a white female zombie, there is a powerful invitation to retranscribe her as analogous to Ben, the black man lynched (at least figuratively) at the conclusion of *Night of the Living Dead*. Ben's body, like that of the female zombie, is destroyed and humiliated by a redneck posse that assumes he is inhuman. Where the female zombie hangs from a tree, Ben's corpse is dragged by meat hooks and ultimately consumed in a bonfire—in both cases, the visual iconography of lynching overwhelms the images. Through retranscription linked across films, coupled with the invocation of traumatic events linked across history, the "pure present tense" of the attraction metamorphoses into the past *as* present tense of the allegorical moment.

When past and present meet in the final scene of *Diary of the Dead*, the connotations attached to lynching radiate not only toward slavery and the civil rights struggle but also toward the disastrously racialized mismanagement of Hurricane Katrina's aftermath in 2005 (footage of which appears earlier in *Diary of the Dead*) and a number of humiliations connected to the Iraq War. The torture of the female zombie by a band of smiling rednecks eager to post their handiwork on the Internet evokes the photographs that exposed the Abu Ghraib torture scandal (April 2004) as well as the widely publicized mutilation, burning, and hanging of bodies belonging to American contractors by Iraqi insurgents in Fallujah (March 2004). At Abu Ghraib, American forces humiliated Iraqis with the same gleeful, grinning pride that often appears in the faces of observers in lynching photographs. In Fallujah, Iraqi insurgents engaged in a practice called *saleh* in Iraqi Arabic, which translates roughly as the lethal public humiliation of an enemy; at least one journalist described saleh as "the act of lynching."[31] When the echoes of these humiliations of Iraqis by Americans and Americans by Iraqis join together with the shame of Hurricane Katrina and a long history of racist violence in America epitomized by lynching, what does this allegorical moment that concludes *Diary of the Dead* become? How do spectators interpret it? What are they afraid of?

The allegorical moment, like any theorized act of spectatorship, can only represent a horizon of possibilities for potential viewer reactions. No physiological sensors or strategic interviews or questionnaire results can ever tell the whole story about a matter as complicated and idiosyncratic as how exactly spectators interact with a film. This is not to say that such approaches are incapable of providing valuable information about certain aspects of the spectatorship experience. Indeed, the increasing interest in cognitivism in film studies over the past twenty years constitutes a contemporaneous and often strikingly different theoretical model to the cinema of attractions.[32] Where the former concentrates on rather basic, empirically observed viewer processes connected to deciphering a narrative or registering an emotion, the latter focuses on more hypothetical, less easily quantified dimensions of spectatorship attached to historical and philosophical concepts such as "modernity."[33]

Cognitivist studies of the horror film in particular have tended to suggest universalist, often ahistorical explanations for what motivates viewer responses of fear and/or horror. For example, Joanne Cantor and Mary Beth Oliver's claim that fright reactions to horror films can be accounted for largely (at least among younger viewers) through theories of stimulus generalization, where "stimuli and events that cause fear in the real world will produce a fear response when they appear in movies," so that "natural" fears of actual "distortions and deformities" will be replicated in viewer responses to similar sights in horror films.[34] Or Noël Carroll's claim that horror film monsters frighten us through their "impurity," their anthropologically defined status as "categorically interstitial, categorically contradictory, incomplete, or formless."[35] For Carroll, zombies inspire fear due to their interstitial nature as both living and dead. But what of the empathic viewer responses to Big Daddy in *Land of the Dead* and the lynched female zombie in *Diary of the Dead* that I have suggested in conjunction with notions of the allegorical moment and retranscription? Cognitive fears of impurity or deformity, bound so tightly to an assumed equivalence between how we process a film and how we process the real world, do not adequately account for the spectatorship possibilities I have outlined: empathy mixed with fear, visceral sensation mixed with historical consciousness.

Robin Wood's influential psychoanalytic and Marxist account of the horror film seems more in line with my concerns than the cognitivist model, at least at first glance. Wood distills the basic structure of the horror film into the formula "normality is threatened by the Monster," where normality stands for "conformity to the dominant social norms" of heterosexual, bourgeois, patriarchal capitalism, and the Monster stands for "all that our civilization represses or oppresses" in the shape of "othered" groups such as women, homosexuals, the working class, foreign cultures, and nonwhite races.[36] The strength of Wood's model is that it allows the horror film to be read in social terms, but its weakness is the rigidity with which the social realm and its cinematic representation are imagined. For Wood, "progressive" or "radical" horror films introduce ambivalence to normality's relationship with the Monster. Normality undergoes critique as the Monster receives sympathy or else normality's dominant ideology is apocalyptically negated through "the recognition of that ideology's disintegration, its untenability, as all it has repressed explodes and blows it apart."[37] In the "reactionary" horror film, by contrast, normality's ideology becomes consolidated through treatment of the Monster with "unmitigated horror," "sexual disgust," and "unremitting ugliness and crudity."[38] Even though Romero's *Dead* films have always held pride of place for Wood as unusually well-realized fulfillments of the genre's progressive potential, Wood's model is finally too inflexible, moralistic, and narrative driven to accommodate the full range of complexities attached to an allegorical moment such as the conclusion of *Diary of the Dead*. Indeed, Wood confesses to "bewilderment" when faced with this scene, even if he finds the film as a whole to be the work of "a great and audacious filmmaker" that confirms Romero as "the most radical of all horror directors."[39]

What confuses Wood about the ending of *Diary of the Dead* are precisely those qualities that pertain to its nature as an attraction. He recognizes the power of its shocking display of spectacle ("its central image is certainly among the most appalling ever produced within fictional cinema"), but he cannot fathom its apparent disconnection from narrative priorities ("the perpetrators of the desecration it depicts are a couple of irrelevant rednecks who played no part in the film").[40] What escapes Wood, here and elsewhere, is the possibility of cinematic significance in registers other than those dominated by narrative. Note, for example, how Wood's judgments of "progressive" and "reactionary" often lean heavily on narrative analysis for their primary criteria, highlighting especially the narrative endpoints of the films ("the 'happy ending,' [when it exists] typically signifying the restoration of repression").[41]

Gunning, as we have seen, points out how the attraction indicates a mode of viewer address that does not necessarily coincide with and may sometimes even oppose conventional narrative development. One way to interpret the final scene of *Diary of the Dead* is to read it as a variation on the attraction Gunning calls "the apotheosis ending." In the apotheosis ending, "which entered cinema from the spectacle theater and pantomime," the film closes with "a sort of grand finale in which principal members of the cast reappear and strike poses in a timeless allegorical space that sums up the action of the piece."[42] The conclusion of *Diary of the Dead* does not reintroduce the principal cast as in the original apotheosis endings of early cinema, but it does provide a spectacular finale that condenses the film into one summarizing image. This image may not make sense as narrative, but it makes profound "sense" as an attraction. It pulls together the confrontational elements aimed at viewers throughout the film and throughout the *Dead* series as a whole. Its evocation and/or retranscription of Iraq, Katrina, Vietnam, the civil rights movement, and slavery characterize its space as allegorical but not timeless. Its temporality depends on the attraction's spectacular "now you see it, now you don't" time of display, but it cannot be limited to the "pure present tense" Gunning assigns to the cinema of attractions.[43]

Instead, this attraction exists in the past as present tense of the allegorical moment, where historical trauma informs the confrontation delivered by sensational spectacle. This is not to say that Gunning's account of an attraction's temporality excludes the possibility of historical reference, for his notion of "timeless allegorical space" is clearly conditioned, like my own, by Walter Benjamin's notion of allegory as a radical disruption of conventional historical continuity.[44] What I am calling attention to here is an important difference in emphasis, rather than disagreement—where Gunning highlights the attraction's allegorical space, I am highlighting its allegorical time.

Given my focus on retranscription, perhaps it is more accurate to describe the allegorical moment's temporality in terms of *pasts* as present tense. The plural "pasts" remind us of the multiple points of contact offered to the spectator between a film and history, as well as between a series of films and histories. By the same logic, the quality of fear provoked by the allegorical moment necessarily encompasses a wide range of possible affect, including (but not limited to) horror, dread, disgust, and anxiety. In fact, this fearful affect may be inseparable from an even more expansive variety of feelings such as empathy, anger, amusement, and admiration. In other words, the allegorical moment demands an approach to fear in film that matches its approach to history in film: attentive to plural, multilayered interactions between spectator and cinema that span cognition and sensation, knowledge and affect, past and present.[45]

For example, viewers may respond to the final scene in *Diary of the Dead* by experiencing a mixture of sense and sensation that could produce very different "answers" to Debra's question, "Are we worth saving?" Sadness and outrage inspired by how history repeats itself, how the lessons of one lynching and one war fail to prevent the occurrence of others, may leave some viewers fearful of a future or a present where something like this female zombie's victimization could happen to them. Other viewers may see the rednecks as a throwback to the posse that kills Ben in *Night of the Living Dead*, making these rednecks closer to a kind of memorial for fears lodged in the past than to an active source of fear in the present. Still others may feel relief that the fearful threat of the "zombies" (Iraqi insurgents? American contractors? Vietcong? U.S. soldiers? Blacks? Whites?) can be controlled, even mocked, by "human" forces—however temporarily. These examples are not meant to be an exhaustive catalog of possible spectator responses but a preliminary list that suggests how the allegorical moment might function. However speculative and incomplete, I hope it is enough to convey how formulations concerning the horror film's production of fear through stimulus generalization, cognitive categorizations of "impurity," or diagnoses of "progressive" and "reactionary" political representation cannot fully explain fear's complexity in the allegorical moment.

Fear in the allegorical moment, when it is filtered through its similarities to and differences from a cinema of attractions, also makes room for viewer responses to films governed by what Gunning calls "an aesthetic of astonishment." When Gunning theorizes how early cinema spectators may have responded to the cinema of attractions, he describes "an attitude in which astonishment and knowledge perform a vertiginous dance, and pleasure derives from the energy released by the play between the shock caused by this illusion of danger and delight in its pure illusion. The jolt experienced becomes a shock of recognition. Far from fulfilling a dream of total replication of reality . . . the experience of the first projections exposes the hollow center of the cinematic illusion."[46] In the case of *Diary of the Dead*'s conclusion, then, an astonished spectator might cringe with fear or disgust at the sight of the mutilated female zombie but simultaneously admire the skillful combination of digital and prosthetic special effects that made this image possible. The point is that viewer responses of fear and knowledge are not mutually exclusive, whether the knowledge stems from awareness of cinematic artifice, as in Gunning's aesthetic of astonishment, or from awareness of historical trauma, as in the allegorical moment. Neither, then, are viewer responses of fear and pleasure mutually exclusive. The allegorical moment insists that traumatic history can be *felt* as well as *known*—and that this knowledge can arrive as a shocking confrontation and/or as a playful encounter with cinematic illusions.

"Playful," "pleasure," and "illusion" need not signal triviality. As Gunning notes, one of the most sophisticated observers of early cinema, the Russian writer and intellectual Maxim Gorky, was already attuned to the double-edged nature of cinema's ability to communicate visceral threat alongside empty illusions.[47] Gorky, writing about his attendance at a projection of Lumière films at the Nizhni-Novgorod Fair in 1896, registers both sensational astonishment ("the extraordinary impression it creates is so unique and complex that I doubt my ability to describe it with all its nuances") and knowing disillusionment ("this mute, gray life finally begins to disturb and depress you").[48] Gorky also experiences fear. When faced with *L'Arrivée d'un train en gare de La Ciotat*, he begins by highlighting its terrifying threat: "It speeds straight at you—watch out! It seems as though it will plunge into the darkness in which you sit, turning you into a ripped sack full of lacerated flesh and splintered bones, and crushing into dust and into broken fragments this hall and this building, so full of women, wine, music and vice." Yet Gorky concludes by highlighting the emptiness of this threat, his knowledge that the train is illusory: "But this, too, is but a train of shadows."[49] His visceral terror and demystifying knowledge exist side by side, without one canceling the other.

In a certain sense, Gorky sees cinema as an encounter with the living dead. His fear emanates from recognizing terrifying life in images freighted with the hollowness of death: "From it there blows upon you something that is cold, something too unlike a living thing."[50] For Gorky, cinema's simultaneous fullness and emptiness are as inextricable as they are frightening. The images carry "a vague but sinister meaning that makes your heart grow faint. You are forgetting where you are. Strange imaginings invade your mind and your consciousness begins to wane and grow dim. . . . But suddenly, alongside you, a gay chatter and a provoking laughter of a woman is heard."[51] In Gorky's experience of cinema, we see the "living dead" projected and may even become "dead" to our immediate surroundings before being jolted back to life. The cinematic experience is death in life, life in death, a procession of living dead images: "Their smiles are lifeless, even though their movements are full of living energy and are so swift as to be almost imperceptible. Their laughter is soundless, although you see the muscles contracting in their gray faces. Before you life is surging, a life deprived of words and shorn of the living spectrum of colors—the gray, the soundless, the bleak and dismal life."[52] One century later, Romero's films testify to how cinema can still provoke the fear and the fascination of seeing and being the living dead. And in a cinema of the living dead, film's fearful attractions partake of history with a timely belatedness.

NOTES

INTRODUCTION

1. The express goal of this book is to reveal what multidisciplinarity can reveal about fear that individual disciplines cannot. This agenda distinguishes it from other collections or journal issues on fear, such as Brian Massumi, ed., *The Politics of Everyday Fear* (Minneapolis: University of Minnesota Press, 1993); Franz Bosbach, ed., *Angst und Politik in der europäischen Geschichte* (Dettelbach: J. H. Roll, 2000); Arien Mack, ed., "Fear: Its Political Uses and Abuses," special issue, *Social Research* 71, no. 4 (Winter 2004); the project "Dealing with Fear" at Akademie Schloss Solitude, Stuttgart (2007–2009), http://www.dealing-with-fear.de/index.html; a thematic cluster on fear in the inaugural issue of *Zeitschrift für Medien- und Kulturforschung*, no. 1 (2009); and Michael Laffan and Max Weiss, ed., *Facing Fear: The History of an Emotion in Global Perspective* (Princeton: Princeton University Press, 2012).

2. See especially William M. Reddy, *The Navigation of Feeling: A Framework for the History of Emotions* (Cambridge: Cambridge University Press, 2001). While anthropology has produced the most vigorous antiessentialist emotions research, it is interesting to note that there are nearly no ethnographies of fear (or fear-like constructs). For an exception to the rule, see an article on precontact Maori fear of combat, Jean Smith, "Self and Experience in Maori Culture," in *Indigenous Psychologies: The Anthropology of the Self*, ed. Paul Heelas and Andrew Lock (London, 1981), 149.

3. Lorraine Daston, oral communication, June 25, 2009; quoted with permission.

4. Jerome Kagan, *What Is Emotion? History, Measures, and Meanings* (New Haven: Yale University Press, 2007), 14.

5. Charles Darwin, *The Expression of the Emotions in Man and Animals* (London: John Murray, 1872), 362. In Darwin's scheme, the emotion of fear was reduced to its corporeal signs, namely "trembling, the erection of the hair, cold perspiration, pallor, widely opened eyes, the relaxation of most of the muscles" (362). To Darwin, the greatest proof of its ancient, evolutionary heritage was that these outer markers obtained in all cultures ("With respect to fear, as exhibited by the various races of man, my informants agree that the signs are the same as with Europeans" [294]) and that primates showed many of them as well ("Monkeys also tremble from fear; and sometimes they void their excretions. I have seen one which, when caught, almost fainted from an excess of terror" [145–46]).

6. See, for example, Thomas Dixon, *From Passions to Emotions: The Creation of a Secular Psychological Category* (Cambridge: Cambridge University Press, 2003), 18–19, 22, 48, 60–61; Daniel M. Gross, *The Secret History of Emotion: From Aristotle's Rhetoric to Modern Brain Science* (Chicago: University of Chicago Press, 2006), 29; Katherine Rowe, "Humoral Knowledge and Liberal Cognition in Davenant's Macbeth," in *Reading the Early Modern Passions: Essays in the Cultural History of Emotion*, ed. Gail Kern Paster, Katherine Rowe, and Mary Floyd-Wilson (Philadelphia: University of Pennsylvania Press, 2004), 181–82; and Nancy J. Chodorow, *The Power of Feelings: Personal Meanings in Psychoanalysis, Gender, and Culture* (New Haven: Yale University Press, 1999), esp. chap. 6.

7. The term "phobic regime" is inspired by Martin Jay's notion of the scopic regime, as elaborated in his "The Scopic Regimes of Modernity," in *Force Fields: Between Intellectual History and Cultural Critique* (New York: Routledge, 1993).

8. Kagan, *What Is Emotion?*, 1. A similar gesture permeates the writings of Antonio Damasio, whose best sellers enjoin readers to "look for Spinoza" by attending to the "feeling brain." See Antonio Damasio, *Descartes' Error: Emotion, Reason, and the Human Brain* (New York: Random House, 1994); and *Looking for Spinoza: Joy, Sorrow, and the Feeling Brain* (Orlando: Harcourt, 2003).

9. Kagan, *What Is Emotion?*, 216. Kagan's injunction is in fact a modern update to an ancient precursor. As rhetorician Daniel Gross reminds us, Aristotle held that emotions such as fear, though often coded as "hardwired," are in fact instigated by "a series of enabling conditions obscured by our platitudes of biology." Gross's survey of the passions from late antiquity through the early modern era to the most recent regime of "brain science"

leaves the concept of "basic emotions" impoverished indeed. See Daniel M. Gross, *The Secret History of Emotion: From Aristotle's "Rhetoric" to Modern Brain Science* (Chicago: University of Chicago Press, 2006), 2.

10. On *Angstlust* from a psychoanalytic perspective, see Michael Balint, *Thrills and Regressions* (New York: International Universities Press, 1959), translated into German as *Angstlust und Regression* (Stuttgart: Klett-Cotta, 1991).

11. On Paul Ekman, see his personal and official website, http://www .paulekman.com, and Antony J. Chapman, Wendy Conroy, Noel Sheehy, ed., *Biographical Dictionary of Psychology* (New York: Routledge, 1997), 161–62. For critiques of emotions scholarship from the life sciences, the best place to get started is the summary by the insider neuroscientist Richard J. Davidson, "Seven Sins in the Study of Emotion: Correctives from Affective Neuroscience," *Brain and Cognition* 52, no. 1 (2003): 129–32.

12. Ruth Leys has used the distinction to supplant distinctions between, say, social psychology (James Averill, Shinobu Kitayama) and basic emotion theory (Silvan Tompkins, Paul Ekman, Paul Griffiths), or between cognitive or appraisal psychology (Magda Arnold, Phoebe Ellsworth, Nico Frijda, Batja Mesquita) and affective neuroscience (Jaak Panksepp). The virtue of the intentionalist-nonintentionalist distinction is that it does not pivot on differences between disciplines (or subdisciplines) as such but on the kind of interpretive work these disciplinary approaches perform. See Ruth Leys, *From Guilt to Shame: Auschwitz and After* (Princeton: Princeton University Press, 2007), chap. 4, esp. 125–26.

13. See Simo Knuuttila, *Emotions in Ancient and Medieval Philosophy* (Oxford: Oxford University Press, 2004), 32, 25. Also see Alexander Nehamas, "Pity and Fear in the *Rhetoric* and the *Poetics*," in *Essays in Aristotle's Poetics*, ed. Amelie Oksenberg Rorty (Princeton: Princeton University Press, 1992), 291–314.

14. See Knuutila, *Emotions in Ancient and Medieval Philosophy*, 248.

15. Deborah Brown, "The Rationality of Cartesian Passions," in *Emotions and Choice from Boethius to Descartes*, ed. Henrik Lagerlund and Mikko Yrjönsuuri (Dordrecht: Kluwer Academic, 2002), 270.

16. For a succinct introduction, see David Sander, "Amygdala," *The Oxford Companion to Emotion and the Affective Sciences*, ed. David Sander and Klaus R. Scherer (Oxford: Oxford University Press, 2009), 28–32. The neuroscientist who more than any other has popularized the amygdala's centrality in fear processing is Joseph LeDoux. See LeDoux's *The Emotional Brain: The Mysterious Underpinnings of Emotional Life* (New York: Simon and Schuster, 1996).

17. For an attempt to undo the category of prehistory, see Daniel Lord Smail, *On Deep History and the Brain* (Berkeley: University of California Press, 2008).

18. Ben Bernanke, "The Macroeconomics of the Great Depression: A Comparative Approach," *Journal of Money, Credit, and Banking* 27, no. 1 (February 1995): 1.

19. On this see, for example, Nikos K. Logothetis, "What We Can Do and What We Cannot Do with fMRI," *Nature* 453, no. 7197 (2008): 869–78.

20. Samuel Taylor Coleridge, "Fears in Solitude," in *Major British Poets of the Romantic Period*, ed. William Heath (New York: Macmillan, 1973), 467–69.

21. Sigmund Freud, "Thoughts for the Times on War and Death," in *The Standard Edition of the Complete Psychological Works of Sigmund Freud*, ed. James Strachey (London: Hogarth Press, 1957), 14: 275.

22. They also moved into popular culture: witness Fox's television show *Lie to Me*: "The truth is written all over our faces." Paul Ekman is scientific consultant; the character of Dr. Cal Lightman is based on Ekman.

23. Paul Ekman, "How to Spot a Terrorist on the Fly," *Washington Post*, October 29, 2006.

24. The historian of emotions Peter Stearns claims credit for this kind of awareness raising in his *American Fear: The Causes and Consequences of High Anxiety* (New York: Routledge, 2006). See Jan Plamper, "The History of Emotions: An Interview with William Reddy, Barbara Rosenwein, and Peter Stearns," *History and Theory* 49, no. 2 (2010): 264. The political scientist Corey Robin's *Fear: The History of a Political Idea* (New York: Oxford University Press, 2004), the medical doctor Marc Siegel's *False Alarm: The Truth About the Epidemic of Fear* (Hoboken: John Wiley and Sons, 2005), the legal philosopher Cass Sunstein's *Laws of Fear: Beyond the Precautionary Principle* (New York: Cambridge University Press, 2005), the medical doctor and historian of science Robert A. Aronowitz's *Unnatural History: Breast Cancer and American Society* (New York: Cambridge University Press, 2007), and the sociologist Robert Wuthnow's *Be Very Afraid: The Cultural Response to Terror, Pandemics, Environmental Devastation, Nuclear Annihilation, and Other Threats* (New York: Oxford University Press, 2010) have had a similar effect.

25. John Locke, *A Letter Concerning Toleration*, ed. James H. Tully (Indianapolis: Hackett Publishing, 1983), 46; John S. Mill, "On Liberty," in *On Liberty and Other Writings*, ed. Stefan Collini (New York: Cambridge University Press, 1989), 13; Schenck v. United States, 249 U.S. 47 (1919).

I. FEAR, ANXIETY, AND THEIR DISORDERS

1. Peter J. Lang, "Anxiety: Toward a Psychophysiological Definition," in *Psychiatric Diagnosis: Exploration of Biological Predictors*, ed. Hagop S. Akiskal and William L. Webb (New York: SP Medical and Scientific Books, 1978), 368.

2. Michael J. Kozak and Gregory A. Miller, "Hypothetical Constructs versus Intervening Variables: A Re-Appraisal of the Three-Systems Model of Anxiety Assessment," *Behavioral Assessment* 4, no. 3 (1982): 347–58.

3. Hilary Putnam, "Minds and Machines," in *Dimensions of Mind*, ed. Sidney Hook (New York: Collier Books, 1960): 148–79.

4. John R. Searle, *The Rediscovery of Mind* (Cambridge: MIT Press, 1992), 14.

5. Searle, *Rediscovery of Mind*, 16.

6. Ibid., 19.

7. Ibid., 94.

8. Jerome Kagan, *What Is Emotion? History, Measures, and Meanings* (New Haven: Yale University Press, 2007), 23.

9. Kagan, *What Is Emotion?*, 26.

10. Searle, *Rediscovery of Mind*, 143–44.

11. Joseph LeDoux, *The Emotional Brain: The Mysterious Underpinnings of Emotional Life* (New York: Simon and Schuster, 1996).

12. Jerome Kagan, *An Argument for Mind* (New Haven: Yale University Press, 2006), 208.

13. Kagan, *What Is Emotion?*, 74.

14. Paul J. Whalen, "Fear, Vigilance, and Ambiguity: Initial Neuroimaging Studies of the Human Amygdala," *Current Directions in Psychological Science* 7, no. 6 (1998): 177–88.

15. Scott L. Rauch, Paul J. Whalen, Lisa M. Shin, Scott C. McInerney, Michael L. Macklin, Natasha B. Lasko, Scott P. Orr, and Roger K. Pitman, "Exaggerated Amygdala Response to Masked Facial Stimuli in Posttraumatic Stress Disorder: A Functional MRI Study," *Biological Psychiatry* 47, no. 9 (2000): 769–76.

16. Jerome Kagan, *Three Seductive Ideas* (Cambridge: Harvard University Press, 1998), 15–38.

17. American Psychiatric Association, *Diagnostic and Statistical Manual of Mental Disorders*, 4th ed., text rev. (Arlington: American Psychiatric Publishing, 2000).

18. Richard J. McNally, *Panic Disorder: A Critical Analysis* (New York: Guilford Press, 1994).

19. Alan J. Goldstein and Dianne L. Chambless, "A Reanalysis of Agoraphobia," *Behavior Therapy* 9, no. 1 (1978): 47–59.

20. David H. Barlow, *Anxiety and Its Disorders: The Nature and Treatment of Anxiety and Panic*, 2nd ed. (New York: Guilford Press, 2002).

21. Donald F. Klein, "False Suffocation Alarms, Spontaneous Panics, and Related Conditions: An Integrative Hypothesis," *Archives of General Psychiatry* 50, no. 4 (1993): 306–17.

22. David M. Clark, "A Cognitive Approach to Panic," *Behaviour Research and Therapy* 24, no. 4 (1986): 461–70.

23. Steven Reiss, Rolf A. Peterson, David M. Gursky, and Richard J. McNally, "Anxiety Sensitivity, Anxiety Frequency and the Prediction of Fearfulness," *Behaviour Research and Therapy* 24, no. 1 (1986): 1–8.

24. Richard J. McNally, "Anxiety Sensitivity and Panic Disorder," *Biological Psychiatry* 52, no. 10 (2002): 938–46.

25. Norman B. Schmidt, Michael J. Zvolensky, and Jon K. Maner, "Anxiety Sensitivity: Prospective Prediction of Panic Attacks and Axis I Pathology," *Journal of Psychiatric Research* 40, no. 8 (2006): 691–99.

26. Ayelet M. Ruscio, Timothy A. Brown, Wai Tat Chiu, Jitender Sareen, Murray B. Stein, and Ronald C. Kessler, "Social fears and Social Phobia in the USA: Results from the National Comorbidity Replication," *Psychological Medicine* 38, no. 1 (2008): 15–28.

27. Christopher Lane, *Shyness: How Normal Behavior Became a Sickness* (New Haven: Yale University Press, 2007).

28. Richard J. McNally and Gail S. Steketee, "The Etiology and Maintenance of Severe Animal Phobias," *Behaviour Research and Therapy* 23, no. 4 (1985): 431–35.

29. Richard J. McNally, "On Nonassociative Fear Emergence," *Behaviour Research and Therapy* 40, no. 2 (2002): 169–72.

30. Martin E. Seligman, "Preparedness and Phobias," *Behavior Therapy* 2, no. 3 (1971): 307–20; Arne Öhman and Susan Mineka, "Fears, Phobias, and Preparedness: Toward an Evolved Module of Fear and Fear Learning," *Psychological Review* 108, no. 3 (2002): 483–522.

31. Harald Merckelbach and Peter J. de Jong, "Evolutionary Models of Phobias," in *Phobias: A Handbook of Theory, Research and Treatment*, ed. Graham C. L. Davey (Chichester: John Wiley and Sons, 1997), 323–47.

32. Richie Poulton and Ross G. Menzies, "Non-Associative Fear Acquisition: A Review of the Evidence From Retrospective and Longitudinal Research," *Behaviour Research and Therapy* 40, no. 2 (2002): 127–49.

33. Richard J. McNally, "Preparedness and Phobias: A Review," *Psychological Bulletin* 101, no. 2 (1987): 283–303.

34. Richard J. McNally, "Disgust Has Arrived," *Journal of Anxiety Disorders* 16, no. 5 (2002): 561–66.

35. McNally and Steketee, "Etiology and Maintenance," 431.

36. Lars-Göran Öst and Ulf Sterner, "Applied Tension: A Specific Behavioral Method for Treatment of Blood Phobia," *Behaviour Research and Therapy* 25, no. 1 (1987): 25–29.

37. Richard J. McNally and Christine E. Louro, "Fear of Flying in Agoraphobia and Simple Phobia: Distinguishing Features," *Journal of Anxiety Disorders* 6, no. 4 (1992): 319–24.

38. Aaron T. Beck, Gary Emery, and Ruth L. Greenberg, *Anxiety Disorders and Phobias: A Cognitive Perspective* (New York: Basic Books, 1985), 202.

39. Gerd Gigerenzer, "Dread Risk, September 11, and Fatal Traffic Accidents," *Psychological Science* 15, no. 4 (2004): 286–87.

40. Richard J. McNally, "On the Scientific Status of Cognitive Appraisal Models of Anxiety Disorder," *Behaviour Research and Therapy* 39, no. 5 (2001): 513–21.

41. Allan Young, *The Harmony of Illusions: Inventing Post-traumatic Stress Disorder* (Princeton: Princeton University Press, 1995).

42. Richard J. McNally, *Remembering Trauma* (Cambridge: Harvard University Press, 2003).

43. Barlow, *Anxiety and Its Disorders*.

44. Richard J. McNally, *What Is Mental Illness?* (Cambridge: Harvard University Press, 2011).

45. Angélique O. J. Cramer, Lourens J. Waldrop, Han L. J. van der Maas, and Denny Borsboom, "Comorbidity: A Network Perspective," *Behavioral and Brain Sciences* 33, nos. 2–3 (2010): 137–93.

2. THE BIOLOGY OF FEAR: EVOLUTIONARY, NEURAL, AND PSYCHOLOGICAL PERSPECTIVES

The author's research has been and is supported by the Swedish Research Council and the U.S. National Institute of Mental Health.

1. For more details, see the Library of Congress's website dedicated to the "Project on the Decade of the Brain," http://www.loc.gov/loc/brain/.

2. James S. Albus et al., "Proposal for a Decade of the Mind Initiative," *Science* 317, no. 5843 (7 September 2007): 1321.

3. Keith Oatley, Dacher Keltner, and Jennifer M. Jenkins, *Understanding Emotions*, 2nd ed. (Malden: Wiley-Blackwell, 2007), 29.

4. Arne Öhman, "Fear," in *Encyclopedia of Stress*, 2nd ed., vol. 2, ed. George Fink (San Diego: Academic Press, 2007).

5. Arne Öhman, Ulf Dimberg, and Lars-Göran Öst, "Animal and Social Phobias: Biological Constraints on Learned Fear Responses," in *Theoretical Issues in Behavior Therapy*, ed. Steven Reiss and Richard R. Bootzin (New York: Academic Press, 1985), 123–75; Arne Öhman and Stefan Wiens, "On the Automaticity of Autonomic Responses in Emotion: An Evolutionary Perspective," in *Handbook of Affective Sciences*, ed. Richard J. Davidson, Klaus Scherer, and H. Hill Goldsmith (New York: Oxford University Press, 2003), 256–75.

6. John M. Allman, *Evolving Brains* (New York: Scientific American Library, 1999), 73.

7. Ernst Mayr, "Behavior Programs and Evolutionary Strategies," *American Scientist* 62, no. 6 (1974): 650–59.

8. See the work of Silvan Tomkins, Paul Ekman et al. For a critical assessment see Ruth Leys's contribution in this edited volume.

9. Martin E. P. Seligman, "Phobias and Preparedness," *Behavior Therapy* 2, no. 3 (1971): 307–20; Arne Öhman and Susan Mineka, "Fears, Phobias, and Preparedness: Toward an Evolved Module of Fear and Fear Learning," *Psychological Review* 108, no. 3 (2001): 483–522.

10. Amy F. T. Arnsten, "Cathecholamine Modulation of Prefrontal Cortical Cognitive Function," *Trends in Cognitive Sciences* 2, no. 11 (1998): 436–47; Joseph E. LeDoux, *The Emotional Brain: The Mysterious Underpinnings of Emotional Life* (New York: Simon and Schuster, 1996).

11. Raymond J. Dolan, "Emotion, Cognition, and Behavior," *Science* 298, no. 5596 (2002): 1191–94.

12. Byron A. Campbell, Gwendolyn Wood, and Thomas McBride, "Origins of Orienting and Defensive Responses: An Evolutionary Perspective," in *Attention and Orienting: Sensory and Motivational Processes*, ed. Peter J. Lang, Robert F. Simons, and Marie T. Balaban (Mahway: Lawrence Erlbaum, 1997).

13. Öhman and Wiens, "On the Automaticity of Autonomic Responses in Emotion."

14. William James, "What is an Emotion?," *Mind* 9, no. 34 (1884): 188–205.

15. For influential critiques of the James-Lange theory, see, e.g., Walter Cannon, "The James-Lange Theory of Emotions: A Critical Examination and an Alternative Theory," *American Journal of Psychology* 39, no. 1/4 (1927): 106–24. For work in the tradition of James-Lange, see, e.g., Stanley Schachter and Jerome Singer, "Cognitive, Social, and Physiological Deter-

minants of Emotional State," *Psychological Review* 69, no. 5 (1962): 379–99; Antonio R. Damasio, *Descartes' Error: Emotion, Reason, and the Human Brain* (New York: Random House, 1994).

16. Hugo D. Critchley et al., "Neural Systems Supporting Interoceptive Awareness: Evidence from Functional and Structural Magnetic Resonance Imaging," *Nature Neuroscience* 7 (2004): 189–95; A. D. Bud Craig, "Human Feelings: Why Are Some More Aware Than Others?" *Trends in Cognitive Sciences* 8, no. 6 (2004): 239–41. For an overview, see Arne Öhman, "Making Sense of Emotion: Evolution, Reason and the Brain," *Daedalus* 135, no. 3 (2006): 33–45.

17. Schachter and Singer, "Cognitive, Social, and Physiological Determinants of Emotional State."

18. Donald G. Dutton and Arthur P. Aron, "Some Evidence for Heightened Sexual Attraction under Conditions of High Anxiety," *Journal of Personality and Social Psychology* 30, no. 4 (1974): 510–17.

19. LeDoux, *Emotional Brain*.

20. Neot N. Doron and Joseph LeDoux, "Organization of Projections to the Lateral Amygdala from Auditory and Visual Areas of the Thalamus in the Rat," *Journal of Comparative Neurology* 412, no. 3 (1999): 383–409; Changjun Shi and Michael Davis, "Visual Pathways Involved in Fear Conditioning Measured with Fear-Potentiated Startle: Behavior and Anatomical Studies," *Journal of Neuroscience* 21, no. 24 (2001): 9844–55.

21. Arne Öhman, Katrina Carlsson, Daniel Lundqvist, and Martin Ingvar, "Neural Mechanisms of Fear: The Central Role of the Amygdala," *Physiology and Behavior* 92 (2007): 180–85.

22. Dutton and Aron, "Some Evidence for Heightened Sexual Attraction under Conditions of High Anxiety."

23. Arne Öhman and Joaquim J. F. Soares, "'Unconscious Anxiety': Phobic Responses to Masked Stimuli," *Journal of Abnormal Psychology* 103, no. 2 (1994): 231–40; Katrina Carlsson et al., "Fear and the Amygdala: Manipulation of Awareness Generates Differential Cerebral Responses to Phobic and Fear-Relevant (but Non-Feared) Stimuli," *Emotion* 4, no. 4 (2004): 340–53.

24. Öhman et al., "Neural Mechanisms of Fear."

25. John S. Morris et al., "Differential Extrageniculostriate and Amygdala Responses to Presentation of Emotional Faces in a Cortically Blind Field," *Brain* 124, no. 6 (2001): 1241–52; Alan J. Pegna et al., "Discriminating Emotional Faces Without Primary visual Cortices Involves the Right Amygdala," *Nature Neuroscience* 8, no. 1 (2005): 24–25.

26. Willem A. Arrindell et al., "Phobic Dimensions: III. Factor Analytic Approaches to the Study of Common Phobic Fears: An Updated Review of

Findings Obtained with Adult Subjects," *Advances in Behaviour Research and Therapy* 13 (1991): 73–130.

27. Seligman, "Phobias and Preparedness"; see also Öhman and Mineka, "Fears, Phobias, and Preparedness."

28. Michael Domjan, "Pavlovian Conditioning: A Functional Perspective," *Annual Review of Psychology* 56 (2005): 179–206.

29. Arne Öhman, "Human Fear Conditioning: Focus on the Amygdala," in *The Human Amygdala*, ed. Elizabeth A. Phelps and Paul J. Whalen (New York: Guilford Press, 2009).

30. Öhman and Mineka, "Fears, Phobias, and Preparedness."

31. Ulf Dimberg and Arne Öhman, "Behold the Wrath: Psychophysiological Responses to Facial Stimuli," *Motivation and Emotion* 20, no. 2 (1996): 149–82.

32. Susan Mineka, "Evolutionary Memories, Emotional Processing, and the Emotional Disorders," *Psychology of Learning and Motivation* 28 (1992): 161–206; Andreas Olsson and Elizabeth A. Phelps, "Social Learning of Fear," *Nature Neuroscience* 10, no. 9 (2007): 1095–102.

33. Andreas Olsson and Elizabeth A. Phelps, "Learned Fear of 'Unseen' Faces after Pavlovian, Observational, and Instructed Fear," *Psychological Science* 15, no. 12 (2004): 822–28.

34. Susan Mineka and Michael Cook, "Mechanisms Involved in the Observational Conditioning of Fear," *Journal of Experimental Psychology: General* 122, no. 1 (1993): 23–38.

35. Öhman, "Human Fear Conditioning."

36. Francisco Esteves et al., "Nonconscious Associative Learning: Pavlovian Conditioning of Skin Conductance Responses to Masked Fear-Relevant Facial Stimuli," *Psychophysiology* 31, no. 4 (1994): 375–85.

37. Arne Öhman and Joaquim J. F. Soares, "Emotional Conditioning to Masked Stimuli: Expectancies for Aversive Outcomes Following Nonrecognized Fear-Relevant Stimuli," *Journal of Experimental Psychology: General* 127, no. 1 (1998): 69–82.

38. David H. Barlow, *Anxiety and Its Disorders: The Nature and Treatment of Anxiety and Panic*, 2nd ed. (New York: Guilford Press, 2002).

39. Lars-Göran Öst, "Rapid Treatment of Specific Phobias," in *Phobias: A Handbook of Theory, Research and Treatment*, ed. Graham Davey (Chichester: John Wiley and Sons, 1997).

40. For accessible reviews on extinction, see Mark Bouton, "Behavior Systems and the Contextual Control of Anxiety, Fear, and Panic," in *Emotion and Consciousness*, ed. Lisa Feldman Barrett, Paula M. Niedenthal, and Piotr Winkielman (New York: Guilford Press, 2005) 205–27; Michael Davis

and Karen M. Myers, "The Role of Glutamate and Gamma-Aminobutyric Acid in Fear Extinction: Clinical Implications for Exposure Therapy," *Biological Psychiatry* 52, no. 10 (2002): 998–1007.

41. Öhman and Mineka, "Fears, Phobias, and Preparedness."

42. Susan Mineka et al., "The Effects of Changing Contexts on Return of Fear Following Exposure Treatment for Spider Fear," *Journal of Consulting and Clinical Psychology* 67, no. 4 (1999): 599–604; Jayson L. Mystkowski et al., "Treatment Context and Return of Fear in Spider Phobia," *Behavior Therapy* 33, no. 3 (2002): 399–416.

3. HOW DID FEAR BECOME A SCIENTIFIC OBJECT AND WHAT KIND OF OBJECT IS IT?

Another version of this chapter has been previously published as "How Did Fear Become a Scientific Object and What Kind of Object Is It?," *Representations* 110, no. 1 (2010): 66–104. My thanks to Jennifer Ashton, Michael Fried, Robert B. Pippin, Jan Plamper, and James A. Russell for their helpful comments on my chapter.

1. "In recent years and with the intensification of anti-terrorism efforts, there has been a clear desire to improve or replace the polygraph technology with something better. There is a real need for administering real-time, highly automated veracity tests inside the country and around the globe, where human intelligence is being collected. At the same time, similar technology may be useful for quick screening of potential suspects in ports of entry" (Panagiotis Tsiamyrtzis et al., "Imaging Facial Physiology for the Detection of Deceit," *International Journal of Computer Vision* 71, no. 2 [2007]: 198). For a popular presentation of the work of Paul Ekman and others on terrorist surveillance and lie detection, see Robin Marantz Henig, "Looking for the Lie," *New York Times Magazine*, February 5, 2006. Ekman has recently served as scientific consultant to the Fox Broadcasting Company's TV series *Lie To Me*, featuring a leading deception expert who studies facial expressions and involuntary body language to discover not only if someone is lying but also why. In its *Time* 100 issue for 2009, *Time* magazine selected Ekman as one of the world's one hundred most influential people.

2. The emotion field has benefited by invoking Charles Darwin's writings on facial expression, but it has frequently misinterpreted his ideas. Darwin is typically thought to have proposed that expressions are selected and adapted for the communication of emotion. But as Alan Fridlund has pointed out, Darwin's conclusion was the opposite: he believed that most facial displays

were not evolutionary adaptations but vestiges or accidents. See Alan Fridlund, *Human Facial Expression: An Evolutionary View* (Cambridge: Academic Press, 1994), 15. For a valuable, nuanced discussion of this point, see Thomas Dixon, *From Passions to Emotions: The Creation of a Secular Psychological Category* (Cambridge: Cambridge University Press, 2003), 159–79.

3. Silvan S. Tomkins, *Affect Imagery Consciousness* (New York: Springer, 1962–63), 1: 248. The recent rise of interest in Tomkins's work in the humanities can be credited to the late Eve Kosofksy Sedgwick who, in *Touching Feeling: Affect, Pedagogy, Performativity* (Durham: Duke University Press, 2003), made the case for the value of Tomkins's nonintentionalist (or materialist) ideas for theorizing affect. I offer a critique of Tomkins's and Sedgwick's ideas about affect in *From Guilt to Shame: Auschwitz and After* (Princeton: Princeton University Press, 2007), chap. 4.

4. Sigmund Freud, "Analysis of a Phobia in a Five-Year-Old Boy," in *The Standard Edition of the Complete Psychological Works of Sigmund Freud*, trans. and ed. James Strachey (London: Hogarth Press, 1953–74), 10: 3-149. For Freud, it is because Hans fears the powerful father's retaliation against his own unmasterable hostility that he (the child) identifies with him to the point of incorporating the father's aggression. That incorporated aggression fuels the child's superego, so that the aggressivity of the scenario is played out in the mode of the subject's experience of a relentless self-reproach. Aggressivity, fear, and guilt in this interpretation thus have a deep connection, one that is lost in modern interpretations of fear, such as those by Tomkins and Ekman.

5. Joseph Wolpe and Stanley Rachman, "Psychoanalytic 'Evidence': A Critique Based on Freud's Case of Little Hans," *Journal of Mental and Nervous Diseases* 131 (1960): 135–48.

6. I use the word "intentionalist" here to describe the position of Freud and all those in the emotion field who call themselves "appraisal theorists" or "cognitivists," because the term "intentionalist" captures what I consider to be the most fundamental aspect of their position, namely, the idea that the emotions are to be understood as states of mind that are directed toward objects and that include cognitions, judgments, and beliefs about the world. "Cognitivism" has been criticized by philosopher of science Paul Griffiths, and others, for two basic reasons: first, it is held to be captive to a particular picture of cognition according to which it involves making propositions or holding "propositional attitudes," thereby tying cognition to the human capacity for producing linguistic propositions, and thus it appears to create a sharp divide between humans and nonhuman animals; second, it is accused of ignoring developments in the life sciences, especially the neurosciences.

See Paul E. Griffiths, *What Emotions Really Are: The Problem of Psychological Categories* (Chicago: University of Chicago Press, 1997), 1–3. Both criticisms seem to me to miss the mark. There is no reason to deny some sort of capacity for cognition and intentionality to nonhuman animals, and, as I try to show in this paper, the reproach that philosophers tend to ignore the findings of the life sciences can serve to distract attention from the inadequacies of the scientific evidence on offer. The conflict between intentionalist and nonintentionalist accounts of emotion, including crucially the nonintentionalist views of Tomkins, Ekman, and others, is the topic of my *From Guilt to Shame*. See also Ruth Leys, "Navigating the Genealogies of Trauma, Guilt, and Affect: An Interview with Ruth Leys," in "Models of Mind and Consciousness," special issue, *University of Toronto Quarterly* 79, no. 2 (Spring 2010): 656–79.

7. As Tomkins wrote in his vision of the "humanomaton" or emotional "animal-machine": "There must be built into such a machine a number of responses which have self-rewarding and self-punishing characteristics. This means that these responses are inherently acceptable or inherently unacceptable. These are essentially aesthetic characteristics of the affective responses—and in one sense not further reducible. . . . If and when the humanomaton learns English, we would require a spontaneous reaction to joy or excitement of the sort 'I like this,' and to fear and shame and distress, 'Whatever this is, I don't care for it.' . . . There must be introduced into the machine a critical gap between the conditions which instigate the self-rewarding or self-punishing responses which maintain them, which turn them off, and the 'knowledge' of these conditions. The machine initially would only know that it liked some of its own responses and disliked some of its own responses but not that they might be turned on, or off, and not how to turn them on, or off, or up, or down in intensity" (Silvan S. Tomkins and Samuel Messick, *Computer Simulation of Personality: Frontier of Psychological Theory* [New York: Wiley, 1963], 18–19).

8. Donald Nathanson, *Shame and Pride: Affect, Sex, and the Birth of the Self* (New York: W. W. Norton, 1992), 66. Griffiths likewise remarks: "The affect program phenomena are a standing example of the emotional or passionate. They are sources of motivation not integrated into the system of beliefs or desires. The characteristic properties of the affect program system states, their informational encapsulation, and their involuntary triggering, necessitate the introduction of a concept of mental state separate from the concepts of belief and desire" (Griffiths, *What Emotions Really Are*, 243). Or as he also states: "The psychoevolved emotions occur in a partially informationally encapsulated modular subsystem of the mind/brain. The processes

that occur therein, the 'beliefs' of the system and the 'judgements' it makes, are not beliefs and judgements of the person in the traditional sense, any more than the 'beliefs' and 'judgements' of the balance mechanisms fed by the inner ear" (Paul. E. Griffiths, "The Degeneration of the Cognitive Theory of Emotions," *Philosophical Psychology* 2, no. 3 [1989]: 298).

9. Because the affect programs are said to be located in primitive, sub-cortical parts of the brain that function independently of knowledge, they are held to bypass the slower cognitive pathways of the higher cortical centers and respond instead in a quick and mindless way to the innate or learned triggers that elicit them. Much recent work on the emotions has been devoted to validating such an approach to the emotions, which has also found its way into the popular media. For example, in an article in *Newsweek* about how people respond to terrorist threats and other situations we find this statement: "The strongest human emotions are fear and anxiety. Crucial to survival, they are programmed into the brain's most primitive regions, allowing them to trump rationality but not for rationality to override them" ("When It's Head Versus Heart, the Heart Wins," *Newsweek*, February 11, 2008, 35).

10. Brian Massumi, "Fear (The Spectrum Said)," *Positions* 13, no. 1 (2005): 37.

11. For Ekman's account of the origins of his research on the emotions, see his afterword, "Afterword: Universality of Emotional Expression? A Personal History of the Dispute," to *The Expression of the Emotions in Man and Animals*, 3rd ed., by Charles Darwin (New York: Oxford University Press, 1998), 363–93. I shall be using this edition of Darwin's *Expression* throughout this chapter. Ekman here states that at the start of his career he did not have a strong commitment as to whether or not the emotions are universal, but his goal was to "settle the matter decisively. Margaret Mead later wrote that it was outrageous for me to have such a goal" (365).

12. For an important assessment from the 1950s, see Jerome S. Bruner and Renato Tagiuri, "The Perception of People," in *Handbook of Social Psychology*, ed. Gardner Lindzey (Reading: Addison-Wesley, 1954), 2:634–56.

13. In "What Are the Primary Affects?" (1964), reprinted in *Exploring Affect: The Selected Writings of Silvan S. Tomkins*, ed. Virginia Demos (Cambridge: Cambridge University Press, 1995), 217–62, Tomkins and his coauthor Robert McCarter reported the results of their own experiments on the judgment of selected facial expressions, experiments carried out in order to test the thesis of universality of the emotions. This paper served as a blueprint for Ekman's subsequent research. As the latter stated: "Tomkins . . . provided a theoretical rationale for studying the face as a means of learning

about personality and emotion. He also showed that observers could obtain very high agreement in judging emotion if the facial expressions were carefully selected to show what he believes are the innate facial affects. . . . Tomkins greatly influenced myself and [Carroll] Izard, helping each of us plan our initial cross-cultural studies of facial expression. The resulting evidence of universality in facial expression rekindled interest in this topic in psychology and anthropology" (Paul Ekman, "The Argument and Evidence About Universals in Facial Expressions of Emotion," in *Handbook of Social Psychophysiology*, ed. Hugh L. Wagner and Antony Manstead (London: Wiley, 1989), 145.

14. For accounts of Ekman's neurocultural model of the emotions, see, for example, Paul Ekman and Wallace V. Friesen, "Nonverbal Leakage and Clues to Deception," *Psychiatry* 32, no. 1 (1969): 88–106; Paul Ekman, "Universals and Cultural Differences in Facial Expressions of Emotion," in *The Nebraska Symposium on Motivation, 1971*, ed. J. Cole (Lincoln: University of Nebraska Press, 1972), 207–83; and "Biological and Cultural Contributions to Body and Facial Movement in the Expression of Emotion," in *Explaining Emotions*, ed. Amelie Oksenberg Rorty (Berkeley: University of California Press, 1980), 73–99, 100–101.

15. Darwin, *Expression*, 19.

16. Of course, "instantaneous" is a relative term in photography, as Phillip Prodger makes clear in *Time Stands Still: Muybridge and the Instantaneous Photography Movement* (New York: Oxford University Press, 2003).

17. Phillip Prodger, "Illustration as Strategy in Charles Darwin's 'The Expression of the Emotions in Man and Animals,'" in *Inscribing Science: Scientific Texts and the Materiality of Communication*, ed. Timothy Lenoir (Stanford: Stanford University Press, 1998), 156.

18. "With exposure times in the tens of seconds, a 'true' rendering of emotional expression would have required the subjects to achieve naturally a representative emotional expression, then hold it unadulterated for the photographer to record on film. This could not be done reliably or with precision" (Prodger, "Illustration as Strategy," 177).

19. Ibid., 169–70.

20. Ibid., 177. However, Prodger continues this passage in a remark suggesting that Darwin was aware of the risk of theatricality or conventionalizing inherent in the situation of being beheld: "Darwin was concerned that an observer might taint a subject's actions through his or her own reaction to the emotion displayed, and that an observer might read into his or her observations because of the circumstances of the occasion" (177).

21. Johann Caspar Lavater, *Von Der Physiognomik* (1772), cited by Richard T. Gray, *About Face: German Physiognomic Thought from Lavater to Auschwitz* (Detroit: Wayne State University Press, 2004), 49–50. In his book, Gray makes many illuminating observations about the ideals of immobility, stasis, and repose in Lavater's physiognomic-observational strategies, ideals that likewise inform the Tomkins-Ekman paradigm—as if only the human form stripped of vital, intentional actions and movements can reveal the authentic, primordial essence of the natural human being.

22. Darwin justifies his study of expression in nonhuman animals by stating that "in observing animals, we are not likely to be biased by our imagination, and we may feel safe that their expressions are not conventional" (Darwin, *Expression*, 24). I take Darwin to mean not that animals are unaware of being seen, but that they are not aware of our specifically human interests and motives in observing them, a point caught by Prodger when he observes of Darwin's statement that "animals are unaware of the scientist's purpose, and are unlikely to modify their behavior in reaction to experimental observation" (Prodger, "Illustration as Strategy," 149).

23. "Until a systematic means of coding facial behaviors had been widely accepted and such drawings as well as a large number of actual photographs and films have been scored, there is no way of knowing to what extent they represented fantasy or reality" (Paul Ekman, Wallace V. Friesen, and Phoebe Ellsworth, *Emotion in the Human Face: Guidelines for Research and an Integration of Findings* [New York: Oxford University Press, 1972], 50–51).

24. For Ekman's denial that his approach bears any relation to the older physiognomic tradition, see his "Duchenne and Facial Expression of Emotion," in *The Mechanism of Human Facial Expression*, G.-B. Duchenne de Boulogne, ed. and trans. R. Andrew Cuthbertson (Cambridge: Cambridge University Press, 1991), 271. But Ekman's fundamental assumption that we can draw a distinction between natural and cultural facial expressions *is* the physiognomic assumption. In a recent study, François Delaporte credits Duchenne with being the discoverer of the means of distinguishing the authentic from the feigned emotional sign—for example, the simulated versus the genuine smile—and appears to defend that distinction in terms similar to those of Ekman, whose work he cites. See François Delaporte, *Anatomy of the Passions*, ed. Todd Myers, trans. Susan Emmanuel (Stanford: Stanford University Press, 2008). For a superb historical discussion of Duchenne's work that critiques Delaporte's interpretation of Duchenne's project, see Stephanie Dupouy, "Le visage au scalpel: L'expression faciale dane l'oeil des savans (1750–1880)" (PhD thesis, Université Paris 1 Panthéon-Sorbonne, 2007). My thanks to the author for allowing me to read her thesis and to

Lorraine Daston and Andreas Mayer for alerting me to its existence. The distinction between "false" versus "true" (or "Duchenne") smiles, a favorite topic of Ekman's, is the target of Alan Fridlund's criticisms in his *Human Facial Expression*, 115–18, 152–55.

25. It is worth noting that Ekman tended to exaggerate the conflict between nature and nurture in pre-Tomkins thinking about faces. He painted his predecessors as extreme cultural relativists, but that portrait was somewhat of a distortion that served his ends.

26. "We believe that some of the impressions of cultural differences in affect display have arisen from a failure to distinguish adequately the pan-cultural elements from the circumstances governing the display of affects which are markedly influenced by social learning and vary within and between cultures. We believe that, while the facial muscles which move when a particular affect is aroused are the same across cultures, the evoking stimuli, the linked affects, the display rules and the behavioral consequences all can vary enormously from one culture to another" (Paul Ekman and Walter V. Friesen, "The Repertoire of Nonverbal Behavior: Categories, Origins, Usage, and Coding," *Semiotica* 1 (1969): 73).

27. See Ekman's early discussion of this issue in "A Methodological Discussion of Nonverbal Behavior," *Journal of Psychology* 43 (1957): 141–49. Ekman recognized that still photographs "freeze" expressions by slicing them out of what is naturally a sequence of movements in time. But in response to complaints by Jerome Bruner and Renato Tagiuri, who criticized the use of such photographs because, as Ekman quoted them as stating, "judgment based on a frozen millisecond of exposure is not representative of the type of judgment made in naturally occurring conditions," Ekman argued that if the purpose of the study did not require a judgment of sequential behavior, then still photographs "may be useful for some research questions" (Ekman, Friesen, and Ellsworth, *Emotion in the Human Face*, 49). He especially defended the use of posed still photographs for their savings in cost and ease of use, remarking that in the case of posed facial behavior, where the poser holds the pose for the camera, "a still will provide the same information as five seconds of film or videotape of the frozen position. Certainly, there is considerable evidence that the frozen few milliseconds of a still photograph *can* provide quite a bit of information" (49)—which was of course precisely the point at issue.

28. Tomkins's theory of "blends" plays an important role here. He and Ekman assume the existence of a core set of affects whose combination ("blends") produce more complex emotions, with the result that much of the time the face expresses an admixture of two or more of the basic emo-

tions. Theirs is an atomistic, combinatorial approach that conceives of the emotions as made up of a limited number of distinct categories or units (or "kinds") out of which the "higher" affects are built up. The approach has the advantage of explaining away any negative results in judgment studies as "confusions" on the part of observers owing to the existence in posed photographs of facial expressions of blends resulting from local, cultural conditions. For the argument about "confusions," see Tomkins and McCarter, "What Are the Primary Affects?" For a discussion and criticism of the applicability of the theory of blends to the whole domain of emotional phenomena, see Griffiths, *What Emotions Really Are*, 101–2.

29. Paul Ekman, Wallace V. Friesen, and Silvan S. Tomkins, "Facial Affect Scoring Technique: A First Validity Study," *Semiotica* 1 (1971): 37–53. Thus if we follow Ekman's writings during these important early years when he was attempting to lay the foundations of a science of emotion, we find him arguing that the facial expressions in the photographs he employed in his experiments must have been free of cultural taint *because* they were universally recognized. At the same time he suggested that those facial expressions were universally recognized *because* they were free of cultural taint. Similarly, Ekman presented FAST as if it were consequent on the finding that photographs of posed expressions could be distinguished correctly by literate and preliterate observers. But there is an important sense in which observers from literate and preliterate cultures were capable of distinguishing these affects correctly *because* FAST (plus subjective intuition) had already predetermined the "correct" or representative posed facial expressions to be used in his judgment tests.

Ekman, Friesen, and Tomkins decided from the outset to develop FAST in terms of emotion categories (happiness, sadness, surprise, anger, disgust, and fear) rather than emotion dimensions (pleasantness-unpleasantness, active-passive, and so on). This decision was based on several considerations, including the claim that the cross-cultural research carried out by Ekman and Izard had suggested the existence of universal categories of facial expression. To develop FAST, Ekman, Friesen, and Tomkins divided the face into three areas (brows-forehead area; eyes-lids-bridge of nose; lower face, consisting of cheek-nose-mouth-chin-jaw). Lists of facial components within each of the three facial areas for each of the six emotions were then compiled. The authors based these lists on the past literature as well as on their own observations and intuitions. To specify the appearance of the relevant components, they obtained "visual-photographic" definitions of each item by requesting several actors to pose the facial movements within each facial area (not the emotions) after they were told and shown what to do with the face. FAST thus consisted of three sets of photographs, one set for each facial area.

The faces to be scored by FAST were selected on theoretical grounds to show only one of the six hypothesized discrete emotions from photographs of posed expressions used by investigators in the past (including most of those used by Ekman and Friesen in their cross-cultural studies), each of which had obtained at least 70 percent agreement among observers about the presence of a single emotion. These selected photographs—the aim was to obtain ten pictures of each of the six emotions, although this proved impossible for disgust and fear—were projected life-size onto a screen, which was masked to show only one facial area at a time, and trained scorers, using the relevant set of FAST items, scored them by selecting the FAST item that best matched the area in question. The results for reliability and validity were found to be "very encouraging" for predicting the recognition of posed faces, although FAST had relatively poor success with fear faces as compared to the other emotion-category faces, owing to the problem of blends. FAST's applicability to spontaneous expressions was justified on the grounds that, since it had been shown by Ekman and Friesen that posed expressions could be judged as showing the same emotions across different cultures, posed expressions must have some intrinsic relation to spontaneous ones. "In light of this evidence," the authors concluded, "it seems reasonable to assume that posed behavior differs little from spontaneous facial behavior in form" (Ekman, Friesen, and Tomkins, "Facial Affect Scoring Technique," 53). For a further discussion of FAST, see also Ekman, Friesen, and Ellsworth, *Emotion in the Human Face*, 114–19.

30. See, for example, Paul Ekman and Erika Rosenberg, ed., *What the Face Reveals: Basic and Applied Studies of Spontaneous Expression Using the Facial Action Coding System*, 2nd ed. (New York: Oxford University Press, 2005), where the issue of posing comes up frequently.

31. Paul Ekman, E. Richard Sorenson, and Wallace V. Friesen, "Pan-Cultural Elements in Facial Displays of Emotion," *Science* 164 (1969), 86.

32. Ekman, Friesen, and Ellsworth, *Emotion in the Human Face*, 106.

33. Paul Ekman and Wallace V. Friesen, "Constants across Cultures in the Face and Emotion," *Journal of Personality and Social Psychology* 17, no. 6 (1971): 128. Or as he also observed: "Posed behaviors differ little from spontaneous facial behavior in form. . . . Posed differs from spontaneous facial behavior in duration, in the lack of attempt to control or otherwise moderate the behavior, and in the frequency of single emotion faces compared to blend faces" (Ekman, Friesen, and Tomkins, "Facial Affect Scoring Technique," 53).

34. Ekman, Friesen, and Ellsworth, *Emotion in the Human Face*, 167.

35. Ibid., 106.

36. Norman L. Munn, "The Effect of Knowledge of the Situation upon Judgment of Emotion from Facial Expressions," *Journal of Abnormal and Social Psychology* 35 (1940): 325.

37. Ekman, Friesen, and Ellsworth, *Emotion in the Human Face*, 81.

38. The phrase "spontaneity without conventionalization" is William A. Hunt's in his discussion of Munn's work in "Recent Developments in the Field of Emotion," *Psychological Bulletin* 38 (1941): 261.

39. Munn, "Effect of Knowledge," 326.

40. Hunt, "Recent Developments in the Field of Emotion," 261.

41. Ekman, Friesen, and Ellsworth, *Emotion in the Human Face*, 94.

42. For example, Ekman insisted that it was important to make sure that adequate sampling procedures had been followed in selecting photos for use in experiments of this kind and that the investigator did not rely on an atypical group of persons to pose expressions, such as those who, because they were "highly extroverted" or specially trained, were particularly good at producing what he continued to call "spontaneous" facial behavior—as if the problem of posing could be solved by avoiding the use of professional actors in experiments of this kind (Ekman, Friesen, and Ellsworth, *Emotion in the Human Face*, 95).

43. Ekman, Friesen, and Ellsworth, *Emotion in the Human Face*, 106.

44. "For this is what Ekman has demonstrated. Given a limited range of semantically designated emotions—grief, happiness, anger, disgust, it is possible to persuade members of different cultures to produce simulations which are mutually intelligible between these cultures," Mead wrote in "Margaret Mead Calls 'Discipline-centric' Approach to Research an 'Example of the Appalling State of the Human Sciences,'" review of *Darwin and Facial Expression: A Century of Research in Review*, ed. Paul Ekman, *Journal of Communication* 25, no. 10 (1975): 212. This left open the question why, if Ekman's experimental findings could be trusted, everybody, regardless of cultural origin, could be "persuaded" to recognize such "simulated" or theatricalized expressions. Mead was prepared to entertain the idea that there must be some universal, presumably innate, element involved, perhaps of the kind Ekman had postulated between the nervous system and specific facial muscles. Recent criticisms by James A. Russell and others of Ekman and Friesen's methods in such cross-cultural studies have now cast doubt on Ekman's universalist claims. Ekman for his part expressed surprise that Mead was willing to suggest that "what is innate would be apparent only in simulation and not in actual emotional experience" and suggested that the

answer must come from data on spontaneous expressions of the kind he had first reported in his hidden camera study of American and Japanese students (Paul Ekman, "Biological and Cultural Contributions to Body and Facial Movement," in *The Anthropology of the Body*, ed. John Blacking [London: Academic Press, 1977], 69).

45. For Ekman's account of his difficult relations with Mead, see also his "Afterword: Universality of Emotional Expression?" where he characterized Mead's review of his 1973 book as a "denunciation" (364). Mead herself adopted a communicative analysis of facial expression, with a debt to cybernetics and kinesics, an analysis that appears closer to recent "paralanguage" theories of communication of the kind advocated by Fridlund than to Ekman's basic emotions approach. Mead's position on this topic was closely aligned with the work of the anthropologist Ray Birdwhistell (1918–1994), who denied the existence of universals in facial and other bodily gestures and movements. Birdwhistell emphasized the need to study body movement as a "language" or form of communication between people, using film and videotape as methods of recording in naturalistic settings and without experimental intervention or manipulation. Birdwhistell's concern with methodology, especially the sensitivity of subjects to being observed, led him to rule out having the camera operator present when they were being filmed. As reported by Martha Davis, a member of Birdwhistell's research circle, by the end of the 1970s, though, Ekman's attempts to apply traditional experimental methods to the study of nonverbal behavior had gained traction, not least because the microstudies of behavior of the kind Birdwhistell advocated took enormous lengths of time compared to Ekman's quicker, more economical procedures. Birdwhistell's criticisms of Ekman's methods, assumptions, and findings ended in the former's defeat when Ekman replaced Birdwhistell in the decisive role of arbiter of the National Institute of Mental Health grants for research on nonverbal communication. Ekman's triumph over Birdwhistell—a triumph at once methodological, intellectual, and institutional—sealed the destiny of emotion research in the United States for the next several decades. What is new today is that criticisms of Ekman's approach are being raised by researchers who have been formed by and trained in Ekman's presuppositions and research methods, and it will be interesting to see whether these critics will have any better success than did Birdwhistell in challenging and dislodging them. See Martha Davis, "Film Projectors as Microscopes: Ray L. Birdwhistell and Microanalysis of Interaction (1955–1975)," *Visual Anthropology Review* 17, no. 2 (fall/winter 2001–2002): 39–49.

46. "A limitation of these cross-cultural experiments is that the facial expressions presented were not genuine but posed by subjects instructed to

show a particular emotion or to move particular facial muscles. One interpreter of this literature [referring to Mead] suggested that the universality in judgments of facial expression might be limited to just such stereotyped, posed expressions" (Paul Ekman and Harriet Oster, "Facial Expressions of Emotion," *Annual Review of Psychology* 30 [1979]: 530). Again in 1987 Ekman acknowledged as one of three limitations of his cross-cultural studies the fact that "the facial expressions were posed, and Mead (1975) argued that establishing that posed expressions are universal need not imply that spontaneous facial expressions are universal" (Paul Ekman, Wallace V. Friesen, et al., "Universals and Cultural Differences in the Judgments of Facial Expressions of Emotion," *Journal of Personality and Social Psychology* 53, no. 4 [1987]: 713).

47. Ekman, "Universals and Cultural Differences in the Judgments of Facial Expressions of Emotion," 713.

48. Ekman, "Biological and Cultural Contributions to Body and Facial Movement," 69. This statement and Ekman's discussion of Mead's criticisms were omitted when in 1980 Ekman republished his paper in Rorty, *Explaining Emotions*, 73–101. In his 1980 version he placed his criticisms of Mead in note 7 on page 100.

49. A few years earlier, *Subincision* had been used to measure the level of castration fear and anxiety it aroused in viewers; in Lazarus's work the emphasis on castration largely disappeared and the film was treated instead as one among others (such as workshop accidents) depicting "bodily mutilation" that could be used to measure stress; in Ekman's work the emphasis shifted yet again from the study of stress to the study of emotions. It is a sign of another cultural shift that when I recently attempted to locate a copy of this film through the Internet, I discovered that the term "subincision," which had formerly referred to a somewhat esoteric Aborigine adolescent initiation ritual held to be deeply upsetting if not traumatic for Western viewers, now chiefly refers to a popular form of penile tattooing.

50. Richard Lazarus, "A Laboratory Approach to the Dynamics of Psychological Stress," *American Psychologist* 19 (1966): 404.

51. For a discussion of the use of this film by Lazarus and Mardi J. Horowitz to study stress and of the question of the image, violence, and appraisal in the development of the diagnosis of posttraumatic stress disorder, see Leys, *From Guilt to Shame*, 93–122.

52. Ekman, Friesen, and Ellsworth, *Emotion in the Human Face*, 163.

53. Over the years Ekman has given several descriptions of this study. The basic sources are Ekman, "Universals and Cultural Differences in Facial Expressions of Emotion," in Cole, *Nebraska Symposium on Motiva-*

tion, 207–83; Ekman, *Darwin and Facial Expression*, 215–18; Wallace V. Friesen, "Cultural Differences in Facial Expressions in a Social Situation: An Experimental Test of the Concept of Display Rules" (PhD diss., University of California, San Francisco 1972).

54. Already in 1981 Tomkins cited Ekman's Japanese-American study as a "brilliant experiment" demonstrating the complex relationships between pancultural universalities and "relativistic transformations" in Silvan S. Tomkins, "The Quest for Primary Motives: Biography and Autobiography of an Idea," *Journal of Personality and Social Psychology* 41, no. 2 (1981): 313. More recently, the emotion theorist Paul E. Griffiths has also endorsed Ekman's experiment in *What Emotions Really Are*, 53–54.

55. In 1990, Andrew Ortony and Terence J. Turner predicted that the basic emotions approach would not lead to significant progress in the field. See Andrew Ortony and Terence J. Turner, "What's So Basic About Basic Emotions?" *Psychological Review* 97 (1990): 315–31.

56. Ross Buck, *The Communication of Emotion* (New York: Guilford Press, 1984), 20.

57. Paul Ekman, "Expression and the Nature of Emotion," in *Approaches to Emotion*, ed. Paul Ekman and Klaus R. Scherer (Hillsdale: Lawrence Erlbaum, 1984), 321.

58. Paul Ekman, Richard J. Davidson, and Wallace V. Friesen, "The Duchenne Smile: Emotional Expression," *Journal of Personality and Social Psychology* 58 (1990): 351.

59. Fridlund, *Human Facial Expression*, 291. For Fridlund's discussion of Ekman's Japanese-American study, see Fridlund, *Human Facial Expression*, 285–93. See also Alan J. Fridlund, "The New Ethology of Human Facial Expression," in *The Psychology of Facial Expression*, ed. James A. Russell and José-Miguel Fernández-Dols (Cambridge: Cambridge University Press, 1997), 103–29. Ekman and his colleagues subsequently carried out two partial replications of the 1972 study of spontaneous expressions, though without including cross-cultural comparisons: Paul Ekman, Wallace V. Friesen, and S. Ancoli, "Facial Signs of Emotional Experience," *Journal of Personality and Social Psychology* 39 (1980): 1125–34; and Erika L. Rosenberg and Paul Ekman, "Coherence Between Expressive and Experiential Systems in Emotion," *Cognition and Emotion* 8 (1994): 201–29, reprinted with an afterword commenting on Fridlund's critique in Ekman and Rosenberg, *What the Face Reveals*, 63–88. For criticisms of these later experiments, see José-Miguel Fernández-Dols and Maria-Angeles Ruiz-Belda, "Spontaneous Facial Behavior During Intense Emotional Episodes: Artistic Truth and Optical Truth," in Russell and Fernández-Dols, *Psychology of Facial Expression*, 260–

62. For a recent assessment of the Fridlund-Ekman debate that finds little evidence for Ekman's emotion-expression link, see Brian Parkinson, "Do Facial Movements Express Emotions or Communicate Motives?" *Personality and Social Psychology Review* 9, no. 4 (2005): 278–311. See also Leys, *From Guilt to Shame*, 188–89, for a discussion of Ekman's replies to Fridlund's criticisms.

60. James A. Russell, "Is There Universal Expression of Emotion from Facial Expression? A Review of the Cross-Cultural Studies," *Psychological Bulletin* 115 (1994): 102–41 (also reprinted as chap. 9, "Cross-Cultural Studies of Facial Expressions of Emotion," in Fridlund, *Human Facial Expression*, 188–268). Ekman replied to Russell's criticisms in "Strong Evidence for Universals in Facial Expression: Reply to Russell's Mistaken Critique," *Psychological Bulletin* 115 (1994): 268–87; and Russell replied in turn in "Facial Expressions of Emotion: What Lies Beyond Minimal Universality?" *Psychological Bulletin* 118 (1995): 378–81. For another of Ekman's replies to the renewal of the debate over universals and his emotion theory, see his "Expression or Communication About Emotion," in *Genetic, Ethological, and Evolutionary Perspectives on Human Development: Essays in Honor of Dr. Daniel G. Freedman*, ed. N. Segal, G. E. Weisfeld, and C. C. Weisfeld (Washington, DC: American Psychological Association, 1997). See also Russell and Fernández-Dols, *Psychology of Facial Expression*, for a useful overview of the issues at stake in this debate; and Pamela J. Naab and James A. Russell, "Judgments of Emotion from Spontaneous Facial Expressions of New Guineans," *Emotion* 7 (2007): 736–44, in which the authors examined the recognition of emotion in twenty "spontaneous" expressions from Papua New Guinea, previously photographed, coded, and labeled by Ekman in 1980. The results showed that spontaneous expressions do not achieve the level of recognition obtained by posed expressions. For a statement of Russell's views concerning the role of "core affect" in the construction of emotional experience, see James A. Russell, "Core Affect and the Psychological Construction of Emotion," *Psychological Review* 110, no. 1 (2003): 145–72.

61. Fridlund, *Human Facial Expression*, 128.

62. Fridlund characterizes his position as a "paralanguage" theory of facial expression in order to emphasize that in humans the role of facial movements is not to express inner emotions but to accompany and supplement speech. Studies of "audience effects" by Fernández-Dols and his colleagues showing, for example, that Olympic gold medalists produce many facial expressions during the medal ceremony but smile almost exclusively when interacting with the audience and officials, have been held to confirm

the situational-transactional character of facial expressions (Fernández-Dols and Ruiz-Belda, "Spontaneous Facial Behavior," 255–74). Fridlund also situates his analysis of facial expression in the context of the post-Tinbergen and post-Lorenz "new ethology," which likewise emphasizes the communicative value of nonhuman animal displays. From the perspective of the new ethology, displays do not necessarily provide "readouts" of internal motivation because it would not be strategically advantageous for animals to automatically signal their future actions. In a large literature on animal displays, whose role in the vicissitudes of emotion research will have to be taken into account in any future history of post–Second World War theoretical and emotional approaches to the affects, see especially J. R. Krebs and R. Dawkins, "Animal Signals: Mind-Reading and Manipulation," in *Behavioral Ecology*, ed. J. Krebs and N. B. Davies (New York: Oxford University Press, 1984), 380–402; R. Hinde, "Was 'The Expression of Emotions' a Misleading Phrase?" *Animal Behavior* 33 (1985): 985–21; and R. Hinde, "Expression and Negotiation," in *The Development of Expressive Behavior: Biology-Environment Interaction*, ed. G. Zivin (New York: Academic Press, 1985): 103–16.

63. I have found the following review articles especially useful: Lisa Feldman Barrett, "Are Emotions Natural Kinds?" *Perspectives on Psychological Science* 1 (2006): 28–58; Lisa Feldman Barrett, "Solving the Emotion Paradox: Categorization and the Experience of Emotion," *Personality and Social Psychology Review* 10, no. 1 (2006): 20–46; Lisa Feldman Barrett et al., "Of Mice and Men: Natural Kinds of Emotions in the Mammalian Brain? A Response to Panksepp and Izard," *Perspectives on Psychological Science* 2 (2007): 297–312 (an article that offers a valuable critique, along lines similar to those stated by Fridlund, of the widespread mistake in emotion research of relying on a hierarchical brain concept, such as Paul MacLean's "triune" brain concept, according to which in humans the neocortex sits atop a more ancient and primitive subcortex "like icing on an already baked cake" [302]—an assumption that leads to the idea that the phylogenetically "older" amygdala and other subcortical structures subserve the "lower" or more primitive emotional functions independently of higher cortical processing); and Lisa Feldman Barrett, Kevin N. Oscher, and James J. Gross, "On the Automaticity of Emotion," in *Social Psychology and the Unconscious: The Automaticity of Higher Mental Processes*, ed. J. Bargh (New York: Psychology Press, 2007), 173–217. As an alternative to the natural kinds approach to the affects proposed by Ekman, Barrett proposes, in terms similar to those offered by Russell, that emotion is a psychological event constructed from the more basic elements of "core affect" and conceptual knowledge. See, for

example, Kristen A. Lindquist and Lisa Feldman Barrett, "Constructing Emotion: The Experience of Fear as a Conceptual Act," *Psychological Science* 19, no. 9 (2008): 898–903.

64. Barrett, "Are Emotions Natural Kinds?," 38.

65. Fridlund, *Human Facial Expression*, 179. Fridlund observes that his performative analysis may be especially applicable to experiments by Ekman in which many of the subjects were actors, and the directed facial actions were obtained using a "coach" (that is, a director) and a mirror (179n6).

66. Russell, "Is There Universal Expression of Emotion," 114.

67. Ian Hacking, "By What Links are the Organs Excited?" *Times Literary Supplement*, July 17, 1998, 11. Hacking here points to the role played by unconscious demands and expectations in the production of facial expressions in terms that are compatible with Fridlund's dramaturgical interpretation of facial displays as determined by (conscious and unconscious) social motives. Seen in this light, Ekman's forced-choice labeling procedures, which oblige experimental subjects to identify emotions in photographs of posed expressions by selecting one label from a limited set of emotion terms, can be understood as methods designed to suppress the social-relational dimension involved in their making by "objectivizing" the emotions in the image and in the "correct" judgment of the objective truth of those representations. Russell has demonstrated that if subjects are encouraged to give a description of such pictures of expression in their own words, they don't use categorical emotion terms but tend to produce a narrative account in terms of the situation they think or imagine is being enacted in the image (Russell, "Facial Expressions of Emotion," 378–81).

68. FACS was modeled on an earlier coding system made by the anatomist C. H. Hjortso. FACS is a "sterile," noninterpretive system that focuses on the visible changes (action units) caused by the underlying facial muscles. The "theoretical" part of Ekman's coding system is Emotion FACS (EMFACS), which makes "predictions" (or pronouncements) about which emotions are expressed by which concatenation of action units. The risk has always been that the "predictions" in EMFACS will tend to get folded into FACS training, since Ekman believes that the truth of EMFACS has been definitively revealed. It is worth noting that the iterative process used by Ekman to select representative portrayals of emotions has not in fact yielded a specific physically characterizable signal for each emotion. Instead, for each emotion a range of signals achieves varying degrees of agreement. For example, in Ekman and Friesen's *Pictures of Facial Affect*, sixty-five different facial signals for anger are specified, yet "no theoretical rationale for this variety has been offered" (James A. Russell, Jo-Anne Bachorowski, and

José-Miguel Fernéndez-Dols, "Facial and Vocal Expressions of Emotion," *Annual Review of Psychology* 54 [2003]: 333).

69. Antonio Damasio, *The Feeling of What Happens: Body and Emotion in the Making of Consciousness* (New York: Houghton Mifflin Harcourt, 2000), 62. I take my subtitle "Have No Fear" from Damasio's subchapter heading "Have No Fear" in *Feeling of What Happens*, 62.

70. Damasio, *Feeling of What Happens*, 53–54.

71. Joseph LeDoux, *The Emotional Brain: The Mysterious Underpinnings of Emotional Life* (New York: Simon and Schuster, 1996).

72. Ralph Adolphs, Daniel Tranel, Hanna Damasio, and Antonio R. Damasio, "Impaired Recognition of Emotion in Facial Expressions Following Bilateral Amygdala Damage to the Human Amygdala," *Nature* 372 (15 December 1994): 669–72. The patient was originally identified as "SM," and this is how she is referred to in most subsequent publications, although in his book, *The Feeling of What Happens*, Damasio calls the patient "S." I shall refer to her as SM.

73. Ralph Adolphs et al., "Fear and the Human Amygdala," *Journal of Neuroscience* 15, no. 9 (September 1995): 5879–87.

74. Damasio, *Feeling of What Happens*, 66.

75. Ibid.

76. Ralph Adolphs, Daniel Tranel, and Antonio R. Damasio, "The Human Amygdala in Social Judgment," *Nature* 393 (June 1998): 470–73. See also Ralph Adolphs and Daniel Tranel, "Emotion Recognition and the Human Amygdala," in *The Amygdala: A Functional Analysis*, 2nd ed., ed. John P. Aggleton (New York: Oxford University Press, 2000), 587–630. In these experiments on SM, ratings of approachability and trustworthiness were analyzed for the fifty faces to which normal controls had assigned the most negative ratings and for the fifty most positive faces. Subjects with bilateral amygdala damage rated the fifty most negative faces more positively than did either normal controls or patients with unilateral amygdala damage. All subject groups gave similar ratings to the fifty most positive faces. On the basis of the results, the researchers suggested that "the human amygdala triggers socially and emotionally relevant information in response to visual stimuli. The amygdala's role appears to be of special importance for social judgment of faces that are normally classified as unapproachable and untrustworthy, consistent with the amygdala's demonstrated role in processing threatening and aversive stimuli" (Adolphs, Tranel, and Damasio, "Human Amygdala in Social Judgment," 472).

77. Damasio, *Feeling of What Happens*, 66–67.

78. As two recent critiques of Damasio's report of the case of SM (or S)

and other neuroscientific studies of the relationship between facial expression and emotion make clear, when they emphasize the bracketing or loss of the social-interpretive dimension of the emotions in Ekman's standardized, image-based approach: Daniel Gross, *The Secret History of Emotion: From Aristotle's Rhetoric to Modern Brain Science* (Chicago: University of Chicago Press, 2006), 28–39. See also John McClain Watson, "From Interpretation to Identification: A History of Facial Images in the Sciences of Emotion," *History of the Human Sciences* 17, no. 1 (2004): 29–51. The latter rightly observes that FACS images "enable researchers to introduce reliability and consistency into their investigation but it is important to remember that these advantages are procured only by bracketing the conceptual quandaries so thoroughly detailed by earlier researchers" (45).

79. Already in 1997, in a discussion of the existing literature on the amygdala's role in the evaluation of emotional stimuli, Elizabeth Phelps raised questions about some of the more extreme claims being made about amygdala-damaged patients, pointing out that such patients are different but that their social deficits are subtle and not as dramatic as had been suggested. She proposed that the amygdala seemed to be activated whenever stimuli were arousing. See Elizabeth A. Phelps and Adam K. Anderson, "Emotional Memory: What Does the Amygdala Do?" *Current Biology* 7 (1997): R312–14. See also Adam K. Anderson and Elizabeth A. Phelps, "Is the Human Amygdala Critical for the Subjective Experience of Emotion? Evidence of Intact Dispositional Affect in Patients with Amygdala Lesions," *Journal of Cognitive Neuroscience* 14, no. 5 (2002): 709–20; and Elizabeth A. Phelps, "Emotion and Cognition: Insights from Studies of the Human Amygdala," *Annual Review of Psychology* 57 (2006): 27–53.

80. In a large and rapidly expanding literature, see especially Ralph Adolphs, James A. Russell, and Daniel Tranel, "A Role for the Human Amygdala in Recognizing Emotional Arousal from Unpleasant Stimuli," *Psychological Science* 10 (1999): 167–71; Ralph Adolphs et al., "Recognition of Facial Emotion in Nine Individuals with Bilateral Amygdala Damage," *Neuropsychologia* 37 (1999): 1111–17; Ralph Adolphs et al., "A Mechanism for Impaired Fear Recognition After Amydala Damage," *Nature* 433 (6 January 2005): 68–72; Ralph Adolphs and Michael Spezio, "Role of the Amygdala in Processing Visual Stimuli," *Progress in Brain Research* 156 (2006): 363–78; D. Tranel et al., "Altered Experience of Emotion Following Bilateral Amygdala Damage," *Cognitive Neuropsychiatry* 11, no. 3 (2006): 219–32; Michael L. Spezio et al., "Amygala Damage Impairs Eye Contact During Conversations with Real People," *Journal of Neuroscience* 27, no. 15 (2007): 3994–97; Ralph Adolphs, "Fear, Faces, and the Human Amygdala," *Current Opinion*

in Neurobiology 18 (2008): 166–72; Matthias Gamer and Christian Buchel, "Amygdala Activation Predicts Gaze Toward Fearful Eyes," *Journal of Neuroscience* 29, no. 28 (2009): 9123–26. In a review of the newer results Adolphs comments: "In summary, the model built by the early lesion and functional imaging results, in which the amygdala was critically involved in the recognition of fear but much less so, if at all, in the recognition of other emotions, has given way to a more complex picture in which fear is but one example of a broader category of stimuli that can recruit the amygdala. . . . Thus the amygdala cannot be conceived as a simple 'fear generator' or even as a 'fear processor'; it plays roles in both the experience and the recognition of a range of negative emotional stimuli, as well as in certain highly arousing positive stimuli. . . . Consistent findings of amygdala involvement in processing fear-related stimuli do not mean that it is *dedicated* to fear-related stimuli. . . . The amygdala, or parts thereof, acts as a detector of salience or relevance" (Andrea S. Heberlein and Ralph Adolphs, "Neurobiology of Emotional Recognition: Current Evidence for Shared Substrates," in *Fundamentals of Social Neuroscience*, ed. E. Harmon-Jones and P. Winkielman [New York: Guilford Press, 2007], 38–39). Of course, the introduction of the notion of "salience" raises the familiar epistemological problem of the frame or the assessment of relevance—in other words, the problem of meaning.

81. See especially Paul J. Whalen et al., "Masked Presentations of Emotional Facial Expressions Modulate Amygdala Activity Without Explicit Knowledge," *Journal of Neuroscience* 18, no. 1 (1998): 411–18; M. Davis and P. J. Whalen, "The Amygdala: Vigilance and Emotion," *Molecular Psychiatry* 6 (2001): 13–34; Paul J. Whalen et al., "Human Amgydala Responsivity to Masked Fearful Eye Whites," *Science* 306 (2004): 2061; and Paul J. Whalen, "Fear, Vigilance, and Ambiguity: Initial Neuroimaging Studies of the Human Amygdala," *Current Directions in Psychological Science* 7 (1998): 177–88, where Whalen observes with reference to Phoebe Ellsworth's appraisal views that "vigilance and emotion are not so much entities that reside within the amygdala as they are processes set in motion by amygdala activation" (183) and concludes: "Most theories of amygdala function, and thus discussions of amygdala neuroimaging results, highlight its role in the production of fear states. Clear animal and human experimental evidence supports this view. Yet such a view may unnecessarily compartmentalize amygdala function, leading us to a categorical understanding of what may be a continuous system. The utility of invoking a process such as vigilance rather than an entity such as fear to explain amygdala function is that it might speak to a greater portion of our daily experience. . . . The present theory offers a more pervasive and generalized role for the amygdala in vigilance evoked by

associative ambiguity to explain its response to a wide variety of biologically relevant stimuli" (185). Whalen draws attention to new experiments suggesting that the stimuli to which the amygdala responds do not even have to be biologically relevant to the organism, but that uncertainty or unpredictability is enough to activate the amygdala (Paul J. Whalen, "The Uncertainty of It All," *TRENDS in Cognitive Sciences* 11 [2007]: 499–500).

82. I am not sure where Adolphs now stands on these issues. For a statement of his position see Ralph Adolphs, "Perception and Emotion: How We Recognize Facial Expressions," *Current Directions in Psychological Science* 15, no. 5 (2006): 222–26, where the author accepts the idea that the amygdala's role in recognizing facial expressions encompasses a broader, more abstract, or perhaps more dimensional rather than categorical aspect, of the emotions, of which fear is only one instance. But this leaves open the possibility that he is still committed to the idea of the existence of a set of "basic emotions" according to the Tomkins-Ekman paradigm. See also Ralph Adolphs, "Fear, Faces, and the Human Amygdala," *Current Opinion in Neurobiology* 18 (2008): 166–72. For a relatively recent statement of Damasio's general position on the affects see his *Looking for Spinoza: Joy, Sorrow, and the Feeling Brain* (New York: Houghton Mifflin Harcourt, 2003).

83. The compatibility between Ekman's hypostatization of the facial image and the hypostatization of the image in new imaging technologies such as PET and fMRI is striking. In this connection, see Joseph Dumit, *Picturing Personhood: Brain Scans and Biomedical Identity* (Princeton: Princeton University Press, 2004), in which the author suggests that PET and fMRI reinforce the notion that we are what our brain images tell us we are.

84. In this connection, in his novel, *Your Face Tomorrow*, vol. 1, *Fever and Spear*, trans. Margaret Jull Costa (New York: Chattus and Windus, 2005), Javier Marías offers a fascinating fictional account of what might be involved in the reading of faces and facial behavior. Indeed, it is striking that this topic is thematized in his book at a time when, post 9/11, these issues are of such urgent concern in contemporary society and psychology. Suffice it to say that María's position is entirely on the side of narrative thick description and the observation over time of multiple aspects of human behavior, not just the observation of isolated faces, much less static depictions of these.

85. Fridlund, *Human Facial Expression*, 137–39. I leave for discussion on another occasion the general question of the role of deceit versus veridical signaling in animal communication. Such a discussion would have to assess the importance of Amotz Zahavi's handicap principle, according to which for animal signals to be effective they must be reliable (that is, believable because truthful), and to be reliable they must impose a cost or handicap on

the signaler. Thus, according to the handicap principle, when a gazelle sights a wolf and jumps high into the air before fleeing it is signaling that it is in top condition, easily able to outrun the predator, and that therefore the wolf should attack another animal. Zahavi suggests that for the gazelle to jump high in this way costs the animal significant energy and as a signal of fitness it is not one that can easily be faked. Zahavi extends the handicap principle to many aspects of human behavior in ways that seem to me too simplistic. See Amotz Zahavi and Avishag Zahavi, *The Handicap Principle: A Missing Piece of Darwin's Puzzle* (New York: Oxford University Press, 1997).

4. SOLDIERS AND EMOTION IN EARLY TWENTIETH-CENTURY RUSSIAN MILITARY PSYCHOLOGY

Research for this article was supported by Sonderforschungsbereich 437 "Kriegserfahrungen: Krieg und Gesellschaft in der Neuzeit" at the University of Tübingen. It was written in 2007–2008 during a fellowship at Historisches Kolleg, Munich, and revised at Ute Frevert's Center for the History of Emotions at Max Planck Institute for Human Development, Berlin, with generous support from a Dilthey Fellowship (Fritz Thyssen Foundation). Another version of this chapter has been previously published as "Fear: Soldiers and Emotion in Early Twentieth-Century Russian Military Psychology," *Slavic Review* 68, no. 2 (2009): 259–83. My greatest debt is to Kim (Jacqueline) Friedlander for extensive comments on substance and style and for letting me read her dissertation before it became publicly available. For their comments, I would also like to thank Dietrich Beyrau, Frank Biess, Ol'ga Edel'man, Jochen Hellbeck, Susan Morrissey, Monique Scheer, Benjamin Schenk, Irina Sirotkina, Mark D. Steinberg, and Glennys Young.

Epigraphs: [V. P.?] Prasalov, "Neskol'ko slov k stat'e V. Polianskogo— 'Moral'nyi element v oblasti fortifikatsii,'" *Voennyi sbornik* 54, no. 5 (1911): 89; A. [M.] Dmitrevskii, "Vospitanie voina mozhet byt' tol'ko v styde nakazaniia, a ne v strakhe nakazaniia," *Voennyi sbornik* 56, no. 10 (1913): 100.

1. Mikhail Petrov, *1812 god: Vospominaniia voinov russkoi armii; iz sobraniia Otdela Pis'mennykh Istochnikov Gosudarstvennogo Istoricheskogo Muzeia*, eds. Fedor A. Petrov et al. (Moscow: Mysl', 1991), 180. Thanks to Ingrid Schierle for pointing me to this source.

2. Petrov, *1812 god*, 183. "Sorevnovanie k chesti" at this point indeed signified "striving for honor" (rather than "ambition").

3. Lev N. Voitolovskii, *Po sledam voiny: Pokhodnye zapiski. 1914–1917*

(Leningrad: Gos. izd-vo, 1925), 69. The opening of the discursive gates regarding soldierly fear was accompanied by professions made by soldiers, officers, and doctors that fear escaped all attempts at verbalization. Consider, for instance, this Russian soldier who suffered a surprise attack by an enemy soldier in the First World War: "He attacked me from behind, and there are no words to describe my fear" (Sofja Fedortschenko, *Der Russe redet: Aufzeichnungen nach dem Stenogramm,* trans. Alexander Eliasberg [Munich: Drei Masken, 1923], 19–20).

4. On the "boundaries of what could be said," see foundational texts of *Begriffsgeschichte,* such as Reinhart Koselleck, *Futures Past: On the Semantics of Historical Time,* trans. Keith Tribe (Cambridge: MIT Press, 1985); Reinhart Koselleck, *The Practice of Conceptual History: Timing History, Spacing Concepts,* trans. Todd Samuel Presner et al. (Stanford: Stanford University Press, 2002); and Willibald Steinmetz, *Das Sagbare und das Machbare: Zum Wandel politischer Handlungsspielräume. England* 1780–1867 (Stuttgart: Klett-Cotta, 1993).

5. Medical case records are the major lacuna in the documentary record; they only become available for the Soviet-Finnish War of 1939–1940 and are used in the publications of D. A. Zhuravlev, such as "Osnovnye etapy razvitiia gosudarstvennogo voennogo zdravookhraneniia Rossii," *Voenno-meditsinskii zhurnal,* no. 2 (2004): 4–12.

6. The literature on shell shock is considerable and still growing. For a study of multiple countries, see Mark S. Micale and Paul Lerner, *Traumatic Pasts: History, Psychiatry, and Trauma in the Modern Age, 1870–1930* (Cambridge: Cambridge University Press, 2001). For Russia, see A. B. Astashov, "Voina kak kul'turnyi shok: Analiz psikhopatologicheskogo sostoianiia russkoi armii v Pervuiu mirovuiu voinu," in *Voenno-istoricheskaia Antologiia: Ezhegodnik,* ed. Elena S. Seniavskaia (Moscow: ROSSPEN, 2002), 268–81; Jacqueline Lee [Kim] Friedlander, "Psychiatrists and Crisis in Russia, 1880–1917" (PhD diss., University of California, Berkeley, 2007); Jacqueline Lee [Kim] Friedlander, "Approaching War Trauma: Russian Psychiatrists Look at Battlefield Breakdown during World War I," *Newsletter of the Institute of Slavic, East European, and Eurasian Studies* (University of California, Berkeley) 21, no. 3 (fall 2004): 3–4, 19–22; Kim Fridlender [Jacqueline Friedlander], "Neskol'ko aspektov *shellshock'a* v Rossii, 1914–1916," in *Rossiia i pervaia mirovaia voina (materialy mezhdunarodnogo nauchnogo kollokviuma),* ed. Nikolai N. Smirnov et al. (St. Petersburg: D. Bulanin, 1999), 315–25; Catherine Merridale, "The Collective Mind: Trauma and Shell-Shock in Twentieth-Century Russia," *Journal of Contemporary History* 35, no. 1 (January 2000): 39–55; Elena S. Seniavskaia, *Psikhologiia voiny v XX veke: Istoricheskii*

opyt Rossii (Moscow: ROSSPEN, 1999); Irina Sirotkina, "The Politics of Etiology: Shell Shock in the Russian Army, 1914–1918," in *Madness and the Mad
in Russian Culture*, ed. Angela Brintlinger and Ilya Vinitsky (Toronto: University of Toronto Press, 2007), 117–29; Laura L. Phillips, "Gendered Dis/
ability: Perspectives from the Treatment of Psychiatric Casualties in Russia's
Early Twentieth-Century Wars," *Social History of Medicine* 20, no. 2 (August
2007): 333–50. For Britain, see Peter Leese, *Shell Shock: Traumatic Neurosis
and the British Soldiers of the First World War* (New York: Palgrave Macmillan, 2002). For France, see Marc Roudebush, "A Battle of Nerves: Hysteria
and Its Treatment in France during World War I" (PhD diss., University of
California, Berkeley, 1995); Susanne Michl, *Im Dienste des "Volkskörpers":
Deutsche und französische Ärzte im Ersten Weltkrieg* (Göttingen: Vandenhoeck
and Ruprecht, 2007), part 3. For Germany, see Paul Frederick Lerner, *Hysterical Men: War, Psychiatry, and the Politics of Trauma in Germany, 1890–1930*
(Ithaca: Cornell University Press, 2003).

7. On the 1874 military reform and Russian mass conscription, see Werner Benecke, *Militär, Reform und Gesellschaft im Zarenreich: Die Wehrpflicht
in Russland 1874–1914* (Paderborn: Ferdinand Schöningh, 2006). One might
also emphasize that in the creation of the national army, service in this army
and death for the nation become endowed with different meaning. If in
armies of paid mercenaries, fear forms part of an act of economic free will,
much as a miner's death is part of his autonomous economic decision and
therefore silenced, the paid soldier does not talk about his economic decision. Only once this risk becomes not his own but part of a decision made
by a larger body—the nation—can a discursive space be opened for talking
about it.

8. This is inspired by Corey Robin, *Fear: The History of a Political Idea*
(New York: Oxford University Press, 2004), 11–12. One might also point to
the emergence of pacifism in the nineteenth century. As soon as a choice
other than war became a thinkable way to solve conflicts, the hardships of
warfare and its ever-looming end, death—as well as the attendant fear—
became options.

9. As Joanna Bourke put it, "psychiatrists, clinical psychologists and
social workers were highly valued for 'curing' men who experienced stress
in killing. These social scientists also provided crucial changes to the military terminology: 'cowardice' (with its accompanying need for execution or
punishment) became 'shell shock' and then 'anxiety states' (which called
for treatment, albeit stigmatizing)" (Joanna Bourke, *An Intimate History of
Killing: Face-to-Face Killing in Twentieth-Century Warfare* [New York: Basic
Books, 1999], 82). The locus classicus for the interiorization thesis is Michel

Foucault, *Madness and Civilization: A History of Insanity in the Age of Reason*, trans. Richard Howard (New York: Pantheon Books, 1965), but also Foucault, *Discipline and Punish: The Birth of the Prison*, trans. Alan Sheridan (New York: Pantheon Books, 1977).

10. See Jeffrey Brooks, *When Russia Learned to Read: Literacy and Popular Literature, 1861–1917* (Princeton: Princeton University Press, 1985); Louise McReynolds, *The News under Russia's Old Regime: The Development of a Mass-Circulation Press* (Princeton: Princeton University Press, 1991). The first Russian crime story (*detektiv*) appeared in 1866. See Norbert Franz, *Moskauer Mordgeschichten: Der russisch-sowjetische Krimi 1953–1983* (Mainz: Liber, 1988), 67. For the establishment of a similar link between the rise of the genre of gothic novels and new fear modes, see Philip Fisher, *The Vehement Passions* (Princeton: Princeton University Press, 2002), 9–11.

11. On the connection between Stendhal and Tolstoy, see Gottfried Schwarz, *Krieg und Roman: Untersuchungen zu Stendhal, Hugo, Tolstoj, Zola und Simon* (Frankfurt am Main: Peter Lang, 1992), esp. 85. Also see Clarence A. Manning, "The Significance of Tolstoy's War Stories," *PMLA* 52, no. 4 (December 1937): 1161–69 (I am grateful to Benjamin Schenk for directing me to this literature). Tolstoy's *Sevastopol' Sketches* were widely received. To get an inkling of how shocking (because realistic) the description of soldiers' emotions seemed to contemporaries, consider writer Aleksei Pisemskii's letter to his friend, the playwright Aleksandr Ostrovskii, about "Sevastopol' in May": "Horror takes hold of you, your hair stands on end just from imagining what is happening there. The story is written in such a relentlessly honest manner that reading it becomes almost unbearable. Definitely read it!" (Aleksei F. Pisemskii, "Pis'mo A. N. Ostrovskomu ot 26 iulia 1855 goda," in *A. F. Pisemskii: Materialy i issledovaniia* [Moscow: Izd-vo Akademii nauk SSSR, 1936], 82).

12. Leo Tolstoy, *The Cossacks and Other Stories*, trans. David McDuff and Paul Foote (New York: Penguin, 2006), 196, 196–97.

13. Tolstoy, *Cossacks and Other Stories*, 242, 231–32, 326, 199.

14. Tolstoy, *Cossacks and Other Stories*, 254–55.

15. This is probably due to the nonmilitary disciplinary backgrounds of most historians of psychiatry. There are exceptions to this downplaying of the military's role. See Friedlander, "Psychiatrists and Crisis in Russia, 1880–1917"; Paul Wanke, *Russian/Soviet Military Psychiatry, 1904–1945* (London: Frank Cass, 2005); Richard A. Gabriel, *Soviet Military Psychiatry: The Theory and Practice of Coping with Battle Stress* (New York: Greenwood Press, 1986). These accounts also differ from the story of professsionalization Julie

Vail Brown tells in her pioneering "The Professionalization of Russian Psychiatry: 1857–1911" (PhD diss., University of Pennsylvania, 1981).

16. This is based above all on Friedlander, "Psychiatrists and Crisis in Russia, 1880–1917." Also see Brown, "Professionalization of Russian Psychiatry"; Gabriel, *Soviet Military Psychiatry*; Irina Sirotkina, *Diagnosing Literary Genius: A Cultural History of Psychiatry in Russia, 1880–1930* (Baltimore: Johns Hopkins University Press, 2002). On psychology, see Daniel Philip Todes, "From Radicalism to Scientific Convention: Biological Psychology in Russia from Sechenov to Pavlov" (PhD diss., University of Pennsylvania, 1981); Seniavskaia, *Psikhologiia voiny v XX veke*. On psychoanalysis, see Aleksandr Etkind, *Eros nevozmozhnogo: Istoriia psikhoanaliza v Rossii* (St. Petersburg: Meduza, 1993); and Martin A. Miller, *Freud and the Bolsheviks: Psychoanalysis in Imperial Russia and the Soviet Union* (New Haven: Yale University Press, 1998).

17. These roots in internal medicine led to the curious fact that such medical journals as *Voenno-meditsinskii zhurnal* continued to feature psychiatric articles under a rubric of "internal diseases" well into the twentieth century and long after psychiatry had become an established branch of medicine.

18. This is attested by its move out of the confines of purely medical and psychiatric "scientific" journals into the premier military journal *Voennyi sbornik* and by its influence on other branches of knowledge and the arts—literature, painting, and theater. On this, see Etkind, *Eros nevozmozhnogo*; and Sirotkina, *Diagnosing Literary Genius*.

19. For the number of shell-shocked soldiers, see Wanke, *Russian/Soviet Military Psychiatry*, 18. For the quote by the American military psychiatrist, see Robert L. Richards, "Mental and Nervous Diseases in the Russo-Japanese War," *Military Surgeon* 26 (1910): 177. The Western reception of the Russian experience with mental illness in the Russo-Japanese War was based not only on the exchange of expert knowledge but also on the treatment of Russian officers in German psychiatric sanatoria. On this, see Hans-Georg Hofer, *Nervenschwäche und Krieg: Modernitätskritik und Krisenbewältigung in der österreichischen Psychiatrie (1880–1920)* (Vienna: Böhlau, 2004), 205. The Russo-Japanese War is often regarded as World War Zero but in fact many wars have been tagged the "first" modern war (most recently the Napoleonic Wars); see David A. Bell, *The First Total War: Napoleon's Europe and the Birth of Warfare as We Know It* (Boston: Houghton Mifflin, 2007). Thus the definition of what constitutes a modern war and, even if one agrees on the criteria, the designation of war are exceedingly difficult as the boundaries are fluid. For a statistics-based argument that premodern wars were more modern

than modern wars if the number of involved civilians is the criterion, see Dieter Langewiesche, "Eskalierte die Kriegsgewalt im Laufe der Geschichte?" in *Moderne Zeiten? Krieg, Revolution und Gewalt im 20. Jahrhundert*, ed. Jörg Baberowski (Göttingen: Vandenhoeck and Ruprecht, 2006), 12–36.

20. According to Angela Brintlinger, "they also aggressively wrote their own history and, by the late nineteenth century, constructing those histories had become a primary source of their legitimacy." Thus history or, rather, a lineage psychiatrists identified for themselves was meant to provide stability for a profession that still felt insecure about itself. See Angela Brintlinger, "Writing about Madness: Russian Attitudes toward Psyche and Psychiatry, 1887–1907," in Brintlinger and Vinitsky, *Madness and the Mad in Russian Culture*, 173.

21. See A. Shcheglov, "Materialy k izucheniiu dushevnykh rasstroistv v armii," *Voenno-meditsinskii zhurnal* 77, no. 11 (1899): 863 (Nasse), 870 (Arndt); M. O. Shaikevich, "K voprosu o dushevnykh zabolevaniiakh v voiske v sviazi s Russko-Iaponskoi voinoi," *Voenno-meditsinskii zhurnal* 85, no. 6 (1907): 276–92; Shaikevich, "K voprosu o dushevnykh zabolevaniiakh v voiske v sviazi s Russko-Iaponskoi voinoi," *Voenno-meditsinskii zhurnal* 85, no. 9 (1907): 86 (fear as a shorthand for a panoply of pathogenic factors).

22. See, e.g., F. Kh. Gadziatskii, "Dushevnye rasstroistva v sviazi s politicheskimi sobytiiami v Rossii," *Voenno-meditsinskii zhurnal* 86, no. 9 (1908): 97.

23. G. Shumkov, "Filosofskaia pokornost' sud'be i boleznennoe malodushie," *Voennyi sbornik* 57, no. 1 (1914): 109.

24. Roman Chetyrkin, *Opyt voenno-meditsinskoi politsii, ili pravila k sokhraneniiu zdorov'ia russkikh soldat v sukhoputnoi sluzhbe* (St. Petersburg: Tipografiia Iversena, 1834), 66. *Politsiia* in the title signified early modern *Policey* rather than the contemporary "police." The very first mentioning of *strakh* was a case unrelated to our concerns, namely a description of a "negro [*negr*]" who lost consciousness in London when lying on the operating table for aneurysm and was found dead after the operation, literally as a result of "fear" ("Deistvie strakha," *Voenno-meditsinskii zhurnal* 2 [1823]: 285–86).

25. Chetyrkin, *Opyt voenno-meditsinskoi politsii*, 62.

26. Ibid., 66.

27. On *organy chuvstv* and *obman chuvstv*, see, e.g., F. Kh. Gadziatskii, "O vliianii dushevno-bol'nykh drug na druga," *Voenno-meditsinskii zhurnal* 76, no. 12 (1898): 1555, 1567.

28. A. I. Kislov, *Voennaia nravstvennost'* (St. Petersburg: Tipografiia Glavnogo Upravleniia putei soobshcheniia i publichnykh zdanii, 1838), 32, 79, 47. Consider also the rich lexicon of an ideal soldier's emotional traits,

presented on a mere two pages: *nenavist'* towards the enemy, *zapal'chivost'*, *smelost'*, *revnost' k dolzhnosti, chuvstvo obiazannosti* (72–73). The taxonomy of feelings, to be sure, is still confused and replete with non sequiturs: despite the religiosity and patriotism with which soldiers are supposedly universally equipped by birth, the decisive, superordinate feeling of "good nature" or "virtue" (*velikodushie*) is variable according to soldier, which is why, when faced with danger, not all soldiers exhibit "fearlessness" (*neustrashimost'*) and some fall prey to the worst of all soldierly feelings, "timidity" (*robost'*) (105–6, 58, 67–68, 77–78). Kislov also distinguishes between *khrabrost'*, which he considers an innate quality, and *muzhestvo*, which he describes as a product of training (69–70).

29. See Kislov, *Voennaia nravstvennost'*, 92, 90, 98. On honor and the duel, see also Ute Frevert, *Men of Honour: A Social and Cultural History of the Duel* (Cambridge: Polity Press, 1995); Irina Reyfman, *Ritualized Violence Russian Style: The Duel in Russian Culture and Literature* (Stanford: Stanford University Press, 1999). The quote by Petrov from the War of 1812 cited at the beginning of this article is a typical expression of this culture of honor. On the pre-Petrine culture of honor, see Nancy Shields Kollmann, *By Honor Bound: State and Society in Early Modern Russia* (Ithaca: Cornell University Press, 1999).

30. Dragomirov came not from psychiatry but from military theory, and yet he belongs in this genealogy because military psychologists (not so much psychiatrists but the borders between psychologists and psychiatrists were fluid anyway, as we have seen) learned and cited from him liberally.

31. See *Encyclopaedia Britannica*, 11th ed. (New York: Encyclopaedia Britannica, 1910–1911), 8:466.

32. Michail I. Dragomirow, "Ausbildung und Erziehung," *Gesammelte Aufsätze: Neue Folge*, trans. Freiherr von Tettau (Hannover: Helwing, 1891), 19. On Dragomirov, see also Joshua Sanborn, "The Short Course for Murder: How Soldiers and Criminals Learn to Kill," in *Violent Acts and Violentization: Assessing, Applying, and Developing Lonnie Athens' Theories*, ed. Lonnie Athens and Jeffery T. Ulmer (Boston: JAI, 2003), 109. To be sure, the axiom of a survival instinct as a soldier's most basic feeling has a longer genealogy, going back to Aleksandr Suvorov and Carl von Clausewitz.

33. Michail I. Dragomirov, "Podgotovka voisk v mirnoe vremia (vospitanie i obrazovanie)," *Izbrannye trudy: Voprosy vospitaniia i obucheniia voisk* (Moscow: Voen. izd-vo, 1956), 625.

34. "The express enemy of self-denial is self-preservation. . . . In fact we are not dealing with two different forces, only with two poles of the same power: the self-denial of the individual is the precondition for the self-pres-

ervation of the masses" (Dragomirow, "Ausbildung und Erziehung," 19). This dialectic proved highly influential and had cameo appearances as, inter alia, the instinct of self-preservation versus patriotism in V. Zaglukhinskii, "Psikhika boitsov vo vremia srazheniia," *Voennyi sbornik* 54, no. 1 (1911): 87.

35. Dragomirow, "Ausbildung und Erziehung," 31. But according to Dragomirov and in line with the liberalism of the reform era, the fear that officers inspired in soldiers could also cause harmful soldierly fear. Only just, law-abiding behavior on the part of officers could keep this particular fear of soldiers in check: "Is there anything we should scorn more in the soldier than the kind of fear that paralyzes spirit and will? This is why soldiers must be led in such a way that the feeling of fear can develop in their souls as rarely as possible, for he who fears his own men, is taught to fear the enemy, too" (Dragomirov, "Podgotovka voisk v mirnoe vremia," 605).

36. This was, at heart, a conservative view. In a similar vein, forty years later one conservative doctor argued that Russia was lucky to boast a 50-plus percent illiteracy rate among its soldiers, because this guarded against the corrosive effects of education, which invariably had such negative consequences as critical attitudes toward officers. See Zaglukhinskii, "Psikhika boitsov vo vremia srazheniia," 89.

37. See Bruce W. Menning, *Bayonets before Bullets: The Imperial Russian Army, 1861–1914* (Bloomington: Indiana University Press, 1992).

38. "Emotional regime" is from William Reddy, who defines it as "the set of normative emotions and the official rituals, practices, and emotives that express and inculcate them; a necessary underpinning of any stable political regime" (William M. Reddy, *The Navigation of Feeling: A Framework for the History of Emotions* [Cambridge: Cambridge University Press, 2001], 129). It is possible that other armies developed similar emotional regimes; the role of *élan* in the French Army is worth studying from this perspective (I owe this point to Chad Bryant).

39. Quoted from Nikolai N. Golovin, *Issledovanie boia: Issledovanie deiatel'nosti i svoistv cheloveka kak boitsa* (St. Petersburg: Ekonomicheskaia Tipo-Litografiia, 1907), 52. Note also Skobelev's pointing to his heart; on "soldier's heart," see Joel D. Howell, "'Soldier's Heart': The Redefinition of Heart Disease and Specialty Formation in Early Twentieth-Century Great Britain," in *War, Medicine and Modernity*, ed. Roger Cooter, Mark Harrison, and Steve Sturdy (Stroud: Sutton, 1998), 85–105. Another general, Petr Parensov, confessed after the Russo-Turkish War: "It was only then that I noticed Turks, only Turks, who were closing in on me from all sides; there were none of our own soldiers in the redoubt. I was all alone. I admit, terror took hold of me [*Priznaius', uzhas okhvatil menia*]" (Petr D. Parensov, *Iz*

proshlogo: Vospominaniia ofitsera General'nogo Shtaba [St. Petersburg: V. Berezovskii, 1901–1908], 2:135; quoted in Golovin, *Issledovanie boia*, 141).

40. See the summary of "O. Kots's" 1873 article in *Berliner klinische Wochenschrift*, "O vliianii strakha na razvitie bolezni," *Voenno-meditsinskii zhurnal* 51, no. 9 (1873): 10–11. In their later historical efforts, Russian psychiatrists came up with a causal link between fear and nervous disorders that dated as far back as Jean Étienne Dominique Esquirol, Johann Christian August Heinroth, and Karl Christian Hille's *Allgemeine und specielle Pathologie und Therapie der Seelenstörungen* (Leipzig: Hartmann, 1827). See Shcheglov, "Materialy k izucheniiu dushevnykh rasstroistv v armii," 862.

41. For the *avtoreferat*, see A. Ozeretskovskii, "Ob isterii v voiskakh," *Voenno-meditsinskii zhurnal* 69, no. 11 (1891): 371. Ozeretskovskii was later often presented as the Russian discoverer of male hysteria. See, e.g., Pospelov, "K voprosu ob isterii u soldat," *Voenno-meditsinskii zhurnal* 76, no. 8 (1898): 1138.

42. Ozeretskovskii, "Ob isterii v voiskakh," 371.

43. See Ia. P. Gorshkov, "K kazuistike psikhozov sifiliticheskogo proiskhozhdeniia," *Voenno-meditsinskii zhurnal* 76, no. 8 (1898): 1168; E. Erikson, "Dva sluchaia tiazheloi isterii na pochve samovnusheniia," *Voenno-meditsinskii zhurnal* 80, no. 11 (1902): 4185 ("Incidentally, the patient himself traces his [fits], not to his head injury or wounds, but to strong fright" [ne ushibu golovy i raneniiam, a sil'nomu ispugu]).

44. M. V. Enval'd, "Dve doktriny boevogo vospitaniia voisk," *Voennyi sbornik* 54, no. 1 (1911): 101–6.

45. Infamously, in Germany the minority opinion of psychiatrist Max Nonne and others that the war merely acted as a catalyst for preexisting psychological disorders, thus freeing the state from its monetary obligation to shell-shocked soldiers, was elevated to majority status at the September 1916 military psychiatry congress in Munich, whereas the majority opinion of Hermann Oppenheim that the war itself was the cause of mental disease, hence the state was responsible for pension claims, was relegated to a marginal position. On this, see Lerner, *Hysterical Men*. It is also important to note that Russia never had the same kind of prolonged debates about compensation for industrial injuries that sowed the ground for German doctors' attitudes during the First World War.

46. See, e.g., Sh— [most likely Grigorii Shumkov], "'Za' i 'protiv' voennoi psikhologii," *Voennyi sbornik* 55, no. 8 (1912): 72.

47. Sh—, "'Za' i 'protiv' voennoi psikhologii," 76. In line with the liberalism of the military psychiatric establishment, Shumkov at times seemed to believe in straightforward enlightenment: if doctors only properly explained

to soldiers that their physiological signs of fear before combat were normal, soldiers would not consider themselves sick and would continue fighting. Shumkov stated that "Sometimes before a battle, during the waiting period when the fighting has yet to start, about 6–8 percent are incapacitated, because they seriously believe they are sick. These are honest people, not shirkers, who are convinced that they have fallen ill (heart, breathing, involuntary defecation). But their illness is the product of ignorance about the psycho-physiological processes in their agitated organisms [*pri volneniiakh*]" ("'Za' i 'protiv' voennoi psikhologii," 81). Shumkov's liberalism might also stem from his peasant background. See G. E. Shumkov, *Vosproizvedenie dvigatel'nykh razdrazhenii aktivnogo kharaktera v zavisimosti ot istekshego vremeni. (Eksperimental'no-psikhologicheskoe issledovanie po metodu ob"ektivnoi psikhologii). Dissertatsiia na stepen' doktora meditsiny. Iz psikhologicheskoi laboratorii Akademika V. M. Bekhtereva* (St. Petersburg: Tipografiia P. P. Soikina, 1909), 163. I am grateful to Kim Friedlander for this source.

48. Sh—, "'Za' i 'protiv' voennoi psikhologii," 80. A. Dmitrevskii basically concurred with Shumkov's views but begged to differ in one aspect: yes, all soldiers experience fear and it is important that they know it; however, not its expression but its suppression must be encouraged, because if expressed, fear becomes like a virus and infects all other soldiers— Dmitrevskii demanded "that nobody express his fear, because this is awfully infectious" (A. Dmitrevskii, "'Za' i 'protiv' psikhologii g-na Sh-a," *Voennyi sbornik* 55, no. 11 [1912]: 96).

49. Consider, for instance, the elaborate catalogue of soldiers' emotions in Sh—, "Emotsii strakha, pechali, radosti i gneva v period ozhidaniia boia," *Voennyi sbornik* 57, no. 2 (1914): 109–18.

50. Shumkov, "Dushevnoe sostoianie voinov v ozhidanii boia. (Po nabliudeniiam ofitserov). Voenno-psikhologicheskii etiud," *Voennyi sbornik* 56, no. 5 (1913): 100 (emphasis in the original), 90, 100, 101.

51. Ibid., 101, 102.

52. K. M. Druzhinin, *Issledovanie dushevnogo sostoianiia voinov v raznykh sluchaiakh boevoi obstanovki po opytu russko-iaponskoi voiny 1904–05 gg.* (St. Petersburg: Russkaia Skoropechatnia, 1910), 4–6.

53. K. M. Druzhinin, *Issledovanie dushevnogo sostoianiia voinov*, 14, 60, 29.

54. Ibid., 17.

55. In 1910 Vladimir Polianskii announced in a footnote that his colleague, Shumkov, was working on a taxonomy of fear: "The doctor and psychiatrist G. E. Shumkov in one of the meetings of the 'military psychology' section of the Obshchestvo revinitelei voennykh znanii aired an approximate

classification of the term of the emotion of *fear* according to its manifestation in the human organism" ("Moral'nyi element v oblasti fortifikatsii," *Voennyi sbornik* 53, no. 11 [1910]: 136).

56. See A. S. Rezanov, *Armiia i tolpa: Opyt voennoi psikhologii* (Warsaw: Varshavskaia esteticheskaia tip., 1910); G. E. Shumkov, "'Vzdragivanie' liudei pri deistvii artileriiskogo ognia (Voenno-psikhologicheskie etiudy)," *Voennyi sbornik* 57, no. 12 (1914): 59–92; G. Shumkov, "Chuvstvo trevogi, kak dominiruiushaia emotsiia v period ozhidaniia boia," *Voennyi sbornik* 56, no. 11 (1913): 95–100; A. Dmitrevskii, "Trevozhnoe ozhidanie—boiazlivoe ili opasnoe ozhidanie," *Voennyi sbornik* 57, no. 1 (1914): 103–6; G. Shumkov, "O vydelenii chuvstva trevogi v samostoiatel'noe chuvstvo," *Voennyi sbornik* 57, no. 4 (1914): 121–26; G. Shumkov, "Psikhika boitsov pod pervym artieleriiskim obstrelom (Voenno-psikhologicheskii etiud)," *Voennyi sbornik* 57, no. 7 (1914): 121; G. Shumkov, "Ugnetenie psikhiki voinov artieleriiskim ognem (Voenno-psikhologicheskii etiud)," *Voennyi sbornik* 57, no. 8 (1914): 105; G. Shumkov, "Rol' chuvstva trevogi v psikhologii mass, kak nachala, niveliruiushchego individual'nosti," *Voennyi sbornik* 57, no. 9 (1914): 85–94.

57. Indeed, the discussion about true heroism often centered on the distribution of medals like the Order of St. George. See, e.g., A. Dmitrevskii, "Mozhno igrat' na slabykh strunakh, no ne vospityvat' v nikh," *Voennyi sbornik* 57, no. 4 (1914): 117–18.

58. As one author put it, there is such a thing as innate bravery, but "natural bravery is seldom sensible bravery" (B. Nikulishchev, "Moral'nyi element v oblasti voennogo iskusstva [Opyt psikhologicheskogo issledovaniia]," *Voennyi sbornik* 55, no. 1 [1912]: 14).

59. G. E. Shumkov, "Geroi terpeniia: Voenno-psikhologicheskii etiud," *Voennyi sbornik* 54, no. 2 (1911): 145.

60. Shumkov, "Geroi terpeniia: Voenno-psikhologicheskii etiud," 148–50.

61. Zaglukhinskii, "Psikhika boitsov vo vremia srazheniia," 87.

62. Ibid., 86. By "soul" he had in mind a transcendental, religiously infused entity.

63. Druzhinin, *Issledovanie dushevnogo sostoianiia voinov*, 42.

64. Polianskii, "Moral'nyi element v oblasti fortifikatsii," 101.

65. Ben Shephard has astutely observed about novelist Pat Barker's Regeneration Trilogy (and the study that served as its inspiration, Elaine Showalter, *The Female Malady: Women, Madness, and English Culture, 1830–1980* [New York: Pantheon Books, 1986], chap. 7) that we tend to overestimate the importance of humane psychiatrists, such as Rivers, the hero of

Barker's novels. See Ben Shephard, *A War of Nerves: Soldiers and Psychiatrists in the Twentieth Century* (Cambridge: Harvard University Press, 2001), 109.

66. See, e.g., Prasalov, "Neskol'ko slov k stat'e V. Polianskogo," 85–95; continued in *Voennyi sbornik* 54, no. 7 (1911): 87–104.

67. This is not to say that the suggested hardline solutions lacked procedural, legal regularity. Much of the discussion focused on forensic medicine, especially the definition of recruits as unfit for military service due to mental feebleness according to paragraph 24, lit. A of the statute military psychiatrists operated with. In a similar vein, imperial Russian officials often ascribed suicides of serfs to fear of (corporeal) punishment by their landlords. See Susan K. Morrissey, *Suicide and the Body Politic in Imperial Russia* (Cambridge: Cambridge University Press, 2006), chaps. 3–5, esp. 126–27.

68. N. Butovskii, *O sposobakh obucheniia i vospitaniia sovremennogo soldata*, vol. 2 (St. Petersburg, 1888), quoted in Shumkov, "Chto delat' s porochnym elementom v armii?" *Voennyi sbornik* 54, no. 11 (1911): 112. This was not yet *dedovshchina*, which emerged later.

69. Shumkov, "Chto delat' s porochnym elementom v armii?," 116.

70. Dmitrevskii, "Vospitanie voina mozhet byt' tol'ko v styde nakazaniia, a ne v strakhe nakazaniia," 100. Also see Dmitrevskii, "Mozhno igrat' na slabykh strunakh," 116.

71. In one author's words, "In periods of imminent combat people turn into machines and, if properly guided, are capable of showing such elemental force, such examples of total self-sacrifice and great heroism, that no obstacles can stop them on their path. In these minutes the quality of leaders becomes ever more important, for unconscious activism, automatism, also has a negative side: under the influence of some negative factor the elemental pushing forward can reverse its direction and turn into running back that is just as hard to stop. Yet the example of the leader, the brave leader, spreads as quickly as a psychological infection (suggestibility is heightened) and can again provoke a forward rush" (Polianskii, "Moral'nyi element v oblasti fortifikatsii," 101–2). Such books as Rezanov's *Armiia i tolpa* and N. A. Ukhach-Ogorovich's *Psikhologiia tolpy i armii* (Kiev: Tipografiia S. V. Kul'zhenko, 1911) are indicative of the new importance of crowd theory. Also see Daniel Beer, "'Microbes of the Mind': Moral Contagion in Late Imperial Russia," *Journal of Modern History* 79, no. 3 (September 2007): 531–71; Daniel Beer, *Renovating Russia: The Human Sciences and the Fate of Liberal Modernity, 1880–1930* (Ithaca: Cornell University Press, 2008).

72. On rumors as viruses in the battle of Mukden, see Zaglukhinskii, "Psikhika boitsov vo vremia srazheniia," 98.

73. A. Dmitrevskii, "Da, voin (rytsar') bez strakha i upreka—dosti-zhimyi ideal (Otvet g-nu Sh-vu)," *Voennyi sbornik* 56, no. 6 (1913): 99.

74. A. Dmitrevskii, "Logika bolgarskikh uspekhov i . . . poeziia russkoi chuvstvitel'nosti," *Voennyi sbornik* 56, no. 7 (1913): 115. This was a shared European sentiment. For Germany, see, e.g., Joachim Radkau, *Das Zeitalter der Nervosität: Deutschland zwischen Bismarck und Hitler* (Munich: Hanser, 1998); Volker Ullrich, *Die nervöse Grossmacht: Aufstieg und Untergang des deut-schen Kaiserreichs, 1871–1918* (Frankfurt am Main: S. Fischer, 1997).

75. Foucault's concept of discourse in the archaeological method up to the 1975 publication of *Surveiller et punir* (*Discipline and Punish*, 1977) was infamously murky about causality, prompting even two sympathetic early interpreters to complain that "the causal power attributed to the rules gov-erning discursive systems is unintelligible" (Hubert L. Dreyfus and Paul Rabinow, *Michel Foucault: Beyond Structuralism and Hermeneutics* [Chicago: University of Chicago Press, 1982], xxiv). His later understanding of dis-course in the genealogical method also elided causality. As one commentator has written, "The genealogist/historian looks for beginnings, not origins. This for Foucault was an essential distinction. Origins imply causes; begin-nings imply differences" (Patricia O'Brian, "Michel Foucault's History of Culture," in *The New Cultural History*, ed. Lynn Hunt [Berkeley: University of California Press, 1989], 37).

76. This potential is embodied, e.g., in Steven Pinker, *The Stuff of Thought: Language as a Window into Human Nature* (New York: Viking, 2007).

77. See my *Geschichte und Gefühl: Grundlagen der Emotionsgeschichte* (Munich: Siedler, 2012), esp. chap. 3.

78. See Catherine Merridale, *Ivan's War: Life and Death in the Red Army, 1939–1945* (New York: Metropolitan Books, 2006), 70–71, 98, 108–10, 135–38.

79. On this, see Seniavskaia, *Psikhologiia voiny v XX veke*; Gabriel, *Soviet Military Psychiatry*.

80. Hints at the connection between espionage, fear-inducing biological weapons, and Western anxiety drugs can be found in Alexander Kouzminov, *Biological Espionage: Special Operations of the Soviet and Foreign Intelligence Services in the West* (London: Greenhill, 2005). Also see the review by Jona-than B. Tucker, *Moscow Times*, no. 3127 (18 March 2005): 4.

81. Mark Glassman, "The Changing Battlefield; When Grace Flees under Fire," *New York Times*, July 25, 2004. Thanks to Susan Morrissey for this reference.

5. FEAR OF A SAFE PLACE

Portions of this chapter appear in Jan Mieszkowski, *Watching War* (Stanford: Stanford University Press, 2012).

1. Susan Sontag, *On Photography* (New York: Farrar, Strauss and Giroux, 1973), 167–68, 168.

2. See Joan Vennochi, "We're in a War—Where are the Media?," *Boston Globe*, May 4, 2008, D9; Brian Stelter, "TV News Winds Down Operations on Iraq War," *New York Times*, December 29, 2008, B1; Alessandra Stanley, "Bob Hope's Spirit, but No Cheesecake," *New York Times*, June 12, 2009, C1; and Joe Garofoli, "Iraq War Is Hell on the Bottom Line at the Box Office," *San Francisco Chronicle*, November 23, 2007, A1.

3. Sontag, *On Photography*, 20–21.

4. This tension in her thought is never reconciled, either in *On Photography* or in her last book, *Regarding the Pain of Others* (New York: Farrar, Strauss and Giroux, 2004), where she revisits the same group of questions and offers yet another set of inconclusive answers.

5. John A. Simpson and Edmund Weiner, ed., *Oxford English Dictionary*, 2nd ed. (New York: Oxford University Press, 1989).

6. Edmund Burke, *A Philosophical Enquiry into the Origin of our Ideas of the Sublime and Beautiful*, ed. James T. Boulton (Notre Dame: University of Notre Dame Press, 1968), 57.

7. Burke, *Philosophical Enquiry*, 57. Burke uses the terms "fear" and "terror" almost interchangeably, with terror perhaps being the more intense form of fear. His terminology stands in stark contrast to Sigmund Freud's well-known efforts in his *Introductory Lectures on Psycho-Analysis* and *Beyond the Pleasure Principle* to distinguish between fear (*Furcht*) and anxiety (*Angst*), the latter refering to an emotional state that has no direct allusion to an object or involves an unknown danger whereas the former has a specific object of apprehension. In fact, one could argue that for Burke fear combines three terms that Freud tries to keep separate: *Furcht*, *Angst*, and *Schreck* (fright).

8. Ibid., 57, 46. Burke understands sympathy as a substitutive process whereby "we are put into the place of another man, affected in many respects as he is affected," hence "we are moved as they [others] are moved" (44). Two years later in his *Theory of Moral Sentiments*, Adam Smith will famously make a similar argument, maintaining that the only reason we have sympathy for our fellow human when he or she suffers is that "by the imagination, we place ourselves in his situation, we conceive of ourselves endur-

ing all the same torments" (Adam Smith, *The Theory of Moral Sentiments*, ed. David D. Raphael and Alec L. Macfie [Indianapolis: Liberty Classics, 1984], 9).

9. Ibid., 39.

10. Immanuel Kant, *Critique of Judgment*, trans. Werner S. Pluhar (Indianapolis: Liberty Classics, 1987), 121, 120 (emphasis added).

11. Kant, *Critique of Judgment*, 129, 121.

12. Ibid., 129.

13. Ibid., 121, 121–22, 122. One could argue that the wars of Kant's day were nothing like the unrestrained conflicts of the Napoleonic era, much less the total wars of the twentieth century, but one can equally well rejoin that the seventeenth-century Wars of Reformation provided abundant examples of the horrors of unrestricted, and interminable, conflict.

14. Edmund Burke, *The Correspondence of Edmund Burke*, 10 vols., ed. Thomas W. Copeland et al. (Cambridge: Cambridge University Press, 1958–78), 6: 10.

15. William Wordsworth, "Preface—Lyrical Ballads," in *Major British Poets of the Romantic Period*, ed. William Heath (New York: Macmillan, 1973), 400.

16. Samuel Taylor Coleridge, "Fears in Solitude," in Heath, *Major British Poets of the Romantic Period*, 467–69; hereafter cited in text by line number.

17. See Barbara E. Rooke, ed., *The Collected Works of Samuel Taylor Coleridge: The Friend II*, vol. 4 (Princeton: Princeton University Press, 1969), 25.

18. François-René de Chateaubriand, *The Memoirs of Chateaubriand*, trans. Robert Baldick (New York: Knopf, 1961), 277.

19. Chateaubriand, *Memoirs of Chateaubriand*, 277–78.

20. Kant, *Critique of Judgment*, 108.

21. Chateaubriand, *Memoirs of Chateaubriand*, 278.

22. Sigmund Freud, "Thoughts for the Times on War and Death," in *The Standard Edition of the Complete Psychological Works of Sigmund Freud*, ed. James Strachey (London: Hogarth Press, 1957), 14: 275, 289.

23. Freud, "Thoughts for the Times," 291.

24. Paul Virilio, *War and Cinema: The Logistics of Perception*, trans. Patrick Camiller (New York: Verso, 1989), 26, 5.

25. Walter Benjamin, "The Work of Art in the Age of its Technological Reproducibility" (third version), in *Walter Benjamin: Selected Writings, Volume 4: 1938–1940*, ed. Howard Eiland and Michael W. Jennings (Cambridge: Belknap Press, 2006), 270.

26. While Kant distinguishes sharply between judgments of beauty and judgments of sublimity, Burke arguably does not—indeed, for him some degree of shock or surprise is characteristic of both.

27. Nicholas Mirzoeff, *Watching Babylon: The War in Iraq and Global Visual Culture* (New York: Routledge, 2005), 67.

6. THE LANGUAGE OF FEAR: SECURITY AND MODERN POLITICS

1. For contemporary theoretical statements of this position, see John Dunn, "Political Obligation," *The History of Political Theory and Other Essays* (New York: Cambridge University Press, 1996), 66–90; Bernard Williams, *In the Beginning Was the Deed: Realism and Moralism in Political Argument*, ed. Geoffrey Hawthorn (Princeton: Princeton University Press, 2005), 3.

2. Even in the case of Stalinist and Nazi mass murder and their accompanying ideologies of anti-Semitism and Marxism, the discourse of security— of safety, threat, danger—played a major role. See J. Arch Getty and Oleg V. Naumov, *The Road to Terror: Stalin and the Self-Destruction of the Bolsheviks, 1932–1939* (New Haven: Yale University Press, 1999); Christopher R. Browning, *The Origins of the Final Solution: The Evolution of Nazi Jewish Policy, September 1939–March 1942* (Lincoln: University of Nebraska Press, 2004).

3. My abbreviated account of Hobbes here draws upon Corey Robin, *Fear: The History of a Political Idea* (New York: Oxford University Press, 2004), 30–50.

4. The analysis in this and the following paragraphs is drawn from Richard Tuck, *Hobbes* (New York: Oxford University Press, 1989), 51–66.

5. Thomas Hobbes, *The Elements of Law, Natural and Politic*, 2nd ed., ed. Ferdinand Tönnies (London: Cass, 1969), I.14.8, 72.

6. Hobbes, *Elements*, I.17.10, 92; Thomas Hobbes, *Leviathan*, ed. Richard Tuck (New York: Cambridge University Press, 1991), chap. 37, 305.

7. Dunn, "Political Obligation," 77–78.

8. Randall Kennedy, *Race, Crime, and the Law* (New York: Pantheon Books, 1997).

9. Eric Foner, *Reconstruction: America's Unfinished Revolution, 1863–1877* (New York: Harper and Row, 1988), 582–85; Jerry M. Cooper, *The Army and Civil Disorder: Federal Military Interventions in Labor Disputes, 1877–1900* (Westport: Greenwood Press, 1980).

10. David Cole and James X. Dempsey, *Terrorism and the Constitution: Sacrificing Civil Liberties in the Name of National Security* (New York: New Press, 2002), x, 210.

11. John Solomon, "Bureaucracy Impedes Bomb Detection Work," Associated Press, August 12, 2006.

12. Cole and Dempsey, *Terrorism*, 177–78, 234.

13. Nancy V. Baker, *General Ashcroft: Attorney at War* (Lawrence: University Press of Kansas, 2006), 67, 82, 106, 108.

14. "Landrieu: We Might Have Been Better Off If Terrorists Had Blown Up the Levees," WWLTV.com, January 29, 2007, http://www.wwltv.com/local/stories/wwl012907tplandrieu.2f011766.html.

15. Hobbes, *Leviathan*, chap. 21, 153.

16. Hobbes, *Behemoth, or the Long Parliament*, ed. Ferdinand Tönnies (Chicago: University of Chicago Press, 1990), iii.

17. Hobbes, *Leviathan*, chap. 18, 129.

18. Cardinal Richelieu quoted in Otto Kirchheimer, *Political Justice: The Use of Legal Procedure for Political Ends* (Princeton: Princeton University Press, 1961), 29.

19. Dennis et al. v. United States, 183 F.2d 212 (1950).

20. George W. Bush, State of the Union address, January 28, 2003, http://www.whitehouse.gov/news/releases/2003/01/20030128-19.html.

21. Transcript of "Chasing Saddam's Weapons," *Frontline*, January 22, 2004, http://www.pbs.org/wgbh/pages/frontline/shows/wmd/etc/script.html.

22. Richard Perle quoted in Seymour M. Hersh, *Chain of Command: The Road from 9/11 to Abu Ghraib* (New York: Harper Collins, 2004), 210.

23. Edmund Burke, *Reflections on the Revolution in France*, ed. J.C.D. Clark (Stanford: Stanford University Press, 2001), 154.

24. George Eliot, *Daniel Deronda* (London: J. M. Dent, 1999), 495–96.

25. See Dunn, "Political Obligation," 78-80.

26. Cass R. Sunstein, *Why Societies Need Dissent* (Cambridge: Harvard University Press, 2003), 81.

27. Joseph Lieberman quoted in "Dean Says Democrats Have United Plan," Cnn.com, December 9, 2005, http://articles.cnn.com/2005-12-08/politics/democrats.iraq_1_howard-dean-iraq-troops?_s=PM:POLITICS.

28. Joseph Lieberman quoted in Thomas E. Ricks, "Leave Politics To Us, Warner Tells General," *Washington Post*, January 24, 2007, http://www.washingtonpost.com/wp-dyn/content/article/2007/01/23/AR2007012301306.html.

29. Transcript of *Fox News Sunday*, January 29, 2007, http://www.foxnews.com/story/0,2933,247844,00.html.

30. Arno J. Mayer, *Why Did the Heavens Not Darken? The 'Final Solution' in History* (New York: Pantheon Books, 1988).

31. Samuel Eliot Morison, "Dissent in the War of 1812," in *Dissent in Three American Wars*, ed. Samuel Eliot Morison, Frederick Merk, and Frank Freidel (Cambridge: Harvard University Press, 1970), 3-31 .

32. John C. Calhoun, *A Disquisition on Government, in Union and Liberty: The Political Philosophy of John C. Calhoun*, ed. Ross M. Lence (Indianapolis: Liberty Fund, 1992), 17.

33. Robert H. Zieger, *America's Great War: World War I and the American Experience* (Lanham: Rowman and Littlefield, 2000); Robert Justin Goldstein, *Political Repression in Modern America: From 1870 to the Present* (Cambridge: Schenkman, 1978), 107; Horace C. Peterson and Gilbert C. Fite, *Opponents of War, 1917–1918* (Seattle: University of Washington Press, 1968), 21–42, 231–34; Seward W. Livermore, *Politics Is Adjourned: Woodrow Wilson and the War Congress, 1916–1918* (Middletown: Wesleyan University Press, 1966), 15–31.

34. Zieger, *America's Great War*, 75, 76, 69; Livermore, *Politics Is Adjourned*, 37–61, 65–73, 81–90, 97–104.

35. Richard Polenberg, *Fighting Faiths: The Abrams Case, the Supreme Court, and Free Speech* (New York: Viking, 1987), 34.

36. John Stuart Mill, *Utilitarianism* (New York: New American Library, 1974), 310. Mill was referring here to the security of persons rather than of nations or states. But his argument about personal security is often extended to nations and states, which are conceived to be persons writ large. See Michael Walzer, *Just and Unjust Wars: A Moral Argument with Historical Illustrations* (New York: Basic Books, 1977), 51–73, though also see, for a qualification of this principle, 74–108. For a useful discussion of the parallels and distinctions between personal security and national security, see Barry Buzan, *People, States and Fear: The National Security Problem in International Relations* (Chapel Hill: University of North Carolina Press, 1983), 18–35. For an excellent discussion of the posited correspondence between individual agents and states in early modern and modern political thought, see Richard Tuck, *The Rights of War and Peace: Political Thought and the International Order from Grotius to Kant* (New York: Oxford University Press, 1999).

37. Raymond Plant makes a similar argument, vis-à-vis negative rights and police protection of those rights, in his critique of the libertarian ideal of a limited state. See Raymond Plant, "Why Social Justice?" in *Perspectives on Social Justice*, ed. David Boucher and Paul Kelly (London: Taylor and Francis, 1998), 274–76.

38. Hannah Arendt's *Eichmann in Jerusalem* (New York: Viking, 1963) remains the most vital statement on this matter; though see Tzvetan Todorov's *Facing the Extreme* (New York: Metropolitan, 1996) for a contrary view.

39. Polenberg, *Fighting Faiths*, 32–33.

40. John Locke, *A Letter Concerning Toleration*, ed. James H. Tully (Indianapolis: Hackett Publishing, 1983), 46; John S. Mill, *On Liberty*, in *On Liberty and Other Writings*, ed. Stefan Collini (New York: Cambridge University Press, 1989), 13; Schenck v. United States, 249 U.S. 47 (1919).

7. THE NEW YORK STOCK MARKET CRASH OF 1929

Another verison of this chapter has been previously published as "1929: The New York Stock Market Crash," *Representations* 110, no. 1 (2010): 129-44.

1. John Maynard Keynes, *The General Theory of Employment, Interest, and Money* (London: Macmillan, 1936), 154, 155, 159.

2. Milton Friedman and Anna J. Schwartz, *A Monetary History of the United States* (Princeton: Princeton University Press, 1963).

3. See Michael D. Bordo, Ehsan U. Choudhri, and Anna J. Schwartz, "Could Stable Money Have Averted the Great Contraction?" *Economic Inquiry* 33, no. 3 (1995): 484–505.

4. Helmut Schmidt, "Vorsicht Finanzhaie," *Die Zeit*, October 8, 1997, 2.

5. George Soros, *The Crisis of Global Capitalism: Open Society Endangered* (New York: Little, Brown, and Company, 1998), 103, 134.

6. George Soros, "Ins and Outs of the Ups and Downs," *Financial Times*, January 25, 2008.

7. "In UBS Vote a Mixed Message," *Wall Street Journal*, February 28, 2008.

8. Eugene Fama, "The Behavior of Stock Market Prices," *Journal of Business* 38 (1965): 34–105; Paul Samuelson, "Proof That Properly Anticipated Prices Fluctuate Randomly," *Industrial Management Review* 6 (1965): 41–49. The theory goes back to the 1900 dissertation of Louis Bachelier, "Théorie de la Spéculation." The most important popular presentation of the theory is Burton Malkiel's bestseller, *A Random Walk Down Wall Street* (New York: W. W. Norton, 1981). See also Burton G. Malkiel, *The Efficient Market Hypothesis and Its Critics* (Princeton: Princeton University Press, 2003).

9. Robert J. Shiller's best seller, *Irrational Exuberance* (Princeton: Princeton University Press, 2000), which was fortuitously but advantageously published on the eve of the dotcom crash, uses history to show the vulnerabilities of market assumptions.

10. Frederick Lewis Allen, *Only Yesterday: An Informal History Of The Nineteen-Twenties* (New York: Harper, 1931); John K. Galbraith, *The Great Crash, 1929* (1955; reprint, Harmondsworth: Penguin, 1975); John Brooks,

Once In Golconda: A True Drama Of Wall Street, 1920–1938 (New York: Harper and Row, 1969); Charles P. Kindleberger, *Manias, Panics, and Crashes: A History Of Financial Crises* (New York: Basic Books, 1978).

11. Eugene White, "The Stock Market Boom and Crash of 1929 Revisited," *Journal of Economic Perspectives* 4, no. 2 (1990): 67–83, argues more moderately that economic data was predicting a (relatively mild) recession and that the stock market reacted to this.

12. Peter Temin, *Did Monetary Forces Cause the Great Depression* (New York: Norton, 1976), 78–83.

13. The most explicit account of 1929 that offers this explanation is Irving Fisher, *The Stock Market Crash—and After* (New York: Macmillan, 1930).

14. "Cotton Futures Decline Sharply," *New York Times*, October 24, 1929, 53.

15. Paul Krugman, "Fear Itself," *New York Times Magazine*, September 30, 2001, 36.

16. Ben Bernanke, "The Macroeconomics of the Great Depression: A Comparative Approach," *Journal of Money Credit and Banking* 27 (February 1995): 1–28.

17. Allen, *Only Yesterday*, 330; Galbraith, *Great Crash*, 123.

18. "Panicky Liquidation on Stock Exchange Partly Checked," *New York Times*, October 25, 1929, 45.

19. "Phones, Radio, Cable Beat All Records," *New York Times*, October 30, 1929, 3.

20. See Barry Eichengreen, *Golden Fetters: The Gold Standard and the Great Depression, 1919–1939* (New York: Oxford University Press, 1992), 251.

21. John Maynard Keynes, *A Treatise on Money* (London: Macmillan, 1930), 2:190; Lionel Robbins, *The Great Depression* (London: Macmillan, 1934), 49.

22. Thomas E. Hall and J. David Ferguson, *The Great Depression: An International Disaster of Perverse Economic Policies* (Ann Arbor: University of Michigan Press, 1998), 66.

23. Temin, *Monetary Forces*, 72.

24. See Ben Bernanke and Mark Gertler, "Inside the Black Box: The Credit Channel of Monetary Policy Transmission," *Journal of Economic Perspectives* 9 (winter 1995): 27–48.

25. Galbraith, *Great Crash*, 147.

26. "Falls Dead at Ticker as Stocks Decline," *New York Times*, October 30, 1929, 3.

27. "Bank Crises Kill, Says Study," *Financial Times*, February 26, 2008, 3.

28. Marek Okólski, "Demographic Processes Before and During the

Ongoing Transition in Poland," *International Journal of Sociology* 34, no. 4 (winter 2004–5): 3–37; see also Marek Okólski, *Reprodukcja ludności a modernizacja społeczeństwa. Polski syndrom* (Warsaw: Książka i Wiedza, 1988).

29. "Heavy Break in Stocks," *New York Times*, October 24, 1929, 43.

30. "Breaks of the Past Recalled in Street," *New York Times*, October 25, 1929, 3.

31. Robert J. Shiller, "Investor Behavior in the October 1987 Stock Market Crash: Survey Evidence," *National Bureaus of Economic Research*, Working paper 2446, November 1987, 24.

32. "The Wall Street Readjustment: Its Present Meaning and Significance for the Future," *New York Times*, October 25, 1929, 36.

33. William Safire, "Fear Itself," *New York Times*, October 21, 1987, A35.

34. Galbraith, *Great Crash*, 140.

35. "Brokers Believe Bottom is Reached," *New York Times*, October 30, 1929, 7.

36. "Calls Stock Crash Blow at Gamblers," *New York Times*, October 29, 1929, 23.

37. Galbraith, *Great Crash*, 128.

38. Keynes, *General Theory*, 159.

39. "The Wall Street Crash A Devastating Slump," *Daily Mail*, May 30, 1998, 12.

40. "Ins and Outs of the Ups and Downs."

41. Paul Krugman, "A Crisis of Faith," *New York Times*, February 18, 2008.

8. LIVING DEAD: FEARFUL ATTRACTIONS OF FILM

This chapter is a slightly revised version of my contribution to the "Fear: Multidisciplinary Perspectives" workshop sponsored by the Shelby Cullom Davis Center for Historical Studies, Princeton University, in April 2008, and another version has been previously published as "Living Dead: Fearful Attractions of Film," *Representations* 110, no. 1 (2010): 105–28. I wish to thank Jan Plamper and Benjamin Lazier, the workshop organizers, for inviting me, and the workshop participants for contributing such thought-provoking discussion. I am grateful also for the earlier opportunities to present some of this material at conferences held at Florida State University and the University of Florida. Special thanks to Tom Gunning, who graciously commented on this chapter and helped me to improve it; of course, I do not wish to imply that he would necessarily agree with all of my claims.

1. Tom Gunning, "An Aesthetic of Astonishment: Early Film and the (In)Credulous Spectator," *Art and Text* 34 (spring 1989): 32. For a different account of this history that places more emphasis on the possibility of actually panicking viewers, see Stephen Bottomore, "The Panicking Audience? Early Cinema and the 'Train Effect,'" *Historical Journal of Film, Radio, and Television* 19, no. 2 (1999): 177–216.

2. For a useful sampling of these alternative approaches to theorizing film spectatorship, see Linda Williams, ed., *Viewing Positions: Ways of Seeing Film* (New Brunswick: Rutgers University Press, 1995).

3. On the influence of the cinema of attractions concept, see Wanda Strauven, ed., *The Cinema of Attractions Reloaded* (Amsterdam: Amsterdam University Press, 2006), which includes a detailed account from Gunning concerning the conceptual genesis of the cinema of attractions and how he developed the term through collaborations and conversations with a number of scholars, especially André Gaudreault. See Tom Gunning's chapter, "Attractions: How They Came into the World," in Strauven, *Cinema of Attractions Reloaded*, 31–39.

4. Tom Gunning, "The Cinema of Attractions: Early Film, Its Spectator and the Avant-Garde," in *Early Cinema: Space, Frame, Narrative*, ed. Thomas Elsaesser (London: British Film Institute, 1990), 58–59.

5. See David Bordwell, Janet Staiger, and Kristin Thompson, *The Classical Hollywood Cinema: Film Style and Mode of Production to 1960* (New York: Columbia University Press, 1985). The critical debates surrounding the concept of classical Hollywood style (along with related notions such as preclassical, postclassical, and nonclassical) have been vigorous and long lasting. See, for example, Jane Gaines, ed., *Classical Hollywood Narrative: The Paradigm Wars* (Durham: Duke University Press, 1992); Steve Neale and Murray Smith, ed., *Contemporary Hollywood Cinema* (London: Routledge, 1998); and David Bordwell, *The Way Hollywood Tells It: Story and Style in Modern Movies* (Berkeley: University of California Press, 2006).

6. David Bordwell and Kristin Thompson, *Film Art: An Introduction*, 8th ed. (Boston: McGraw-Hill, 2008), 94–96.

7. Bordwell, Staiger, and Thompson, *Classical Hollywood Cinema*, 3.

8. In this spirit, some scholars have argued against the assumption that classical Hollywood style adheres more closely to norms grounded in "realist" conventions rather than "excessive," melodramatic ones. See, for example, Rick Altman, "Dickens, Griffith, and Film Theory Today," in Gaines, *Classical Hollywood Narrative*, 9–47; Linda Williams, "Film Bodies: Gender, Genre, and Excess," *Film Quarterly* 44, no. 4 (summer 1991): 2–13; and Linda Williams, "Melodrama Revised," in *Refiguring American Film Genres: Theo-*

ry and History, ed. Nick Browne (Berkeley: University of California Press, 1998), 42–88.

9. Gunning, "Cinema of Attractions," 57.

10. Adam Lowenstein, *Shocking Representation: Historical Trauma, National Cinema, and the Modern Horror Film* (New York: Columbia University Press, 2005), 2.

11. For my divergence from Gunning on this score and related discussion, see Lowenstein, *Shocking Representation*, 46–47; and Adam Lowenstein, "Spectacle Horror and *Hostel*: Why 'Torture Porn' Does Not Exist," *Critical Quarterly* 53, no. 1 (April 2011): 42-60.

12. For a brief summary of the origins and influence of the series, as well as an argument for *Night of the Living Dead* as one of the most important American films ever produced independently, see Adam Lowenstein, "*Night of the Living Dead*," in *Fifty Key American Films*, ed. John White and Sabine Haenni (London: Routledge, 2009), 142–47.

13. I do not make this turn to Freud casually or mechanically but with the conviction that his work continues to provide a valuable stimulus for certain kinds of research in both the humanities and the social sciences, particularly in relation to trauma studies. For an eloquent statement (and enactment) of this position, see E. Ann Kaplan, *Trauma Culture: The Politics of Terror and Loss in Media and Literature* (New Brunswick: Rutgers University Press, 2005), esp. 24–41.

14. Jean Laplanche and Jean-Bertrand Pontalis, *The Language of Psychoanalysis*, trans. Donald Nicholson-Smith (1967; New York: Norton, 1973), 111.

15. See Sigmund Freud, letter to Wilhelm Fliess, December 6, 1896; quoted in Laplanche and Pontalis, *Language of Psychoanalysis*, 112.

16. Ibid.

17. See Janet Walker, "The Vicissitudes of Traumatic Memory and the Postmodern History Film," in *Trauma and Cinema: Cross-Cultural Explorations*, ed. E. Ann Kaplan and Ban Wang (Hong Kong: Hong Kong University Press, 2004), 123–44.

18. It is important to note that Big Daddy is never shown participating in the most "monstrous" aspect of zombie behavior: eating the flesh of the living.

19. See, for example, Romero's comments in the documentary *Undead Again: The Making of* Land of the Dead, *Land of the Dead* DVD (Los Angeles: Universal, 2005).

20. George A. Romero quoted in Michael Rowe, "*Land of the Dead*: Home of the Grave," *Fangoria* 244 (June 2005): 97.

21. See Lowenstein, *Shocking Representation*, 153–64. See also Sumiko

Higashi, *"Night of the Living Dead*: A Horror Film About the Horrors of the Vietnam Era,"* in *From Hanoi to Hollywood: The Vietnam War in American Film*, ed. Linda Dittmar and Gene Michaud (New Brunswick: Rutgers University Press, 1990), 175–88; and Ben Hervey, *Night of the Living Dead* (London: British Film Institute, 2008).

22. Sigmund Freud, "Project for a Scientific Psychology," *The Standard Edition of the Complete Psychological Works of Sigmund Freud*, ed. and trans. James Strachey (London: Hogarth Press, 1957), 1:356. As an editorial footnote (356n1) points out, this early account of prepubescent sexuality would itself be revised by Freud soon afterward with his discovery of infantile sexuality.

23. Of course, this retranscription may also be understood as channeled through *Dawn of the Dead* and *Day of the Dead*—both of these sequels, it should be noted, also include central black male characters. For a related analysis that focuses particularly on issues of gender in Romero's zombie films and their revision in the 1990 remake of *Night of the Living Dead* (written by Romero, directed by Tom Savini), see Barry Keith Grant, "Taking Back the *Night of the Living Dead*: George Romero, Feminism, and the Horror Film," in *The Dread of Difference: Gender and the Horror Film*, ed. Barry Keith Grant (Austin: University of Texas Press, 1996), 200–12.

24. In the documentary *Undead Again*, Romero speaks about how he and Dennis Hopper connected immediately as "guys who were disappointed that the '60's didn't work out the way we expected they would." When Hopper offered to play Kaufman like Secretary of Defense Donald Rumsfeld, Romero responded, "That's exactly where I'm going with this; this is the Bush administration."

25. On horror fandom, see Matt Hills, *The Pleasures of Horror* (London: Continuum, 2005). On goth subculture, see Lauren M. E. Goodlad and Michael Bibby, ed., *Goth: Undead Subculture* (Durham: Duke University Press, 2007). The prominence of Romero's name in advertising for all of the *Dead* sequels indicates an expectation of auteurist recognition and series knowledge among viewers.

26. On cult films, see Mark Jancovich, Antonio Lázaro Reboll, Julian Stringer, and Andy Willis, ed., *Defining Cult Movies: The Cultural Politics of Oppositional Taste* (Manchester: Manchester University Press, 2003); J. P. Telotte, ed., *The Cult Film Experience: Beyond All Reason* (Austin: University of Texas Press, 1991); J. Hoberman and Jonathan Rosenbaum, *Midnight Movies* (New York: Harper and Row, 1983); and Danny Peary, *Cult Movies* (New York: Dell, 1981).

27. For a study of the implications of cinema as a home viewing experi-

ence, see Barbara Klinger, *Beyond the Multiplex: Cinema, New Technologies, and the Home* (Berkeley: University of California Press, 2006).

28. Tom Gunning, "'Now You See It, Now You Don't': The Temporality of the Cinema of Attractions," *Velvet Light Trap* 32 (fall 1993): 7.

29. Gunning, "'Now You See It, Now You Don't,'" 7, 11.

30. For examples of lynching photographs, see James Allen, ed., *Without Sanctuary: Lynching Photography in America* (Santa Fe: Twin Palms, 2000).

31. Nir Rosen, "Fallujah—Inside the Iraqi Resistance: Part 1, Losing It," *Asia Times*, July 15, 2004, http://www.atimes.com/atimes/Front_Page/FG16Aa02.html.

32. For important examples of cognitivist research in film studies, see David Bordwell, *Narration in the Fiction Film* (Madison: University of Wisconsin Press, 1985); and Carl Plantinga and Greg M. Smith, ed., *Passionate Views: Film, Cognition, and Emotion* (Baltimore: Johns Hopkins University Press, 1999). For a polemical argument in support of cognitivism as a superior alternative to film theory of the 1970s and 1980s dominated by psychoanalytic and Marxist approaches, see David Bordwell and Noël Carroll, ed., *Post-Theory: Reconstructing Film Studies* (Madison: University of Wisconsin Press, 1996). For a valuable compendium of 1970s and 1980s film theory, see Philip Rosen, ed., *Narrative, Apparatus, Ideology: A Film Theory Reader* (New York: Columbia University Press, 1986). On psychoanalytic approaches to the horror film, see Steven Jay Schneider, ed., *Horror Film and Psychoanalysis: Freud's Worst Nightmare* (Cambridge: Cambridge University Press, 2004); and Carol J. Clover, *Men, Women, and Chain Saws: Gender in the Modern Horror Film* (Princeton: Princeton University Press, 1992).

33. These differences in theoretical stance have fueled an ongoing critical debate in film studies around the "modernity thesis." For accounts of this debate, see Ben Singer, *Melodrama and Modernity: Early Sensational Cinema and Its Contexts* (New York: Columbia University Press, 2001), esp. 17–35, 101–30; and Adam Lowenstein, "Cinema, Benjamin, and the Allegorical Representation of September 11," *Critical Quarterly* 45, nos. 1–2 (spring/summer 2003): 73–84. One particularly significant branch of the modernity thesis involves a redefinition of classical Hollywood style as "vernacular modernism." See, for example, Miriam Bratu Hansen, "The Mass Production of the Senses: Classical Cinema and Vernacular Modernism," in *Reinventing Film Studies*, ed. Christine Gledhill and Linda Williams (London: Arnold, 2000), 332–50.

34. Joanne Cantor and Mary Beth Oliver, "Developmental Differences in Responses to Horror," in *The Horror Film*, ed. Stephen Prince (New Brunswick: Rutgers University Press, 2004), 225–26. See also James B. Weaver III

and Ron Tamborini, ed., *Horror Films: Current Research on Audience Preferences and Reactions* (Mahwah: Erlbaum, 1996).

35. Noël Carroll, *The Philosophy of Horror, or Paradoxes of the Heart* (London: Routledge, 1990), 32. For complications and extensions of Carroll's argument, see David J. Russell, "Monster Roundup: Reintegrating the Horror Genre," in Browne, *Refiguring American Film Genres*, 233–54; and Steven Jay Schneider and Daniel Shaw, ed., *Dark Thoughts: Philosophic Reflections on Cinematic Horror* (Lanham: Scarecrow Press, 2003).

36. Robin Wood, "An Introduction to the American Horror Film," in *Planks of Reason: Essays on the Horror Film*, rev. ed., ed. Barry Keith Grant and Christopher Sharrett (Lanham: Scarecrow Press, 2004), 117, 113, 111–13.

37. Wood, "Introduction to American Horror Film," 119, 134.

38. Ibid., 135, 136.

39. Robin Wood, "Fresh Meat," *Film Comment* 44, no. 1 (January/February 2008): 31, 29. For Wood on Romero's first three *Dead* films, see his *Hollywood from Vietnam to Reagan . . . and Beyond* (New York: Columbia University Press, 2003), 63–119, 287–94. For arguments that complicate Wood's claims, see Murray Smith, "A(moral) Monstrosity," in *The Modern Fantastic: The Films of David Cronenberg*, ed. Michael Grant (Westport: Praeger,2000), 69–83; Lowenstein, *Shocking Representation*, 154–64; and Adam Lowenstein, "A Reintroduction to the American Horror Film," in *The Wiley-Blackwell History of American Film*, vol. 4, ed. Cynthia Lucia, Roy Grundmann, and Art Simon (Oxford: Wiley-Blackwell, 2012), 154–76.

40. Wood, "Fresh Meat," 31.

41. Wood, "Introduction to American Horror Film," 113.

42. Gunning, "'Now You See It, Now You Don't,'" 10.

43. Ibid., 11, 7.

44. See Walter Benjamin, *The Origin of German Tragic Drama*, trans. John Osborne (1928; London: Verso, 1998).

45. In this sense, my formulation of the allegorical moment challenges more narrowly focused attempts to isolate certain spectator reactions to horror films as if feelings of "fear" and "horror," for example, can be definitively specified and separated. See Steven Jay Schneider, "Toward an Aesthetics of Cinematic Horror," in Prince, *Horror Film*, 131–49.

46. Gunning, "Aesthetic of Astonishment," 42.

47. See ibid., 31–45; and Tom Gunning, "'Animated Pictures': Tales of Cinema's Forgotten Future, After 100 Years of Films," in Gledhill and Williams, *Reinventing Film Studies*, 316–31.

48. Maxim Gorky, review of Lumière program, *Nizhegorodski listok*, July

4, 1896; reprinted (trans. Leda Swan) in Jay Leyda, *Kino: A History of the Russian and Soviet Film* (New York: Collier Books, 1973), 407, 408. See also Gorky's related review from the same year reprinted as "Gorky on the Films, 1896," trans. Leonard Mins, in *New Theatre and Film 1934 to 1937: An Anthology*, ed. Herbert Kline (San Diego: Harcourt Brace Jovanovich, 1985), 227–31. For related context and discussion, see Yuri Tsivian, *Early Cinema in Russia and Its Cultural Reception*, trans. Alan Bodger (London: Routledge, 1994).

49. Gorky, review of Lumière, 408.

50. Gorky, "Gorky on the Films, 1896," 228.

51. Gorky, review of Lumière, 408.

52. Ibid., 407.

CONTRIBUTORS

HAROLD JAMES holds a joint appointment at Princeton as professor of history and as professor of international affairs in the Woodrow Wilson School. He is also Marie Curie Visiting Professor at the European University Institute in Florence. His books include *The German Slump: Politics and Economics, 1924–1936* (Oxford University Press, 1986); *A German Identity, 1770–1990* (Routledge, 1989); *International Monetary Cooperation Since Bretton Woods* (Oxford University Press, 1996); *The Deutsche Bank and the Nazi Economic War Against the Jews* (Cambridge University Press, 2001); *The End of Globalization: Lessons from the Great Depression* (Harvard University Press, 2001); *Europe Reborn: A History, 1914–2000* (Longman, 2003); *The Nazi Dictatorship and the Deutsche Bank* (Cambridge University Press, 2004); *The Roman Predicament: How the Rules of International Order Create the Politics of Empire* (Princeton University Press, 2006); *Family Capitalism: Wendels, Haniels, and Falcks* (Belknap of Harvard University Press, 2006); *The Creation and Destruction of Value: The Globalization Cycle* (Harvard University Press, 2009); and *Krupp: A History of the Legendary German Firm* (Princeton University Press, 2012).

BENJAMIN LAZIER is associate professor of history and humanities at Reed College. His interests include intellectual history, the history of technology, the environment, globalisms, religious thought, political thought, political economy, animality, the emotions, and movements for social action. He is the author of *God Interrupted: Heresy and the European Imagination between the World Wars* (Princeton University Press, 2008).

For his current work on the history of the notion of the "Whole Earth," see "Earthrise; or, the Globalization of the World Picture," *American Historical Review* 116, no. 3 (June 2011): 602–30.

RUTH LEYS is the Henry Wiesenfeld Professor of Humanities in the Humanities Center at Johns Hopkins University. Her books include *Trauma: A Genealogy* (University of Chicago Press, 2000) and *From Guilt to Shame: Auschwitz and After* (Princeton University Press, 2007). For recent publications on aspects of her current work in progress on the history of post–Second World War experimental and theoretical approaches to emotion and affect, see "The Turn to Affect: A Critique," *Critical Inquiry* 37, no. 3 (spring 2011): 434–72; "Affect and Intention: A Reply to William E. Connolly," *Critical Inquiry* 37, no. 4 (summer 2011): 799–805; and "'Both of Us Disgusted in My Insula': Mirror Neuron Theory and Emotional Empathy," nonsite.org, issue no. 5 (spring 2012), http://non-site.org/article/"both-of-us-disgusted-in-my-insula"-mirror-neuron-theory-and-emotional-empathy.

ADAM LOWENSTEIN is associate professor of English and film studies at the University of Pittsburgh. He is the author of *Shocking Representation: Historical Trauma, National Cinema, and the Modern Horror Film* (Columbia University Press, 2005) and is completing a book on cinematic spectatorship, surrealism, and the age of digital media.

RICHARD J. MCNALLY is professor and director of clinical training in the Department of Psychology at Harvard University. He is the author of more than 350 publications, including the books *Panic Disorder: A Critical Analysis* (Guilford Press, 1994); *Remembering Trauma* (Belknap of Harvard University Press, 2003); and *What Is Mental Illness?* (Belknap of Harvard University Press, 2011). He served on the *DSM-IV* posttraumatic stress disorder and specific phobia committees and has served as a consultant to the *DSM-V* committee addressing panic disorder and posttraumatic stress disorder.

JAN MIESZKOWSKI is professor of German and humanities at Reed College. He is the author of *Labors of Imagination: Aesthetics and Political Economy from Kant to Althusser* (Fordham University Press, 2006) and *Watching War* (Stanford University Press, 2012), and he has published articles on a wide range of topics in literary and cultural theory, continental philosophy, and modern art.

ARNE ÖHMAN is senior professor and professor emeritus of psychology in the Department of Clinical Neuroscience, Karolinska Institutet, Stockholm. From 1997 to 2010 he served on the Nobel Assembly, an elected body that chooses Nobel laureates in Medicine. In 2001 he received the Award for Distinguished Contributions to Psychophysiology and in 2011 the Wilhelm Wundt–William James Award. His research is concerned with an evolutionary perspective on emotion, especially the interplay of nonconscious perceptual mechanisms, psychophysiological responses, and the neural underpinnings of emotion (above all fear), as well as the relevance of these processes for an understanding of anxiety disorders. He has published more than fifty chapters in edited books and in a dozen major handbooks and encyclopedias, including the *Handbook of Emotions* (Guilford Press, 1993, 2000, and 2008), the *Handbook of Cognition and Emotion* (Wiley, 1999), the *Handbook of Psychophysiology* (Cambridge University Press, 2000), the *Handbook of Affective Sciences* (Wiley, 2003), and the *Handbook of Neuroscience for the Behavioral Sciences* (Wiley, 2009). He has also published 160 scientific articles in such journals as *Nature*, *Proceedings of the National Academy of Sciences of the United States of America*, *Daedalus*, *Emotion*, and *Psychological Review*.

JAN PLAMPER is professor of history at Goldsmiths, University of London. He is the author of *The Stalin Cult: A Study in the Alchemy of Power* (Yale University Press, 2012) and *Geschichte und Gefühl: Grundlagen der Emotionsgeschichte* (*History and Feeling: Foundations of the History of Emotions*) (Siedler, 2012; forthcoming in English with Oxford University Press).

COREY ROBIN is associate professor of political science at Brooklyn College and the CUNY Graduate Center. He is the author of *Fear: The History of a Political Idea* (Oxford University Press, 2004) and *The Reactionary Mind: Conservatism from Edmund Burke to Sarah Palin* (Oxford University Press, 2011). His articles have appeared in the *New York Times*, *Harper's*, the *London Review of Books*, and elsewhere. His blog, www.coreyrobin.com, has won the Charm Quark award (otherwise known as third prize) for "best writing in politics and social science" from 3 Quarks Daily and a Cliopatria award for best writer.

INDEX